CLARENDON AND CULTURAL CONTINUITY

GARLAND REFERENCE LIBRARY
OF THE HUMANITIES
(VOL. 168)

Edward Hyde, 1st Earl of Clarendon
from a portrait by Adriaen Hannerman (c. 1648–55)

CLARENDON AND CULTURAL CONTINUITY
A Bibliographical Study

Graham Roebuck

GARLAND PUBLISHING, INC. • NEW YORK & LONDON
1981

Library of Congress Cataloging in Publication Data

Roebuck, Graham.
   Clarendon and cultural continuity.

   (Garland reference library of the humanities ; v. 168)
   Includes bibliographical references and indexes.
   1. Clarendon, Edward Hyde, Earl of, 1609–1674—
Bibliography. 2. Great Britain—History—Puritan Rev-
olution, 1642–1660—Bibliography. I. Title. II. Series.
Z8172.5.R63 [DA447.C6]   941.06′092′4   78-68260
ISBN 0-8240-9769-6   AACR2

Printed on acid-free, 250-year-life paper
Manufactured in the United States of America

FOR MY MOTHER AND FATHER

CONTENTS

ACKNOWLEDGMENTS

If I could claim to be, like Johnson's lexicographer, nothing worse than a harmless drudge, I need apologize to none but the reader of this work for the tedium inflicted. But it is not so, for I have drawn heavily on the time, energy and talents of many people in the course of compiling it. I wish to express my thanks to all those on whom I have imposed in this task, and to exonerate them from the faults and errors of it, which are mine.

Numerous debts to scholars whose arguments have helped to shape my discourse will be apparent in the following pages, particularly in the final section. But I would especially mention B.D. Greenslade of University College, London, whose elucidation of seventeenth-century cultural continuity, both in conversations a number of years ago and in writings outside the scope of my essay, represents an ideal of clarity and elegance. A.S.G. Edwards of the University of Victoria, B.C., first suggested this project, and Lawrence Davidow, formerly of Garland, helped greatly in giving it initial shape. The informed conversation and judgment of Richard Newman have been most useful, and the protracted labors of Barbara Bergeron to rescue the manuscript from flocks of egregious errors have been heroic.

I am indebted to my friends and colleagues at McMaster who have graciously ridden along with my conversational hobby horse, and particularly to George Paul, Kevin Berland, David Blewett and Robert Johnston for specific suggestions. To Suzanne Robicheau I am grateful for research assistance in the preliminary stages, and to Susan Hardy, for whose preparation of the main index, proofreading and support in the crucial and wearying final stages I am deeply indebted.

Typing and word-processing have been admirably tackled at various stages of composition by Lynn Rabkin, Cheryl Sherry, Lucy Lade, Eileen Millington, Audrey Alexander, Kathy

Greenall and my mother, Vera Roebuck. I appreciate their dedicated work. Grants from the Faculty of Humanities and the Arts Research Board of McMaster University have helped to defray the expenses involved in research and typescript preparation, and are gratefully acknowledged.

Oxford University Press has kindly granted permission for quotations from Clarendon, and the National Portrait Gallery for reproduction of the fine portrait of the subject of this book. Similarly, many libraries on both sides of the Atlantic have been most obliging, especially the Beinecke Rare Book and Manuscript Library, Yale University; the Folger Shakespeare Library, Washington, D.C.; the Houghton Library, Harvard University; the Humanities Research Center, University of Texas at Austin; the Huntington Library, San Marino, California; the Robarts Library, Toronto; the Thomas Fisher Rare Book Room, Toronto; the library of Osgoode Hall, Toronto; the library of York University, Toronto; the John Rylands Library, University of Manchester. To the staffs of the British Library and the Bodleian Library on many occasions, and to that of the Mills Memorial Library, McMaster University, particularly its Rare Book Room, I remain especially indebted for their unflagging courtesy.

W.G.R.
McMaster, 1981

INTRODUCTION

As a young man, a student of law, Edward Hyde enjoyed the patronage and friendship of a number of those most eminent in Church and State. That his future as a public figure was at that time already very bright may be inferred from the fact that he was chosen to be one of the managers of an elaborate staging of James Shirley's masque *The Triumph of Peace* (February, 1634), notable for the vehement loyalty of its sentiments, as well as for its extravagance. Each of the four Inns of Court chose two representatives. Of the eight men thus appointed, six were to achieve illustrious careers. From Middle Temple along with Hyde came Bulstrode Whitelocke, who left an account of the event, from Inner Temple Sir Edward Herbert and John Selden, from Lincoln's Inn Sir William Noy, later to be Attorney General, and from Gray's Inn, Sir John Finch, later Lord Keeper.[1] Hyde was also proud to number himself among the Tribe of Ben. On the threshold of a legal or administrative career, he also courted the Muse. His account of this period in his life in the autobiography, *Life* [150], was written at a very much later date, and is, so some critics charge, smugly self-approving. Yet he admits to his irresolution as he "stood at gaze" wondering which course of life to take. Ben Jonson had "for many years an extraordinary kindness for Mr. Hyde, till he found he betook himself to business, which he believed ought never to be preferred before his company" (*Life*, 1857 ed., p. 28). And there, with a brief tribute to Jonson's genius and his reformation of the language, the irresolution ends.

---

1. For an account of the masque and an estimate of its cost (a million U.S. dollars at the 1930 value) see A. Wigfall Green, *The Inns of Court and Early English Drama* (New York: Benjamin Blom, 1965; first published by Yale University Press, 1931), pp. 123–132.

xi

His predilection for business and graver subjects over the rakish life of a gentleman of poetry and pleasure is clear enough in the pages of this same autobiography. Although he hints at his appearance in that kind of company, he makes much more of abstracting himself from the debauched company of soldiers and others who took advantage of the liberty of those times, in order to retire to his books and answer the legal problems posed to him almost every day by his diligent and attentive uncle. His reading, we gather, like that of the young John Donne (whose pattern of life Hyde's somewhat resembles at this time), was voracious, much inclined to classical history and to theology, but not wholly excluding the politer learning. Unlike Donne, however, he could not give himself over more than superficially to a rakish existence, and so, in keeping with his inclinations, sought out for himself more profitable pursuits, such as speaking plain truths to Archbishop Laud.

However, he appears as one of the dozen contributors of elegiac verses to the memorial edition of Donne's poems.[2] On the evidence of this work the young poet cannot be said to speak in an inimitable accent, or to have achieved a personal idiom— indeed, his point, like that of most poems on the great poet's death, is that poetry must henceforth steal from Donne's accumulated riches. Although his sentiments are conventional enough, and do not presage a brilliant poetic career, he enunciates at one point a preference for good conscience over the prospects of fame, which was to become a constant theme of his mature philosophy. Compressed by strict meter the idea is most awkwardly conveyed:

> Fate hath done mankinde wrong; vertue may aime
> Reward of conscience, never, can, of fame,
> Since her great trumpet's broke, could onely give
> Faith to the world, command it to beleeve;

The poem is then swiftly concluded in a paradoxical couplet, which seems to say that the arts are the best divinity, a view which his later outlook certainly did not condone. Perhaps at this

---

2. "On the death of Dr DONNE," *POEMS, By J.D. WITH ELEGIES ON THE AUTHORS DEATH* (London: Iohn Marriot, 1633), p. 377.

time he saw the door to poetic fame as closed to him. There was demanding business of state in the offing, troubled waters through which a secure conscience could navigate better than an ephemeral wit. Still, he had courted the Muse, and many years later Dryden reminded the then Lord Chancellor Clarendon of his earlier affinities with polite learning, and of his enthusiasm for poetry and poets:

> The Muses (who your early courtship boast,
> Though now your flames are with their beauty lost)
> Yet watch their time, that if you have forgot
> They were your Mistresses, the World may not:
> Decay'd by time and wars, they only prove
> Their former beauty by your former love;
> And now present, as antient Ladies do
> That courted long at length are forc'd to woo.[3]

Hyde's brief flirtation with poetry had, however, an earlier date, when he wrote commendatory verses to William D'Avenant's *The Tragedy of Albovine*. Later, when writing his autobiography, Clarendon does not remember D'Avenant as being a member of the illustrious circle of his youth, including as it did Selden, Cotton, John Vaughan, Kenelm Digby, Thomas May and Thomas Carew. The poem is brief, and runs thus:

> Why should the fond ambition of a friend,
> With such industrious accents strive to lend
> A Prologue to thy worth? Can aught of mine
> Enrich thy Volume? th'ast rear'd thyself a Shrine
> Will out-live Pyramids; Marble Pillars shall,
> Ere thy great Muse, receive a funeral:
> Thy Wit hath purchas'd such a Patron's name
> To deck thy front, as must derive to Fame
> These tragic raptures, and indent with Eyes
> To spend hot tears, t'enrich the Sacrifice.[4]

3. "To my Lord Chancellor Presented on New-years-day [1662]," *The Poems of John Dryden*, ed. James Kinsley (Oxford: Clarendon Press, 1958), pp. 28–32.
4. See James Maidment and W.H. Logan, eds., *The Dramatic Works of Sir William D'avenant* (New York: Russell & Russell, 1964), vol. i, pp. xliii–xlvi and 13–14 for a discussion of Clarendon's relationship with D'Avenant.

The admiration of poetic achievement which moved Hyde to this hyperbolic praise of D'Avenant's muse evaporated in the sterner realities of civil war. Indeed, he contracted a distaste for poets in general, and came to disapprove of the pursuit of poetry in men of mature age, as a frivolous and trivial concern. Thomas May (author of a rival history of the Long Parliament) and the politically meddlesome Edmund Waller are especially disliked. In the *Life* Jonson and Carew alone are excepted from this pervasive coolness, but the accounts he gives of them scarcely arrest the onward narrative of Mr. Hyde's life.

We do not know what his library in these years at Middle Temple may have contained, for it was seized by parliamentary ordinance, but the magnificent and beautifully bound collection of his maturity was, as Professor Hardacre has shown [234], notably devoid of belles-lettres. As his surviving commonplace books (Bodleian MSS Clarendon 126, 127) attest, Hyde's imagination was more strongly engaged by the prose of business, especially that of Bacon and of the historians, ancient and modern.

From his youth on, if the retrospective angle of *Life* is not misleading, Clarendon was inclined by temperament and conservative upbringing to that kind of view of the world which could be labelled, if the anachronism be allowed, "natural Toryism." That is to say, he reflected on the decay in manners, morals and, generally, culture of his nation. Although a true and tough-minded Baconian, interested in, if not personally proficient in, the new physical sciences, and more especially in a rational account of human affairs, Clarendon found in modernism no attraction. In his maturity and old age particularly he was given to expressing regret over the inroads of modern—often equated with licentious or atheistic—habits of thought, which he saw as undermining the good old-fashioned English cheerfulness and decorum which graced the days of his youth. The reign of Queen Elizabeth, in which the landmarks of the national destiny were, as he supposed, firm and evident, the establishment of the law and of the Church secure, is frequently treated or invoked for the nostalgic light it sheds, although the old Queen was dead before he was born. This is, of course, a not uncommon attitude in his generation, and is used for its propaganda value by writers of quite different political persuasion. However, he did have genuine cause to dislike the cast of mind of the new generation of politicians at Court, forerunners of the Cabal administration, who unscrupulously engineered his downfall in 1667. Whether their actions resulted from simple and natural enmity and ambition, or whether they really represented the forces of modernist reform, is a question still addressed by historians of the Restoration period.

Whatever kind of reformist Hyde, as a young MP, became—and this too is a matter of scholarly debate—he revered what he took to be the ancient constitution of the land. So did his eventual political opponents. Refurbishing that structure, so strained by Charles I's many years of mismanagement, which amounted to a form of despotism, was the limit of his ambition. When he saw the Long Parliament reformists, with whom he had been in accord, going too far and undermining essential foundations, he decisively broke with them. Then he took up his pen in the royalist cause. In *Life* he is anxious to represent his actions as disinterested (see [3]), although one may reasonably suspect that this young, talented and highly articulate lawyer saw himself as especially well-prepared to enter the public stage and play a decisive role in the looming struggle for his nation's culture. His situation then suggests comparison with that of Milton, almost his exact contemporary, who was consciously preparing for his own greatness, not only in poetry.

When, in December, 1641, Hyde resolved to lend his talents to the King, the royal cause was in disarray, ineffectually presenting its case to Parliament and public. There ensued the most far-reaching conflict in post-medieval English constitutional history. It was, at first, a contest conducted by means of declararations, protestations, manifestos and pamphlets—"Paper-bullets" Hyde calls them [67B], and "paper skirmishes," the preludes of "sharper actions." The character of the contest was without precedent in English history, in that both sides ostensibly sought the same goal, and used the same rhetorical fictions. But writers on both sides, led by Hyde, learned the arts of polemic, and, by degrees, of forgery, counterfeiting, composing of centos and satires. The paper battle was at its climax in 1643 when Sir Thomas Browne complained of the universal tyranny of the press to which he had fallen victim, although a single and private man. His plight (unauthorized publication of *Religio Medici*) is not to be compared, he says, to the highest perversion of the times: "the name of his Majesty defamed, the honour of Parliament depraved, the writings of both depravedly, anticipatively, counterfeitly imprinted."[5] In the world of political propaganda—for Hyde's work had become propaganda, rather than disinterested argument[6]—encomia are not as freely lavished as in the former world of witty poetry. However, parliamentary writers began to suspect that the royalist cause was being propagated and coordinated by an evil genius. One of these writers ("a just complainer") presents an encomium of sorts, which probably amused and gratified him: "Reader (before we enter the List with this bold Pamphletiere) we must informe thee that we are to contend with a Tongue and Pen, tipt with so saucy, peremptory, railing and false a Dialect, that we are confident, all the past, present, and future Ages, will be non-plust to produce a parallel" [63B]. Even in his own party there was misgiving about Hyde's wit. In thoughtful words Sir Philip Warwick considers its drawbacks and advantages [105].

Hyde had become one of the master propagandists of English history. Very few statesmen, if any can be called into comparison, had undergone such an apprenticeship. In the view of some historians his greatness is to be found here, in the years when his work clearly changed the course of English history. They argue that he effectively created mixed monarchy, the idea of a constitutionally responsible king, an idea so potent that it survived even the practice of Charles I and Charles II, each by his nature greatly averse to observing constitutional restrictions. Here is the basis of a pattern in British history which kept it apart from absolutism, on the one hand, and outright repub-

5. "To the Reader," in his *Religio Medici*, Sir Geoffrey Keynes, ed., *Sir Thomas Browne: Selected Writings* (Chicago: University of Chicago Press, 1970), p. 5.

6. Some modern scholars who have recognized his role as royal penman argue that, when writing the *History*, he came to believe this same propaganda as objectively true.

licanism on the other, and thus made possible much of the British legacy to the modern world. In this respect Clarendon deserves well of Whig opinion, and has sometimes received qualified endorsement from that quarter. (The remarks of Horace Walpole [148] are an instance.) It is a strong argument and, however, its details may be disputed, gives some color to Ranke's famous assertion that "Clarendon belongs to those who have essentially fixed the circle of ideas of the English nation" [297].

As the Civil War drew toward its close, and having been made responsible for the safety of the Prince of Wales, Hyde retreated to Jersey. He was not at a loss. One of the most awesome and admirable aspects of the man is his refusal to repine under the most adverse of circumstances. As his letters written in this onset of a protracted exile frequently demonstrate, he seized the ancient ideal of retirement as a positive blessing, and urged other defeated royalists remaining in England to do the same. His bookishness, his wide learning, his own acute sense of the fragility of cultural continuity, led him to shift his energies from propaganda applied to current exigency into reflective history. He began to write the *History*, which, as he declared in a private letter, would make "mad work" among friends and enemies, and quickly realized that his grander purpose was to transmit to posterity the meaning of the things he had experienced, and to preserve the memories of worthy men on both sides who had fallen in the conflict, as his preamble to his most famous piece, the portrait of Falkland, makes quite clear.[7]

It was perhaps in the years 1646 to 1648 that Hyde most clearly saw that his nation was at a fateful juncture, and understood his duty to preserve its inheritance. The Church stood in danger of annihilation, the common law as a stronghold of personal liberty was about to yield to martial diktat, and the robust good humor of England to the last vigil of the saints, Oxford to enthusiasts, and social hierarchy to levelling. Such consequences

---

7. It is interesting to note that this passage, which has been so much commented upon, provided Boswell with a model for the *Life of Johnson*.

are foreshadowed in some of the civil war propaganda, and with especial vividness in *The Difference and Disparity* [73], which probably belongs to that period. What he actually achieved in the *History*, and by his statesmanship, is thereafter a subject of ceaseless debate. This debate resembles in some of its characteristics a "battle of the books"; the values of antiquity pitched against modernism. What the *History* shows by means of forensic analysis is how the dynamic of change is always more effective than the passivity of secure traditionalism, and how it is all too easily controlled by the unscrupulous and the unfixed in principle. The author may not always appreciate just how dynamic the forces of change can be, and nineteenth-century historians especially berate him for underestimating the power and the seriousness of Puritanism. Similarly, twentieth-century historians see him as discounting the force of egalitarian aspirations.

How good, or accurate, or unbiased is the *History*? These questions have kept his reputation alive, not solely on grounds of what is sometimes called "academic" interest, but also because they point a perennial and more important problem of how to understand history. For many readers today the work in its entirety is not as accessible as it was to readers of a more leisured age for reason of length and because of the detailed grasp of historical occurrences needed to appreciate much of it. This problem is not entirely new, as one surmises from the number of times that excerpts and abridged versions have been published. Ever since its first publication as, in effect, a *vade mecum* of high Toryism, it has been subjected to misunderstanding and partisan scrutiny. Thus it takes a central position in the Whig-Tory battles of the eighteenth and nineteenth centuries.

During those centuries the stature of the *History*[8] ensured that interest in his other writings for their own merits remained slight and marginal, so that whenever they are cited or referred to it is with the purpose of supporting a judgment on the *History* and its accuracy. The *Life*, for instance, enjoyed no very great interest for its own sake, and was, perhaps for this reason, never

8. Professor Trevor-Roper describes it as the best-seller of the eighteenth century [327].

adequately presented. Twentieth-century fondness for autobiography has led some scholars to express a preference for the *Life* over the *History*, which may finally result in an accurate version. In the eighteenth and nineteenth centuries the essays, sometimes printed singly, as in [152, 153 and 154], enjoyed some vogue, and the *State Papers* [155] have continued to be used by historians since their publication. These, and other works, such as the refutation of Hobbes [101], the *Contemplations* [129A], and *Religion and Policy* [161], show the reflective and philosophical sides of a man who, if not himself a philosopher, responds with broad and substantial learning, tempered by experience, to many of the issues exercising the best minds of the time. Not readily available outside of research libraries, they appeal now almost exclusively to the coterie interests of specialist scholars. In recent years there are signs of a freshening of scholarly interest afforded them. Clarendon's political achievement as Lord Chancellor, however, continues to provoke a more widespread controversy, yielding vastly dissimilar assessments.

After having become, in the nineteenth century, a recognized classic of our literature, Clarendon's reputation fell into the neglect commonly attendant on that exalted status. T.S. Eliot in his well-known essay "Religion and Literature" remarks on the dangers of this occurrence. Gibbon and Clarendon he regards as "our two great English historians," whose writings have too often for his taste been regarded as "literature," as distinct from their values as history, which, he adds, probably indicates an end to their real literary influence. Better to be mauled by Whigs than accepted by the literary establishment.

When preparing his memorial lecture for the tercentenary of Clarendon's birth [219], Sir Charles Firth expected to be able to assume a popular impression of Clarendon. He discovered that there really wasn't one. The *History* had become an English classic; beautifully bound volumes on the shelves of a cultivated man's library, its prose used in small parcels for academic exercises, the work itself essentially unread.

Unread masterpieces on bookshelves make for ideal local coloring in works of fiction. It may be that prose fiction, in the twentieth century especially, has assumed some of the burden of cultural transmission carried by historiography in the eighteenth.[9] Although this study makes no claim to treat prose fiction, it is worth mentioning here one curious and revealing use of Clarendon's reputation in a novel. In Ford Madox Ford's *No More Parades* (1925) (the second novel in the *Parade's End* tetralogy), Christopher Tietjens, immensely conscious of being the "last Tory," and given to recurrent meditation on George Herbert, Bemerton, and the ideals of Anglican sainthood, tries to account for his stubborn integrity:

> [General Campion:] "You think all generals are illiterate fools. But I have spent a great deal of time in reading, though I never read anything later than the seventeenth century." Tietjens said: "I know sir. . . . You made me read Clarendon's *History of the Great Rebellion* when I was twelve."[10]

Last Tories persist, of course. Indeed, the sense of living in the welter of a dissolving culture, rather than in the heigh-day of progress, is a most potent ingredient of the Tory temperament. Clarendon himself could without misgiving actively support the scientific progress of the Royal Society, or praise the advancement of modern scholarship (as he does in *Religion and Policy* [161]), but he was also the precursor of the Tory party, and anticipated Tietjens' bleak vision of standing at a great cultural watershed, on the far side of which all would be utterly changed.

This bibliographical study is written in the belief that Clarendon is of more than merely antiquarian interest; that his wisdom is

9. The distortion caused by an excessive emphasis on "literary" values is argued by James William Johnson, *The Formation of English Neo-Classical Thought* (Princeton: Princeton University Press, 1967), pp. 31–32. Here he observes that nothing has been more neglected in studies of classical thought in England than historiography. The pervasiveness of reference in the eighteenth century to historians from Herodotus to Clarendon is dismissed by literary critics as "trite usage, empty homage to an ideal." To study the influence of historiography on literary tradition is to cut across academic disciplines. After the Restoration, enthusiasm for historiography was enormous, and its significance ought not to be ignored.

10. *The Bodley Head Ford Madox Ford* (1963), vol. iv, p. 230.

valuable, and that to recall the importance of his life's work for our predecessors is not merely arcane. It is not, however, a strident appeal for revaluation. It was undertaken in the green expectation that it would be quite brief, and that, as an account of Clarendon's own works, it could be definitive. This has proved to be quite impossible. Since it has to do not only with many of Clarendon's presumed writings, but also with the responses to them, and to his career as statesman, it cannot hope to be complete. Books dealing with Clarendon as their major subject are relatively few. Books and articles which deal with him and his works in larger contexts are legion, and not confined to one or two disciplines. How to deal with this situation as it concerns the question of inclusion has made for many difficult decisions. As a rule of thumb I have attempted to include works which assess one or another aspect of his life and writing over and above simply citing him. The success of this *ad hoc* policy is, of course, for the individual reader to gauge.

Doubtless there are omissions from the list of works about Clarendon caused by my ignorance of their existence. In the sections treating his career as a surreptitious pamphleteer are numerous inclusions the authorship of which I assert, but cannot prove. Nevertheless, it seems better to present this account, inadequate though it may be, than to wait indefinitely upon a distant ideal.

Bibliographic methods, sufficiently detailed to obviate confusion, but not aspiring to descriptive bibliography, are sketched at the beginnings of sections. Here also may be found introductory considerations, given in hope that they may help to guide the reader through a long and sometimes tangled story.

Section A

Speeches and Apologetics
in the Royalist Cause, 1641–1643

It is well known, and attested to by contemporaries, that from late 1641 Edward Hyde was the penman of most royalist propaganda. Not only at the time, but also in retrospect, he was proud of the services he performed in this capacity-- proud enough to include or at least to refer to most of his pamphlets from that period in *The History of the Rebellion*. Indeed, the arguments which he propounded in the period from 1641 to 1643 were to form the basis upon which he erected his account of the English Civil Wars. From his responses to the exigencies and day-to-day crises of this time English constitutional monarchy was forged. Not all his political pamphlets achieved the recognition implied by inclusion in *The History of the Rebellion*. Those omitted--recorded in the following list--did not wholly meet the requirements of his mature political philosophy.

As a lawyer of reformist sympathies Hyde joined the resistance to what he saw as Strafford's tyrannical administration, attempting first to curb the excesses of royal prerogative, and later to dismantle the very apparatus of tyranny. It is in this role that we first encounter him on the public stage (see [1 and 2] below). For whatever reasons-- scholarly opinion is divided--he desisted from a course of action which, if it had been continued, might have induced him into the same path as that followed by Pym and Hampden. He became instead the leading figure of the newly emerging royalist party in the Commons. Had he not acted in this way, the King's constitutional position would have been threadbare, and his popular appeal very limited.

However, as it happened, Hyde, with remarkable success, disguised his activities as the King's adviser until it was eventually impossible for him to remain an active member of the Westminster Parliament. Throwing in his lot with the King's party, he, with aims essentially different from those of the King himself, established himself as acknowledged theorist and apologist of the royal cause, attempting to pursue a policy which, on the one hand, required moderation and constitutional obedience of the King, and, on the other, called for a spirit of accommodation in the remaining Parliament.

It has frequently been observed that whereas Hyde believed, or grew to believe, in his own propaganda (a theory which Hobbes called "mixarchy") Charles I did not. Or rather, did so only intermittently, when it served the turn, for he continued to be swayed by the counsels of his queen, and those whom Parliament called "Cavaliers." The strains of these conflicting purposes at work in the royalist cause are graphically illustrated in some of the pamphlets recorded and discussed in this section.

What has interested me as much as these tokens of a political battle, and is therefore reflected in the commentaries, is Hyde's special wit and the swift evolution of a language of polemic superior in effectiveness to that of his parliamentary opponents. Theirs was a difficult position. In the name of Parliament and King they sought to redress an imbalance of constitutional power, which left them in the logical dilemma of arguing that what Charles did, or attempted to do, was under the influence of malignant counsels. Thus they attempted to preserve an older constitutional equilibrium. In fact, the situation was the reverse. Charles attempted a *coup d'état* in the endeavor to arrest five members of the Commons and one member of the Lords--a move deplored by Hyde. This, and allegations of the King's inclination to Popery (probably wholly unfounded), are hardened into staples of Parliament's propaganda, and the quick-witted Hyde made maximum use of them. The following pamphlets are the record of a campaign which must be regarded as highly successful, in the context of polemic. But their ultimate result was to enable the King to wage war, as a result of having gained some measure of public support. And that, at least in the short term, was a defeat to Hyde's policy. The reader of the *History*, however, will recognize time and again in these pamphlets positions, attitudes, even phrases, which Hyde was to put together in a wider and masterful work, the *History*. The propaganda was to be transformed into historical philosophy of the highest order.

I have identified the individual works of Hyde's pen, so far as that may be done with reasonable expectation of accuracy, down to November, 1643. For a number of compelling reasons it seemed impossible to continue the attempt beyond that date. The propaganda war had ground nearly to a halt. The adversaries' positions were clearly identified and formed, and the would-be neutral ground was as committed as it ever would become. A war, which was now for conquest, not accommodation, was joined in earnest. Propaganda continued to be written, of course, but by this time the characteristic arguments and rhetoric, at least, of the royalists was established, largely by Hyde. The slogans and watchwords of

Hyde's making were now the common currency of polemic. His
own influence from that time, as he admits in *The History of
the Rebellion*, had been eclipsed by the King's military advisers. His own efforts, he now realized, had achieved no accommodation, but rather served as instruments to make possible
the waging of war which, for the King, would have been in
1641 unthinkable. About this time, as he observes in the
History, the barbarities of the royalist military made them
indistinguishable from the enemy. Also Falkland had died on
the battlefield, signifying the destruction of that enlightened,
liberal Anglican viewpoint nurtured at Great Tew in pre-war
calm. Hyde's heart, for a while, was alienated.

But despite the many argumentative victories of these
pamphlets, and the practical failure of the cause, Hyde, as
we know, did not withdraw from the contest. In 1646 he retired
to Jersey to begin work on a royalist apology meant for publication, which evolved, perhaps as a result of Charles I's
wishing him to counter Tom May's history of the Parliament,
into a monumental work of history. In the meantime his
energies, now as Chancellor, were engaged in tending the King's
shrunken exchequer, and in sustaining correspondence with
Royalist sympathizers. He was, in addition, charged with the
heavy responsibility of conducting the affairs of the heir to
the throne.

In those works of 1641-1643 there remain difficulties in
the way of an exact bibliography. There are some declarations,
even more proclamations, and a few speeches in which Secretary
Nicholas and Lord Falkland must have had a share, but which
seem to me to bear insufficient evidence of his own style to
warrant inclusion. Sometimes the same form of words issued in
one proclamation would be reissued in different regions, adapted
somewhat to fit the circumstances. Such reissues I do not
attempt to record. Similarly, a number of speeches, especially
in the months following the raising of the royal standard in
August, 1642, are repeated and printed in various parts of
England. Such are the King's speech to the army at Wellington
on September 19, and the King's speech to Shropshire on September 28, 1642, variations of which are delivered in formulaic
manner in the weeks following. When the King became established in Oxford it became customary to issue centos of speeches,
declarations, etc., not always authorized, from an earlier date.
These may have been, often clearly were, work originally by
Hyde. It seemed likely to complicate further an already complicated picture to attempt to record them. Finally there is
a great difficulty, and little likelihood of certainty, in
exactly distinguishing other editions of pamphlets from reissues. As Steele observes in his bibliography of royal
proclamations, editions might often be regarded as "settings

up" of type, which makes it very difficult to establish
chronological sequences.

METHOD

1. In the following entries the number in the left-hand
    margin indicates the main entry. Subsidiary entries
    (e.g., other editions with variants, and related docu-
    ments) may be indicated by number and letter.

2. In each main entry the full title as it appears on the
    title page is given, but information concerning printers
    and publishers is sometimes given in shortened form when
    no confusion is likely to arise.

3. Entries are in presumed chronological sequence of composi-
    tion, not of publication.

4. Probable dates of composition are sometimes provided in
    square brackets preceding the title.

5. When possible the title pages of the most accessible
    versions of each pamphlet have been cited (e.g., Thomason
    items).

6. Entries are related to other appropriate bibliographies:
    Wing, Thomason, Madan, Steele.

7. Where pamphlets are referred to, discussed or quoted (in
    part or in full) in *The History of the Rebellion*, the
    volume and page numbers of the reference are noted.

8. In transcribing title pages peculiarities of font are not
    noticed. Larger or smaller, italic or roman capitals are
    all rendered similarly as capitals. All lower-case
    letters, italic or otherwise, are rendered as lower case.
    I am aware of no instance in which confusion of edition
    is likely to arise for lack of more sophisticated dis-
    crimination.

9. Line endings are not indicated. Neither is the long 's'
    distinguished from the short. The two common forms of
    upper case j--'j' and 'J'--are given as 'J.'

10. I have distinguished VV from W because in some instances this difference is important in identifying editions.

11. The number of pages in each main entry is given in parentheses following the title. This is the number of printed pages, irrespective of peculiarities of pagination.

12. Printers' ornaments, borders, devices, etc., are not noted.

13. It will be immediately clear that other features of descriptive bibliography, such as an account of gatherings, signatures, etc., have not been employed.

The features outlined above were devised with the aim of identifying as simply as possible, but with the avoidance of confusion, the titles of works by Hyde. As anyone who has attempted to find his way through Civil War propaganda will know, the short-title method of Wing is frequently too sparse. The admirable and much more comprehensive method of Madan, on the other hand, involves more complexity than can be coped with in typescript. The method here employed, therefore, is an attempt to reach an intermediate level of bibliographical description.

ABBREVIATIONS

1. Information Pertaining to Title Pages

brs.	broadside
n.p.	no place of publication
[s.n.]	*sine nota.* Where [s.n.] alone appears, no place of publication, no publisher or printer and no date of publication are given. Where [s.n.] followed by a year is given, only the year is to be found on the title page.
Barker	a short form of "Robert Barker and the Assignes of John Bill." In some works bearing this imprint occur also the words "Printer to the Kings most Excellent

Majesty." All variants of these notations
are rendered simply as "Barker."[1]

Leonard Lichfield   a short form of all variant imprints used
by Lichfield, the University of Oxford
printer.

2. Bibliographies and Books Regularly Cited

Hist. Reb.   *THE HISTORY OF THE REBELLION AND CIVIL
WARS IN ENGLAND.* Edited by W.D. Macray.
6 vols. Oxford: Clarendon Press, 1888.
(Volumes, not books, are indicated by
lower-case roman numerals, and pages by
arabic numerals.)

Life   *THE LIFE OF EDWARD EARL OF CLARENDON.* 2
vols. Oxford: University Press, MDCCCLVII.
(Volumes, not sections, are indicated by
lower case roman numerals, and pages by
arabic numerals.)

Lister   *LIFE AND ADMINISTRATION OF EDWARD, EARL
OF CLARENDON.* 3 vols. London: Longman,
Orme, Brown, Green, and Longmans, 1838.
(Volumes are indicated by lower-case roman
numerals, pages by arabic numerals.)

Madan   *OXFORD BOOKS: A BIBLIOGRAPHY OF PRINTED
WORKS RELATING TO THE UNIVERSITY AND CITY
OF OXFORD, OR PRINTED OR PUBLISHED THERE.*
3 vols. Oxford: Clarendon Press, 1895–
1931.

Steele   *A BIBLIOGRAPHY OF ROYAL PROCLAMATIONS OF
THE TUDOR AND STUART SOVEREIGNS AND OF
OTHERS PUBLISHED UNDER AUTHORITY 1485–
1714.* 2 vols. (Vol. 1: England and
Wales; Vol. 2: Scotland and Ireland.)

1. In fact, Robert Barker has little to do with these
works. By 1635 he was imprisoned as a debtor in King's
Bench Prison, where he died in 1645. In 1615 he had assigned
his interest in the King's Printing House to, among others,
John Bill. By 1618 he had begun litigation to recover it.
Bill died in 1630, when the imprint became Robert Barker
and the Assignes of John Bill. (See Henry E. Plomer, *A DIC-
TIONARY OF THE BOOKSELLERS AND PRINTERS WHO WERE AT WORK IN
ENGLAND SCOTLAND AND IRELAND FROM 1641-1667.* Bibliographical
Society, 1968 [a reprint of the 1907 first edition].)

New York: Burt Franklin, 1967. This is
a reprint of the Clarendon Press edition
of 1910, sometimes referred to as
*Bibliotheca Lindesiana Vol. V. The Late
Earl of Crawford's Catalogue of Proclamations.*

Thomason

CATALOGUE OF THE PAMPHLETS, BOOKS, NEWS-
PAPERS, AND MANUSCRIPTS RELATING TO THE
CIVIL WAR, THE COMMONWEALTH, AND
RESTORATION, COLLECTED BY GEORGE
THOMASON, 1640-1661. 2 vols. in 4 parts.
[London]: The trustees [of the British
Museum], 1908.

Wing

SHORT-TITLE CATALOGUE OF BOOKS PRINTED IN
ENGLAND, SCOTLAND, IRELAND, WALES, AND
BRITISH AMERICA, AND OF ENGLISH BOOKS
PRINTED IN OTHER COUNTRIES 1641-1700.
3 vols. New York: Columbia University
Press, 1945, 1948, 1951. Vol. 1 is re-
vised and published by the Index Committee
of the Modern Language Association of
America, 1972. (The remainder is in
process of revision.)

1 Mr: HIDES ARGVMENT BEFORE THE LORDS IN THE VPPER HOVSE
of Parliament. Aprill 1641. (12 pp.)

[London]: 1641

Wing C 4419
Thomason E. 157 (14)

    This is of interest as an expression of Clarendon's
legal and oratorical skills in the service of reformist
zeal. Its target is the oppressive power of the Council
of the North, sometimes called the Court of York, which
(along with those of other similar institutions) were seen
as encroaching on the common law privileges of a large
segment of the populations of England and Wales.
    In December, 1640, Hyde had been appointed chairman of
a committee to inquire into grievances against these
courts, and on April 26, 1641, delivered the speech here
recorded. It has relevance to the proceedings against
the Earl of Strafford, who was beheaded the following
month (May 12). Although at this stage a leader of reformist sentiment, Hyde wished proceedings against Strafford
to stop short of a death sentence. (See *Hist. Reb.*, i,

317-21.) In *Life*, i, 72, he candidly pictures himself at
this time: "the greatest chairman in the committee of the
greatest moment."
    Modern scholarship has laid more emphasis on Clarendon's
early reformist sympathies than hitherto, which is supported
by this evidence.

2   [July, 1641]
M^r· EDVVARD HYDES SPEECH AT A Conference betweene both
Houses, on Tewsday the 6th. of July, 1641. At the
Transmission of the severall Impeachments against the Lord
Chiefe Barron Damport, Mr. Barron Trevor, and Mr. Barron
Weston. (12 pp.)

London: for Abel Roper, 1641.

Wing C 4426
Thomason E. 198 (36)

    Davenport, Trevor and Weston, Barons of the Exchequer,
were accused by Hyde of illegally exercising their powers
in (among other matters) the levy of ship-money and tonnage
and poundage. Here, on the side of John Hampden, he insists on the sanctity of common law and, in language
repeatedly echoed in the Civil War tracts, rigid adherence
to the known laws of the land. Continued injustice will
bring about the ravages of war on a "people prepared for
destruction and desolation."
    Lister comments on the quality of his rhetoric: "In
his oratory, argument and irony were the most effective
instruments. The passages that were intended to rise
into eloquence are somewhat forced, fanciful, and pon-
derous, and infected with the bad taste which too much
characterised the forensic oratory of that period" (i,
86-7).
    The speech was reprinted under a much more aggressive
title to point its applicability to mid-eighteenth-
century affairs:

A warning to time-servers, and corrupt administrators of
justice. Being a speech ... at the bar of the Lords house,
on the Commons impeachment of the judges, the 6th of July,
1641.... (22 pp.)

London: S. Slow [1731?]

3 [Dec., 1641]
   HIS MAJESTIES Declaration, To all His loving SUBJECTS:
   Published with the advice of His Privie Councell. (25 pp.)

   London: Barker, 1641

   Wing C 2251
   Thomason E. 131 (1)
   Hist. Reb., i, 493-6

   This edition is by the King's official printer, Robert
Barker, and set in Gothic letter, as is often the case.
There are other editions, including an unauthorized London
one, hastily printed, Cambridge and Edinburgh (Wing C 2249A,
C 2249B, C 2250, C 2252, C 2253).
   This answer to the Grand Remonstrance is perhaps the
most important declaration Hyde composed in the royal name.
The first literary service he performed for Charles I, it
presents in the regal voice Hyde's own reasons for parting
company with the reformist faction: "many excellent Lawes
passed by Us in this Parliament, which in truth (with very
much content to Our Selfe) We conceive to be so large and
ample, that very many sober men have very little left to
wish for."
   The Remonstrance, devised in the King's absence from
London, and presented to him on December 1, had been opposed
by an emergent royalist group in the Commons, where it
passed by the margin of eleven votes. Hyde objected to the
illegality of publishing it. In *Life* he provides a dramatic
retrospective account of his recruitment to the King's
service, and of the circumstances in which he composed
this declaration:

   As soon as the remonstrance ... was printed, Mr.
   Hyde, only to give vent to his own indignation, and
   without the least purpose of communicating it, or that
   any use should be made of it, had drawn such a full
   answer to it, as the subject would have enabled any
   man to have done who had thought of it: and the Lord
   Digby, who had much conversation and friendship with
   him, coming accidentally and suddenly into the room,
   where he was alone among his books and papers; con-
   ferring together of the extravagant proceedings of
   the parliament, he ... read the answer to him which
   he had prepared to the remonstrance; with which he
   seemed much pleased, and desired him, that he would
   permit it to be made use of by the king, and that he
   might shew it to his majesty; who found it absolutely
   necessary to publish some answer in his own name to

that remonstrance, which had so much poisoned the
hearts of the people.

Under protest, and after an unavailing attempt to preserve
his anonymity, Hyde delivered the document requiring a

> promise of secrecy, and, likewise, that his majesty
> would not publish without first communicating it to
> his council, and as done with their advice. And to
> that purpose he affixed that title to it, before he
> delivered the papers out of his hands.... and it was
> very apparent to all men, that the king's service was
> very much advanced by it; and it was not more evident
> to any than to the house of commons, who knew not how
> to make any expostulation upon it, it being in the
> king's own name, and published with the advice of his
> privy-council: so that all they could do was, to en-
> deavour to discover who was the penner of it; to which
> discovery they were most intent by all their secret
> friends in court, who found means to discover most
> other secrets to them, but in this they could do them
> no service. [i, 79-81]

In *Hist. Reb.* he describes the tone of the declaration
as "without the least sharpness or return of that language
which he [the King] had received" (i, 493). Here are
established the fundamental, recurrent elements of the
royalist position: insistence on the known laws, defense
of the Protestant religion (divested of its more provocative Laudian characteristics), and eagerness to protect
the Irish Protestants against Catholic rebels. Failure to
condemn the latter had seriously weakened the King's
credibility.

Lister judges the declaration to be "firm, temperate,
and judicious, retorting without acrimony, condescending
without meanness, and blending conciliation with reproof"
(i, 137).

4 [Jan., 1642]
   The Kings Message to both Houses. January 12. 1641. (brs.)

   London: Barker, 1641 [1642]

   Wing C 2449
   Thomason 669.f.3 (34)
   Steele 1934

   This brief message is rather the product of Hyde's
moderating influence than a certainly identifiable product

of his pen. It seeks to undo the disastrous effects
of the King's attempt on the five members, January 4,
1642, which many scholars regard as an abortive *coup
d'état*. His newly recruited advisers, Falkland, Colepeper and Hyde, were not consulted before the event.
It stresses the King's care of the privileges of
Parliament, which he had so recently breached.

In this edition of the broadside is another message
to similar effect, [5] below

5 His Majesties Profession and Addition to His last Message
to the Parliament. Jan. 14. 1641.

London: Barker, 1641 [1642]

Wing C 2718
Thomason 669.f.3 (34)
Steele 1940

This addition to [4] above is rather better organized,
suggesting a regained nerve. Along with concern for Parliament's privilege goes an admonition that care be taken
for the lawful prerogative, and stress is laid on the
King's care of religion with hopes of a speedy resolution
of the Irish crisis.

6 20. Januarii 1641. His Majesties Letter to both Houses
OF PARLIAMENT. (brs.)

London: for F.C. and T.B., 1641 [1642]

Wing C 2398
Thomason 669.f.3 (35)
Steele 1950
Hist. Reb, i, 529-30

Another edition, [London]: for John Thomas
(Wing C 2399), may be found in the Crawford Collection.

The King seemed to have damaged irreparably the prospect of accommodation with Parliament by his attempt on
the five members. Seeking to recover trust in the King's
motives, Hyde here represents Charles as initiating a
settlement of differences in the disputes on privilege,
prerogative, revenue, liberty of the person, and the
Church. The opening (omitted from *Hist. Reb*.) remarks
with typical irony that it would be usual to expect remedies for evils to proceed from Parliament, but in the

event the King finds that he must propose them to a dila-
tory assembly. In *Hist. Reb.* the strategy of the paper is
declared: "divide those who desired the public peace from
the ministers of confusion" (i, 529).

There are several later editions, suggesting that it
was thought to continue to be the most effective means of
countering Parliament's indignation. It occurs in the
collection of related materials below [7], and is appended
to [8] below.

7 [Feb., 1642]
   HIS MAJESTIES MESSAGE To both Houses of Parliament,
   JANUARY 20. And the Petition of the House of COMMONS,
   Jan. 26. With His Majesties Answer, Jan. 28. Together
   with the Scots Commissioners Propositions for IRELAND,
   And the resolution of both Houses of Parliament therein:
   With His Majesties Answer thereunto. (24 pp.)

   London: Barker, 1641 [1642]

   Wing C 2450
   Thomason E. 133 (3)

   It is also appended to [8] below.

8 [June?, 1642]
   A VINDICATION OF THE KING, WITH Some OBSERVATIONS upon the
   TWO HOVSES: By a true Son of the Church of England, and a
   lover of his Countries Liberty. 1642. (14 pp.)

   [Oxford]: for William Webb, 1642

   Wing V 507
   Madan 1010

   Madan also records a reissue of this pamphlet
   (Madan 1011, Wing V 508), and there is a third version
   collected by Thomason (E. 118 (3)), Wing V 509.
   The author of the "Vindication" is probably not Hyde.

9 [Jan., 1642]
   HIS MAJESTIES LETTER IANVARY the 24th. IN ANSVVER TO THE
   PETITION OF BOTH HOVSES Of Parliament, as it was presented
   by the Earle of New-port, and the Lord Seymer. Ian. 21.
   1641. (brs.)

   London: For Henry Twyford.

Wing C 2389
Thomason 669.f.3 (36)
Steele 1955
Hist. Reb., i, 530

Parliament continued to press the matter of the five
members, requiring the King's proof of the treason
charged against them. This reply, no doubt advised if
not directly penned by Hyde, puts the onus on Parliament
to advise whether the King should proceed by way of
impeachment or by common law. The question, difficult
to resolve, was intended to allow Charles to abandon his
prosecution.
This letter is omitted from the collection of related
matters, [7] above.

10 [Jan., 1642]
The Kings Maiesties Answer to the Petition of the House
of Commons, sent on Saturday last, the nine and twentieth
of this instant January, 1642. (brs.)

London: for Iohn Burroughes, 1642

Wing C 2132
Thomason 669.f.3 (37)
Steele 1966
Hist. Reb., i, 536–7

There are four other editions recorded in Wing:
C 2132A, C 2133, C 2134, and C 2135. Steele notes that
in some the date is given as 28th of January.
The Commons, worried by the more accommodating posture of the Lords, decided to press for control of the
militia, demanding installation in the Tower, and in
other military strong points, officers sympathetic to
their views.
This reply, described in *Hist. Reb.* as "very soft and
dispassioned" (i, 536), is marked by Hyde's adroitness
of expression. The King will deny only those motions
which "would alter the fundamental Laws, and endanger the
very foundations." The Commons "ask more than subjects
ever asked" of a King who has granted more than "ever
King Hath granted." It ends by reminding the Commons of
a previous message, presumably [6] above. This message
is reprinted in [7] above, pp. 9–16.

11   [Feb., 1642]
     TWO PETITIONS Of the Lords and Commons to His Majestie.
     Febr. 2. 1641. With His Majesties gracious Answer : Also
     His Majesties consent for the Princess MARIES going to
     HOLLAND, and Her Majestie to accompany Her. Together
     with Her Majesties Answer to a Message of both Houses.
     (18 pp.)

     London: Barker, MDCXLI [1642]

     Wing E 2429
     Thomason E. 134 (20)
     Hist. Reb., i, 557

         The two petitions concern the question of the militia,
     and that of the five members plus Lord Kimbolton. The
     royal answer to the latter is submissive inasmuch as the
     grounds which the King once thought sufficient he now
     abandons, along with any further thought of prosecution.
     It ends, however, with offer of pardon to any who "happly
     may be involved in some unknowing and unwilling Errors."
         The former matter Hyde admits to be more difficult
     (*Hist. Reb.*, i, 557). He had been dismayed by the attempt
     on the five members, but nevertheless sought legal means
     to excuse the King's action. In the question of the con-
     trol of the militia he believed that any challenge to the
     power of the Crown in this regard was encroachment on the
     just prerogative. In the event he found the King willing
     to concede somewhat (or appear to), the reasons for which
     are to be found in the title of the document: fear for
     the safety of the Queen and the Princess if the petition-
     ers should march to Windsor. Hyde probably penned this
     royal reply, although it seems that he regarded the con-
     cessions involved in what was essentially a delaying
     tactic as being of dubious advantage. The answer to the
     other petition was much more to his taste, and seems,
     although brief, to convey his style.

12   [Feb., 1642]
     His Majesties Message to the House of Commons, February 7.
     1641. (brs.)

     London: Barker, 1641 [1642]

     Wing C 2473
     Thomason 669.f.3 (42)
     Steele 1977
     Hist. Reb., i, 560

Wing records two other editions: C 2474, by Barker, and C 2475 by Iohn Franke. This sharp and amusing broadside signals Hyde's attack on Pym in particular, and the intemperance of parliamentary language in general. He had hoped that the strategy of firm but temperate rebuttals would betray the more radical leaders of reform into a tone of address likely to alienate sympathy. This message notes that Pym had accused the King of providing with passes persons who subsequently appeared in the leadership of the Irish rebellion. But since Pym's speech of accusation had not been previously printed, the King could take no official notice of it for fear of breach of privilege. Now that the speech is in print, it caustically concludes, it must be regarded either as a forgery or the result of misinformation, because the King is certain of having used great discretion in the giving out of passes. Thus the message concludes with a demand that the abuse of royal authority be explained.

The tactic of the paper is to isolate Pym by making him appear a fool or a rogue. It provides also an opportunity to assert the King's concern for Protestantism in Ireland.

13 [Feb., 1642]
    HIS MAJESTIES MESSAGE Concerning Licences granted to persons going into IRELAND. And the ANSVVER of the House of COMMONS. With His Majesties Reply to the House of COMMONS Answer. (14 pp.)

    London: Barker, 1641 [1642]

    Wing C 2430
    Thomason E. 134 (27)
    Hist. Reb., i, 561-2

    The first two pages are a reprint of [12] above.
    The Commons' answer stands by Pym's allegations, adding the names of prominent persons who had obtained licences to proceed to Ireland, and concludes with the suggestion that the King must have evil counsellors near his person who subvert his declared intentions. This answer must have been given on February 10.
    The King's reply shows evidence of Hyde's influence in its opening remarks concerning the King's care not to breach parliamentary privilege, and then offers explanation of the specific instances cited by the Commons. This is essentially to the effect that they received

passes prior to the order of restraint, and that the persons named were well affected to the King's legitimate
service in Ireland. It repeats the demand for a public
apology.
In *Hist. Reb.* the specific names are omitted.

14 [Feb., 1642]
A MESSAGE From both HOUSES of PARLIAMENT unto His
MAJESTIE, Concerning the PRINCE, His SON. With the
ANSVVER of His Majestie thereunto. Together with His
Majesties Answer to the desire of both Houses concerning
the MILITIA. (13 pp.)

London: Barker, 1641 [1642]

Wing E 1654
Thomason E. 136 (3)
Hist. Reb., i, 577

Wing E 1655 is another edition.
Hist. Reb., i, 565-71, is an impassioned but rigorously argued treatment of the circumstances which gave
rise to this remarkable royal *volte face*. Bills for the
removal of bishops from Parliament and for conceding control of the militia had actually received royal assent on
February 14--two weeks before this 'Answer' of the King.
Both actions were vigorously opposed by Hyde, but the
influence of the Queen easily prevailed. In other respects February 14 was disastrous: an intercepted letter
of Lord Digby was used to destroy his and the Queen's
political credibility, and the Commons resolved on impeach-
ing the Attorney General for allegedly advising the attempt
on the five members. Pursuing the advantages so easily
won, the Commons pressed the matter of Ireland. At the
end of the month was published a royal answer (not, it
seems, Hyde's work) which summarizes the series of defeats
which the royal cause suffered that month:

HIS MAIESTIES MOST GRATIOVS ANSWER To the Proposition of
both houses of Parliament, for Ireland sent the Twenty
fourth of February 1642. (brs.)

London: Iohn Franke, MDCXLII

Wing C 2502
Steele 1999

Thomason 669.f.3 (49) is another edition, similar but not
identical to Wing C 2501. Pp. 1-2 of Thomason E. 136 (2)
also reproduce the same material under the title:

CERTAINE REASONS PRESENTED TO THE KINGS MOST EXCELLENT
MAIESTIE, Feb. 24. 1641. by the Lords and Commons in
Parliament touching the Princes stay at Hampton Court
[etc.]

London: R. Olton and G. Dexter, for John Wright, MDCXLII

It is a desperate response, agreeing to everything proposed, and no doubt intended to gain time and secure the
safety of the Prince.
   The Message here in question, [14] above, is different
entirely. It seems to represent a resurrection of Hyde's
influence, and thus a steadying of the King's reactions.
It rejects both the Commons' request that the Prince not
be sent abroad, and the King's capitulation over the issue
of the militia. This is a clever and closely-worded
defense which once again reverts to the matter of the
five members, and proceeds to argue that the Parliament's
ordering of the militia by ordinance encroaches upon the
just rights of the prerogative, and the authority invested
in the City of London and other corporations.
   This edition by the official printer appears to be
the one which Hyde consulted when composing the *Hist. Reb.*
Another edition, containing the same answer to the Parliament's petition, has slight verbal variations and a much
more explicit (and damaging) title:

HIS MAIESTIES LETTER TO THE LORD KEEPER. TOGETHER WITH
His Message to both Houses of Parliament, in answer to
their Petition Concerning the Militia, Feb. 28. 1641.
Declaring the Reasons why his Majestie doth not conceive
himself obliged by any promise formerly made, to yeeld to
the same. (6 pp.)

London: for Iohn Franke, 1642

Wing C 2406
Thomason E. 136 (14)

Hist. Reb. reports that at the publishing of this message
the Commons "were marvellously transported," voting that
those who advised it were "enemies to the State." The
circumstances of Hyde's composition of this answer are
too complex to be summarized here. Lister, i, 163-166,
gives a good account based on *Life*, i, 99-103.

15 [March, 1642]
    THE Message and Resolution. of both Houses of PARLIAMENT,
    Presented to the KINGS Majestie at Theobalds, March 1.
    1641. WITH HIS MAJESTIES ANSWER to the Message and Reso-
    lution of both Houses of Parliament, March 2. 1641.
    Whereunto is added the Petition of divers CITIZENS of
    London, concerning the Militia of the City. (6 pp.)

    London: by T.F. for J. Thomas, 1641 [1642]

    Wing E 1647
    Thomason E. 136 (5)
    Hist. Reb., i, 580-81

        At Theobalds the committee of both Houses presented a
    petition which reiterates in forceful language the demand
    that the King with the Prince return to Whitehall. It
    rejects his reply, [14] above, on the militia. The King's
    brief (2 pp.) reply looks on the face of it like an unre-
    hearsed verbal response rather than a prepared document.
    The circumstances of this reply revealed in *Life* are
    interesting and warrant its being regarded as Hyde's work.
    Hyde was in the House when the proposed message was framed:
    "that the king might not be surprised with the sight of
    the message before he heard of it, he [Hyde] sent instantly
    to the lord Grandison (in whom he had entire confidence)
    to speak with him.... He writ to the king, that such per-
    sons would be presently with him, and the substance of the
    message they would bring to him; which in respect of the
    length of it, and of many particulars in it, would require
    some time to answer, which he should receive soon enough;
    and for the present, he might upon the delivery make some
    short resentment of the houses' proceeding with him; and
    conclude, that he would send an answer to their message
    in due time" (i, 104).

16 [March, 1642]
    His Majesties Speech to the Committee, the 9th of March,
    1641. when they presented the Declaration of both Houses
    of Parliament at New-market. (brs.)

    London: Barker, 1641 [1642]

    Wing C 2801
    Thomason 669.f.3 (53)
    Steele 2017
    Hist. Reb., i, 589

The new declaration to which this is an answer is
given in *Hist. Reb.*, i, 582-86, and an account of the
debate on it follows. As in [15] above, the King's answer
is sharp, citing as grievances Pym's speech (see [12]
above) and the proliferation of seditious pamphlets and
sermons which has gone unchecked by Parliament. Clearly
the King was troubled by direct confrontations with the
representatives of Parliament, preferring to have his
replies prepared in advance by Hyde. He therefore urges
Parliament to proceed in future according to the method
outlined in his reply of January 20, [6] above. The
King's reply also promises a full answer, [17] below, in
his own time. No doubt the difficulty of communication
with Hyde (see commentary on [15] above) made the King
reluctant to deal face to face with committees. On this
occasion he seems to have lost some of his composure.
Another edition of the same reply under a different title
concludes with the damaging editorial comment, "After hee
had consummated his Speech in a satisfactory period, he
seemed to be respectively discontented, notwithstanding
in his Majesties due pleasure, season, and time, hee will
returne a correspondent Answer to their Declaration without any dubious suspitition." In:

16A THE KINGS MAIESTIES ANSWER TO THE DECLARATION OF THE
LORDS AND COMMONS in PARLIAMENT. With a Gracious Answer
to the French Kings Royal Letter. Mar. 10. 1641.

[London]: for Roger Garthwaite, 1641 [1642]

Wing C 2117

17   [March, 1642]
HUNTINGTON 15° Martii, 1641. His Majesties Message to
both Houses of Parliament, upon His removall to the City
of York. (brs.)

London: Barker, 1641 [1642]

Wing--unrecorded; it is another edition of C 2467.
Steele 2030
Hist. Reb., i, 591-2

Thomason 669.f.3 (55) is another edition by Barker
(Wing C 2467).
Though no doubt composed by Hyde, this was issued
officially from Huntington on the King's northward journey.
It requires the King's subjects to withhold obedience to
ordinances and orders of Parliament which lack the royal

assent. The intention is to frustrate Parliament's attempt
to legitimize its effective control over the militia, the
details of which were being settled in the Commons on the
15th.

Suspecting that the King's replies were being framed
in London, the Commons resolved on the 16th that whoever
advised this message was an enemy of the kingdom.

18   [March, 1642]
     By the King. A Proclamation for putting the Laws against
     Popish Recusants in due execution.   (brs.)

     [York]: Barker, 1641 [1642]

     Wing C 2593
     Steele 2039

          There is no specific indication of this being Hyde's
     work. In *Hist. Reb.* he does not quote it, but some of
     the language of the proclamation is echoed in his brief
     reference to it (i, 595). It is possible that Hyde,
     Colepeper, and Falkland advised this attempt to minimize
     the damaging allegation that there was an internationally
     supported Papist plot, encouraged by the Queen, which is
     found in the Parliament declaration of March 9, to which
     [16] above is an answer.

          It was thought sufficiently important to reprint in
     August, 1642, in

18A TWO PROCLAMATIONS By the KING. The first declaring His
     Majesties expresse Command, That no Popish Recusant, nor
     any other, who shall refuse to take the two Oathes of
     Allegiance and supreamacy, shall serve Him in His Army
     [....] The second, for putting the Lawes against Popish
     Recusants in due execution. (5 pp.)

     [London]: reprinted for Iohn Thomas, 1642

     Wing C 2858
     Thomason E. 112 (22)

19   [March, 1642]
     HIS MAJESTIES DECLARATION To both HOUSES of Parliament;
     (Which He likewise recommends to the consideration of all
     His loving Subjects) In Answer to That presented to Him
     at New-market the 9th of March 1641.   (18 pp.)

London: Barker, 1641 [1642]

Wing C 2268
Thomason E. 140 (26)
Hist. Reb., ii, 1-6

There are numerous editions, including official ones
by Barker at York (Wing C 2266, which gives the date as
"Martii 21," Wing C 2267; six editions probably in London:
Wing C 2269, C 2270, C 2270A, C 2271, C 2272, C 2272A;
and an Edinburgh edition, Wing C 2273).

This is a major statement of the royal position at a
crucial juncture, and clearly the work of Hyde. It is a
complete answer to the Parliament declaration of March 9
(to which [16] above is the first response), an answer
which the Parliament had long expected. Opening remarks
refer to the time-lapse between the March 9 document and
this reply, arguing that a much longer period might reasonably have been expected in which to reply to an address
in such indecorous language.

It proceeds in confident manner to answer each alleged
grievance of the preceding several months, stressing the
extent to which the King had consented to acts of Parliament intended to remedy real problems.

In this declaration Hyde's sense of the importance of
a style to contrast with that of parliamentary manifestos
is abundantly clear. In *Hist. Reb.* he justifies his tone
in the following words:

They who now read this Declaration, and remember
only the insolent and undutiful expressions in that
Declaration to which this was an answer, and the more
insolent and seditious actions which preceded, accompanied and attended it, may think that the style was
not answerable to the provocation, nor princely enough
for such a contest.... But they, again, who consider
and remember that conjuncture of time, the incredible
disadvantage his majesty suffered by the misunderstanding of his going to the House of Commons ... I
say, whoever remembers this, and that, though it might
be presumed that the exorbitancy of the Parliament
might be very offensive to some sober and discerning
men, yet his majesty had no reason to presume of their
eminent and vehement zeal in his behalf, since he saw
all those (two or three only excepted) from whom he
might challenge the duty and faith of servants *usque
ad aras*, and for whose sake he had undergone many
difficulties, either totally alienated from his

service and engaged against him, or, like men in a
trance, unapplicable to it; he will conclude that it
concerned his majesty by all gentleness and condescen-
sion to undeceive and recover men to their sobriety
and understanding before he could hope to make them
apprehensive of their own duty or the reverence that
was due to him; and therefore, that he was to descend
to all possible arts and means to that purpose, it
being very evident that men would no sooner discern
his princely justice and clemency than they must be
sensible of the indignities which were offered to him,
and incensed against those who were the authors of
them. [ii, 6-7]

20 [March, 1642]
His Majesties Answer To the Petition of both Houses of
PARLIAMENT, Presented to Him at York on Saturday the 26
of March, 1642. by the Lord Willoughby, Lord Dungarvan,
and Sir Anthony Irby.

This is pp. 7-15 of:

THE PETITION OF Both Houses of Parliament, Presented to
His MAJESTIE at York, March 26. 1642. With His Majesties
Answer thereunto. And the Petition of the Noblemen and
Gentlemen estated in Ireland, and now in London. And
likewise the Petition of the Countie of LINCOLN, With His
Majesties severall and respective Answers thereunto.
(22 pp.)

London: Barker, MDCXLII

Wing E 2164
Thomason E. 141 (23)
Hist. Reb, ii, 10-12

   According to Hyde's reconstruction of events, Parliament chose to send a new petition on March 22 in answer
to the King's sharp, unprepared reply of March 9 ([16]
above) before they should receive a fuller statement ([19]
above) which might "answer, and so prevent, some other
scandals they had a mind to lay to his majesty's charge"
(*Hist. Reb.*, ii, 7). This is the answer to that new petition, presented "immediately" and returned to Parliament
by the same messengers.
   It is undoubtedly Hyde's work, characterized by
scathing irony in its opening salvo:

> If you would have the patience to have expected Our
> Answer to your last Declaration (which, considering
> the nature of it hath not been long in coming) We
> beleeve you would have saved your selves the labour
> of saying much of this Message

It continues with pointed remarks on the language of such
petitions and on the degree of their encroachment on
royal prerogative:

> you will reduce all Our Answers hereafter into a very
> little room; In plain English, It is to take away
> the Freedome of Our Vote, which were We but a Subject,
> were High Injustice; but being your King, We leave
> all the world to judge what it is.

Objections to seditious sermons and pamphlets, three
of which are cited, further emphasize Hyde's concern with
the superior effectiveness as propaganda of a reasonable
(although sharp and witty) style in contrast with the
language of parliamentary edicts. Hyde liked (as in this
instance) to print Parliament documents and the replies
to them side by side to provoke comparison, such was his
confidence in the effectiveness of his work. In *Hist.
Reb*. he estimates the value of these "paper skirmishes,"
thinking them likely to persuade people "that the King
was in the right" (ii, 13).

21 [March, 1642]
    At the Court at York. 28. Martii. 1642 (brs.)

    York: Barker, 1642

    Wing C 2150
    Steele 2063

    Although signed by Secretary Edward Nicholas, this
brief answer to the Lincoln petitioners clearly derives
from the answer to the Parliament petition of March 26
([20] above) to which it refers the petitioners, as well
as to the answer to the declaration presented to the King
at Newmarket ([19] above). It suggests that the petitioners "may find reason to petition the Parliament to
comply with his Majesties just Desires, and gracious
Offers."
    It is identical with *THE PETITION OF Both Houses of
Parliament*, etc. ([20] above), pp. 18-19 and 21-22.

NOTE: Hyde's judgment of the success of the King's pamphlet
   campaign at this time is given in *Hist. Reb.* Considerable
   attention was now being given to the dissemination of royalist documents, and their effect began to redress the balance
   of sympathy in favor of the King, partly as a result of in-
   sisting that the will to resist Parliament was founded on
   the law rather than on the arbitrary exercise of royal power.
   "The King's Declarations, which were now carefully published,
   gave them some trouble, and made great impression in sober
   men who were moved with the reason, and in rich men who were
   startled at the commands in them" (ii, 23).

22   [April, 1642]
   HIS MAJESTIES MESSAGE Sent to the PARLIAMENT, April 8. 1642.
   Concerning His Resolution to go into Ireland for suppress-
   ing the Rebells there.   (6 pp.)

   London: Barker, 1642

   Wing C 2447
   Thomason E. 143 (4)
   Hist. Reb., ii, 33-34

      There are other editions--including one by Barker at
   York, which gives "Rebellion" for "Rebells," Wing C 2444--
   which suggest the marketable value of this surprise move:
   Wing C 2445, C 2446, C 2448, C 2448A, and C 2448B.
      This message proposes two interesting royal initia-
   tives. The first is the King's intention to lead in person an army, to be armed and equipped from the military
   stores in the magazine of Hull, against the Irish rebels
   now popularly known as the Queen's army. The second is a
   promise that his Attorney will present a bill to Parliament to settle the militia.
      In *Hist. Reb.* Hyde states that Parliament "neither
   before nor after ever received any message from his
   majesty that more discomposed them" (ii, 34). It had the
   effect of forcing the parliamentary leaders into maintain-
   ing rhetorical fictions in their declarations, unable to
   express their real fears about the King's intentions.
   Parliamentary actions, however, such as refusing the King
   access to Hull were eloquent of genuine apprehensions.
   In the rhetoric of debate it was necessary to maintain
   that such obstructions were done in the royal service.
   Hyde exploited this weakness in Parliament's position, no
   longer in the hope of persuading members, but in appeal
   to a suspicious and uncommitted public. Hyde also remarks
   that Parliament secretly feared that if the King's

proposal took effect Ireland could no longer continue "a
nursery for soldiers of their own" (*Hist. Reb.*, ii, 35).
Nevertheless, he did not approve of either of these
tactics, and implies that he was one who strongly opposed
this course (*Hist. Reb.*, ii, 42).

23   [April, 1642]
The humble PETITION OF The Lords and Commons in PARLIAMENT,
Sent to His MAJESTIE at YORK. Concerning the Removall of
His Majesties Arms, Cannon, and Ammunition, in His Magazin
at Hull. And the taking off the Reprive of six con-
demned Priests, prisoners in Newgate. With His Majesties
Answer thereunto. 14. April. 1642. (10 pp.)

York: Barker, 1642

Wing E 1582
Thomason E. 144 (11)
Hist. Reb., ii, 30-32

The London edition by Barker is Wing E 1583 (Thomason
E. 143 (15)). Other later editions are Wing E 1582A of
June 21, E 1583A.
The Parliament petition, sent the day after the King's
message [22] above, also uses the argument of Ireland as
its reason for wishing to appropriate the magazine. The
question of the six priests is cleverly introduced to keep
alight suspicions of the King's covert love of Popery.
Hyde's reply is a detailed exposé of false logic in the
petition, and in its turn it charges Parliament with dissimulation in sending "this Message out of Compliment and
Ceremony, resolving to be your own Carvers at last." The
final stage of his answer develops the concept of law as
arbiter of good and evil, illustrated by quotation from a
speech made in Parliament on the topic: "'Twas well said
in a speech made by a private person, but published by
Order of the House of Commons this Parliament: [section
of speech quoted] So said that Gentleman, and much more,
very well in defence of the Law, and against Arbitrary
power." A marginal gloss identifies "Pym's speech against
the Earle of Strafford." Hyde's irony is elsewhere evident, as in his supposing that Parliament finds the execution of the six priests "so very necessary to the great
and Pious work of Reformation."
It is likely that Hyde consulted a copy of this York
edition when composing *Hist. Reb.* The London edition by
Barker reads "complimentall Ceremony" rather than "Compliment and Ceremony," which is the reading of the MS of
Hist. Reb.

24 [April, 1642]
    THE PETITION OF The LORDS and COMMONS, PRESENTED To His
    Majestie By the Earle of Stamford, Master Chancellour of
    the Exchequer, and Master Hungerford, April 18. 1642. To-
    gether with His MAJESTIES Answer thereunto. (14 pp.)

    London: Barker, 1642

    Wing E 2179
    Thomason E. 144 (19)
    Hist. Reb., ii, 38-41

        Wing records three other editions under this title:
    E 2179A, 2179B, and 2179C. The same pamphlet was printed
    by Barker in York under a somewhat different title, pre-
    sumably at just about the same time:

24A The humble PETITION Of the Lords and Commons assembled in
    PARLIAMENT, Presented to His MAJESTIE at YORK, 18. April.
    Concerning His Message lately sent unto them, touching
    His Resolution of going into Ireland. VVith His Majesties
    Answer thereunto. (25 pp.)

    York: Barker, 1642

    Wing E 1577

        Another edition was the reprint by Lichfield, the
    official Oxford printer, in June: Wing E 1578, Madan 1009.
        The Parliament's petition replies to [22] above.
    Although the King's answer contains an agreement to post-
    pone his Irish expedition, its tone is not one of capitu-
    lation to parliamentary demands. Rather it opens on a
    note of exasperation, wondering whether anything the King
    could say or do would be free of misunderstanding, and
    then, gradually coming to specific objections, point by
    point, establishes a tone of superior patience and fore-
    bearance, being unwilling to "be tempted, (in a just
    indignation,) to express a greater passion than he was
    yet willing to put on." Hyde admits that the King has
    been threatened out of this (ill-advised) venture (*Hist.
    Reb.*, ii, 42).

25 [April, 1642]
    HIS MAJESTIES Message TO Both Houses of Parliament,
    April 28. 1642. Concerning his Refusall to passe the
    Bill for the Militia. (5 pp.)

    London: Barker, 1642

Wing C 2453
Thomason E. 145 (13)

Wing C 2453A is another, London, edition. Some copies
of the Barker, London, edition (not Thomason's) use Roman
numerals: MDCXLII. Wing C 2454 is the York edition by
Barker, in which the title is somewhat different.

Hyde regretted the King's proposal for the settling
of the militia ([22] above), which was sent to Parliament
April 8. It was considerably altered and returned to the
King, April 28, for his assent. This message is once
again an instance of Hyde's having to make the best of a
bad job: "Though no sober man could deny the reasonable-
ness of that answer ... yet it had been better for his
majesty that that overture had never been made" (*Hist.
Reb.*, ii, 45).

The argument for rejecting the amended bill is that
the amendments are so extensive that they wholly distort
the original purpose. It is conducted soberly enough,
with insistence on the King's right to order the militia
and warnings of what might happen if such powers were to
be legally invested in particular people by the example
of Sir John Hotham at Hull who, even in the absence of
legal authority, conducted himself with "high Insolency."
There are flashes of Hyde's characteristic sarcasm as when
he hopes that "this Animadversion will be no breach of
your Priviledges in this throng of Businesse."

26   [April, 1642]
His Majesties second Message to the Parliament,
concerning Sir Iohn Hothams Refusall to give His MAJESTIE
Entrance into His Town of HULL.   (brs.)

London: Barker, 1642

Wing C 2769
Thomason 669.f.5 (10)
Steele 2096
Hist. Reb., ii, 51

The King's humiliation before Hull occasioned two
messages. The first, of April 24, is a flustered, indignant
statement, little more than a bald recital of events with
no sense of the larger issues and principles at stake.
It was sent by express to Parliament. The second one,
which is the title above, of April 28, looks like an
attempt by Hyde once again to retrieve that which hasty
and aggressive royal actions had lost. Its tone is still

firm enough, deploring the indignity caused the King by
Hotham's actions, and requiring a prompt and satisfactory
answer. It offers Parliament a means of avoiding confrontation without losing face by expressing confidence that
Parliament put a garrison into Hull against an attempt by
Papists, not against the lawful requirements of the King.
His purpose is to recover by law his just privileges, and
he has no other end in view than defense of the Protestant
religion, the law of the land and the liberty of the
subject.

   This message betokens a small victory Hyde won over
those who advised military confrontation. *Hist. Reb.*
blandly records that instead of an assault on Hull, the
King chose to send this, a second message, "for many
reasons" (ii, 51).

27 [May, 1642]
    HIS MAIESTIES ANSWER To the DECLARATION OF BOTH HOVSES
    Concerning Hull. Sent 4. May 1642. With his Majesties
    Expresse Warrant to the High Sheriffe of the County of
    Yorke concerning the proceedings of Sir John Hotham in
    Hull. (7 pp.)

    London: for S.E., 1642

    Wing C 2112
    Hist. Reb., ii, 52-56

    Instead of a reply to [26] above, Parliament immedi-
ately published a declaration which widened the scope of
the issue with reference to what it conceived to be new
aggravations, such as the intercepted letter of Lord
Digby.

   This answer, touching on each of the new grievances,
is typical of Hyde's work. Particularly interesting are
quotations from Pym's speech against Strafford which
stress the law as a safeguard of liberty. The second of
these quotations, particularly apposite in the circumstances, is used to conclude the answer: "If the Prerogative of the King overwhelm the Liberty of the People, it
will be turn'd to Tyranny; if Liberty undermine the Prerogative, it will grow into Anarchy, And so We say, Into
Confusion." The final clause is omitted from the *Hist.
Reb.* report.

28   [May, 1642]
     THE ANSWER OF Both Houses of Parliament, Presented to His
     Majestie at YORK the ninth of May, 1642. To two Messages
     sent to them from His Majestie, concerning Sir Iohn
     Hothams Refusall to give His Majestie Entrance into His
     Town of HULL. WITH His Majesties REPLY thereunto.
     (5 pp.)

     London: Barker, 1642

     Wing E 1219
     Thomason E. 147 (5)
     Hist. Reb., ii, 57-8

          There is another official edition by Barker at York,
     Wing E 1219A, and a third, probably London, "for I.T.,"
     Wing E 1219B. The title of Thomason's copy differs
     slightly from that given above ("PARLIAMENT"; "Hull";
     "MDCXLII") although it appears to be the same edition.
          The parliamentary answer, delivered by a small com-
     mittee instructed to remain at York, is described in *Hist.
     Reb.* as "being in a mould unusual, and a dialect higher
     and rougher than even themselves had yet used." The
     reply presses the illegality of Parliament's assuming
     authority without the King's consent, and declaring Sir
     John Hotham guiltless without reference to the opinions
     of the judges. It threatens that those who obey parlia-
     mentary ordinances on the militia put themselves in
     danger of being called to make legal account.

29   [May, 1642]
     His Majesties ANSWER, BY VVAY OF DECLARATION To a PRINTED
     PAPER, ENTITULED, A Declaration of both Houses of Parlia-
     ment, in Answer to His Majesties last Message concerning
     the Militia. (11 pp.)

     London: Barker, 1642

     Wing C 2090
     Thomason E. 148 (13)
     Hist. Reb., ii, 64-9

          The answer appears to have been printed and published
     May 23 in an edition lacking the printer's name
     (Wing C 2089) and in two editions simultaneously at York
     (Wing C 2090A) and London by the official printer.
          It marks a further deterioration in relationships.
     The Parliament declaration which it answers was published
     May 5 or 6, but was not sent to the King. Hyde represents

the King as anxious to "apply some antidote to this
poison," but troubled by the problem of taking notice of
it without breaching parliamentary privilege (*Hist. Reb.*,
ii, 64). These declarations are described as "infallible
symptoms of sharper actions" (ibid., ii, 69) and Hyde
complains (here and elsewhere) of the wide dissemination
of parliamentary manifestos and the suppression of those
of the King--a complaint which seems to have some substance, and reflects the inconvenience to the King of
having lost the use of London. He also remarks that the
King desired that his and Parliament's manifestos should
be published side by side. In fact that practice had already commenced (see commentary on [20] above). That the
"paper skirmishes" now constituted propaganda warfare,
that is, appealed to an otherwise wary and neutral populace whose response might ultimately determine the outcome, is recognized by Hyde in *Hist. Reb.*, ii, 69. For
an appraisal of Hyde's contribution to making possible
the option of warfare for the royalist party (although
this was not Hyde's intention), see B.H.G. Wormald,
Clarendon, Politics, History, and Rebellion [359].

This answer, therefore, marks an important stage in
the slide towards civil war. The opening dwells on the
necessity of the King's indulging to a greater degree
than any monarch hitherto in the arts of printed persuasion.

30   [May, 1642]
     HIS MAJESTIES ANSWER TO THE PETITION AND Three VOTES of
     Parliament, Presented to Him at York May 23. 1642.
     Concerning the disbanding of His MAJESTIES Guard.   (6 pp.)

     London: Barker, MDCXLII

     Wing C 2128
     Thomason E. 149 (7)
     Hist. Reb., ii, 78-80

     There are other editions of this title by a variety
of London printers: Wing C 2129, C 2130, C 2131, C2131A,
C 2131B. This edition, issued both in London and York by
the official printer, carries the rubric "Published together by His Majesties Command" in pursuance of the
policy of publishing Parliament's and the King's manifestos
side by side for comparison (see commentary on [29] above).
The same materials appear also in:

30A THE PETITION Of both Houses of Parliament. Presented to
His Majesty at YORK, the 23 of May 1642. Concerning the
disbanding of His Guard. With the three Votes of both
Houses of the 20. And His Majesties Answer thereunto.

London: reprinted for Richard Lownes, 1642

Wing E 2167

Also Wing E 2165 (the York edition by Barker) and
E 2166, a London reprint for Edward Husbands.
The King's raising of a troop of horse and a regiment
of train-band infantry (600 according to Hyde) is construed as making war against Parliament. The three votes
condemn this development, and the petition requests its
reversal. In his answer Hyde turns to good effect the
Parliament's deployment of military power: the King has
not claimed that "all those Pikes and Protestations, that
Army on one side, and the Navie on the other" constitute
war levied on him. It goes on to argue the need of protection against Sir John Hotham's menaces, and the in-
validity of statutes cited in the third of the votes.
Typically, the final section expands the scope of the
answer to include complaints against seditious literature, and the strain Parliament has been imposing on the
proper constitutional balance of King and Parliament which
will see "this well founded Monarchy be turned to a
Democracy."

31   [May, 1642]
His Majesties ANSWER TO A BOOK, ENTITULED, The Declaration,
or Remonstrance of the LORDS and COMMONS, of the 19th of
May, 1642. (30 pp.)

London: Barker, 1642

Wing C 2092
Thomason E. 150 (29)
Hist. Reb., ii, 135-149

There is an official York edition by Barker,
Wing C 2093; one by the Cambridge University Printer,
R. Daniel, Wing C 2096; two London reprints, Wing C 2094
and C 2095.
This is as full an answer, point by point, to the
Remonstrance as that is a compendious recapitulation of
all grievances since the beginning of the current Parliament. The argument of the Remonstrance is of particular
interest in illustrating the refinement of tactics in the
"paper skirmishes." Some of Hyde's methods are answered

in their own kind, and some of his characteristic arguments turned upon the King's position. There are complaints against the language of the royal declarations
and answers, against the use and abuse of the press opera-
ting in York, and against the dissemination of royalist
propaganda, and aspersions are cast on the legal expertise
of the penner of the royal documents. It seems that Parliament considered the attempt on the five members and
Lord Kimbolton as its single most effective complaint: it
is mentioned no fewer than four times in this remonstrance.
Hyde's answer, longer even than the Remonstrance, opens
in a tone of mock exasperation: the King might as well
cease from the labors of his pen and leave it to God to
enlighten the understanding of his subjects, but that he
is unwearied in taking pains on behalf of his people. It
concludes by remarking that although the language of his
answers is sharper than would be his habit, yet in consideration of the provocation, he would be more reasonably suspected of too much mildness. His response in the
five members debacle is intended to disarm the force of
Parliament's repeated criticism by allowing that it "in
truth was an errour (Our going to the House of Commons),"
and then providing a low-keyed explanation of his intentions.

32   [May, 1642]
     His Majesties ANSWER To a Printed Book, ENTITULED, A
     Remonstrance, or, The Declaration of the LORDS and COMMONS
     now assembled in Parliament, May 26. 1642. In Answer to
     a Declaration under His Majesties Name, concerning the
     businesse of HULL.   (30 pp.)

     London: Barker, 1642

     Wing C 2103
     Thomason E. 150 (20)
     Hist. Reb., ii, 149-164

         Wing records six further editions: C 2103A, C 2104,
     C 2105, C 2106, C 2107, and C 2108. The latter, an Oxford
     reprint, probably from the York original, is dated by
     Madan, 1006, as "about June 25."
         It is interesting that this answer was thought impor-
     tant enough to merit a Latin translation, indicative,
     perhaps, of growing European interest in the causes of
     the crisis:

32A RESPONSVM SVAE MAIESTATIS Ad Librum editum, inscriptum, REMONSTRANTIA aut DECLARATIO Dominorum & Communium nunc congregatorum in Parlamento. XXVI Maij 1642. (44 pp.)

Eboraci: Robertvm Barkervm [etc.]

A Declaration and Profession of the King along with one by the Lords of his Council are appended. (See also [33] below.)

This answer was prepared "with all imaginable haste" (*Hist. Reb.*, ii, 164), and appeared some few days after June 3, the date on which the King received the *Nineteen Propositions*,[1] to which the answer refers in passing. The matter in contention is that of the Militia, on which topic the Remonstrance of May 26 cites and interprets several statutes, especially the preamble to a statute of 25 Edw. III. Hyde objects to the parliamentary interpretation of "consuetudines ... quas vulgas elegerit" in the following manner: "for, unlesse they have a power of declaring Latine, as well as Law, sure Elegerit signifieth Hath chosen, as well as Will chuse." The crux of the matter is that Parliament insists that the King's duty, sworn on oath, is to assent to such good laws as the people shall choose; whereas Hyde, stressing the continuity of custom, argues that the royal oath is to maintain the existing laws, in which the "Authority of the perpetuall practice of all succeeding Ages" is a better guide than present votes in Parliament, which are concocted to suit the exigencies of the situation. The legal argument is, of course, arcane, and of limited value as propaganda --a recognition Hyde turns to advantage in remarking that they attempt to use a Latin document which many subjects (and indeed many members of Parliament) could not understand. He then quotes the English-language coronation oath, which unequivocally supports the view.

The main point of the Answer, however, lies not in legal legerdemain, but in miniature rehearsal of the central argument of *Hist. Reb.*: namely, that a "faction of Malignant, Schismaticall, and Ambitious Persons" intends to "alter the whole frame of Government both of Church and State, and to subject both King and People to their own Lawlesse Arbitrary power and Government." This analysis is pursued with great energy and acerbity in several

1. The answer to the Nineteen Propositions, which was received in the Lords June 21, was the work of Falkland--the only significant royal document not by Hyde at this time.

different ways. One of the more interesting is a brief
rendition of Hooker's description of the rise of Anabaptism in Germany, which concludes with "This Story is worth
the reading at large, and needs no Application."

The Answer supposes that those in Parliament who have
come to recognize the deceptions practiced would not be-
have accordingly, while for the others, the King "shall
now expect the worst Actions these Men have power to
commit against Us: (Worse words they cannot give Us)."

33 [June, 1642]
His MAJESTIES DECLARATION To all His loving SUBJECTS,
Occasioned by a false and scandalous Imputation laid upon
His Majestie, of an Intention of Raising or Leavying War
against His Parliament, and of having raised Force to
that end. ALSO, His Majesties Declaration and Profession,
together with that of the Lords and others of His Councell
there present, disavowing any Preparations or Intentions
of Leavying War against His two Houses of Parliament.
(13 pp.)

London: Barker, MDCXLII

Wing C 2237
Thomason E. 151 (27)
Hist. Reb., ii, 186-190

The layout of the title page is altered slightly for
different issues of this edition. The declaration was
made June 16 and the first edition is by Barker at York
(Wing C 2238). There are two other London editions,
Wing C 2239 and C 2240, a Cambridge edition C 2238A and
an Oxford reprint which includes a proclamation of June 18
under the title *HIS MAIESTIES PROCLAMATION AND DECLARATION*
[etc.], Wing C 2548, Madan 1008. The second part, the
Declaration and Profession, together with that of ... *His
Councell* [etc.] also appears in [32A] above, there dated
June 15.

The *Nineteen Propositions* signalled an important
shift in parliamentary tactics. In effect, Parliament
abandons the paper controversy, which had clearly
assumed the character of an appeal for popularity, because
Hyde and associates had gained the advantage. Parliament
now begins to present in a bare form calculatedly unaccept-
able demands in order to bring the crisis to a head as
swiftly as possible. Further postponement of the appeal
to arms would be likely to work to the King's advantage.
On June 10 Parliament published orders for the collection

of money and plate to raise forces ostensibly in defense of King and Parliament against the malignant party which was said to be "ready to commit all manner of outrage and violence."

It is, then, in this context that the royal declaration also proposes to raise money and plate at interest on the security of the royal demesnes. The argument, written in caustic tone, is intended to reveal that Parliament is controlled by a ruthless and seditious faction who

> assume to themselves (meerly upon the Authority of the name of Parliament) a Power monstrous to all understandings, and to do Actions, and to make Orders Evidently and Demonstrably contrary to all Known Law and Reason, (As to take up Arms against Us under colour of defending Us; To cause Money to be brought in to them, and to forbid Our own Money to be paid to Us, or to Our use, under colour that We will imploy it to ill; To beat Us, and sterve Us for Our own good, and by Our own Power and Authority) which must in short time make the greatest Court, and greatest Person cheap, and of no Estimation.

The opening represents the King as not surprised that his opponents "having spent all their Stock of bitter and reproachful Language ... should now break out into some bold and disloyal Action against Us." This is an important tract in the attempt to make the King's military preparations seem strictly self-defense.

34   [June, 1642]
His Majesties ANSWER TO THE PETITION OF The LORDS and COMMONS in PARLIAMENT assembled: Presented to His MAJESTIE at YORK, June 17. 1642.   (14 pp.)

London: Barker, 1642

Wing C 2137
Thomason E. 152 (2)
Hist. Reb., ii, 200-205 n.   This is in the MS History,
   but omitted from the final *History*.

The title of the Thomason copy is capitalized differently from the above title (Crawford Collection copy): "HIS MAJESTIES" and "Majestie." Wing C 2136 is the York edition by Barker, and there are two reprints, Wing C 2137A and C 2173B. Although it is not mentioned in the title, the petition of June 15 is printed, pp. 1-3. Madan 1009 is an Oxford reprint by Lichfield.

The King's alleged refusal to accept a petition of
the gentlemen and freeholders of Yorkshire is the cause
of a petition of the Lords and Commons, principally com-
plaining of discontented persons, recusants, cavaliers
and others who, having "little Interest or Affection to
the publike good" congregate at York, "to the great
terrour and amazement of Your Majesties peaceable Subjects." They urge the King to take counsel of his Parliament, and warn against any action tending to its dissolution.

Hyde's strongly worded answer is skeptical of the
Yorkshire petition, believing it "framed and contrived
(as many others of such nature have been) in London, not
in Yorkshire," and that it was far from being a popular
protest, but rather "solicited by a few, mean, inconsiderable persons" and offered June 3 by Sir Thomas Fairfax, a
lone malcontent among "the greatest, and the most cheerful
concourse of people that ever was beheld of one County."
Each point of the Parliament petition is answered at
length in a manner which stresses the King's single-minded
adherence to the law and, by contrast, dissimulation,
intimidation and lawlessness of the petitioners. They
are made to appear innovators by contrasting their actions
and language to the "innocency of former times." Thus
Hyde condemns a newly-coined phrase, "Enemies to the
Common-wealth," and interestingly remarks on the use of
"Cavaliers"--"a word, by what mistake soever it seems,
much in disfavour." This word enters the arena in Parliament's orders for money and plate of June 10, to signify
men without respect for God, the law, religion, liberty,
property, or Parliament.

35   [June, 1642]
     His Majesties ANSWER To a printed Paper, intituled, A
     new Declaration of the Lords and Commons in Parliament,
     of the 21. of June, 1642. In Answer to His Majesties
     Letter dated the fourteenth of June, and sent to the Lord
     Major, Aldermen, and Sheriffs of the City of London. (8 pp.)

     York: Barker, 1642

     Wing C 2109
     Hist. Reb., ii, 207-209 (shortened version)

     This answer also appears under the title:

35A HIS MAJESTIES DECLARATION CONCERNING LEAVIES. (13 pp.)

     London: Barker, MDCXLII

Wing C 2190
Thomason E. 153 (24)

There are three reprints, Wing C 2191, C 2192, and
C 2193. The latter is the work of Lichfield at Oxford
(Madan 1012).

The King's letter, mentioned in the title of [35],
warned City officials not to lend money, plate, or horses
to Parliament, and the Parliament's response, a declaration to the City, to which this is an answer, argues that
defense of Parliament is necessary to protect the charter
of the City, and the lives and property of its citizens.

In *Hist. Reb.* Hyde remarks, "These paper-skirmishes
left neither side better inclined to the other; but, by
sharpening each other, drew the matter nearer to an issue"
(ii, 206). The sharpness is especially evident in the
opening sentences which emphasize the arbitrary power of
those who "think such Declarations and Votes to be such
unresistable Engines of Batterie against Us and the Law."
It is a wonder "that since they have usurped the Supream
Power to themselves, they have not taken upon them the
Supream Style too, and directed this very new Declaration,
To their trustie and welbeloved, their Subjects of the
Citie of London."

The theme of the answer is common to a number of earlier tracts, namely the discrepancy between Parliament's
verbal professions and its actions. Other complaints echo
those of earlier tracts. It is interesting that here Hyde
attempts to take the offensive in the matter of the Protestant religion in order to counteract the still persistent charge of the King's inclination to Popery, and in
order to give some substance to the claim that the King's
military preparations are on behalf of established
religion:

> [all men] see the Protestant Religion, and the Pro-
> fessors thereof miserably reproached, and in danger
> of being destroyed by a vicious and Malignant Party
> of Brownists, Anabaptists, and other Sectaries, (the
> principal ring leaders of whom have too great a
> power, even with some Members in both Our Houses of
> Parliament) Our Authority despised, and, as much as
> in them lies, taken from Us, and reviled in Pulpits
> and Presses by persons immediately in their Protec-
> tion.

36   [July, 1642]
      His Maiesties MESSAGE TO Both Houses of PARLIAMENT, of
      the eleventh of Iuly. 1642. Together With his MAJESTIES
      Proclamation declaring His Majesties purpose to goe in
      His Royall Person to Hull: and the true occasion and end
      thereof. (6 pp.)

      London: for Andrew Coe, 1642

      Thomason E. 107 (24)
      Hist. Reb., ii, 228 (part of the message quoted, and the
        proclamation is summarized)

      This edition is not recorded in Wing. Other editions
      are Wing C 2455, C 2457, and C 2456, which is the official
      London version by Barker (Thomason E. 155 (14)).
      The message demands a satisfactory answer by July 15.
      In the proclamation the King complains that his own town
      of Hull has been wrested from him "if We shall be allowed
      to call any thing Our owne." It continues by charging
      that

          instead of repairing Our Honour for this Indignity,
          severall Orders and Votes of the Major part, then
          present, have beene made to justifie all this as Legall;
          which Orders and Votes would have Us, and others to
          beleeve, upon the many Protestations in Print, That
          there hath beene nothing done therein (as in many
          other things of that nature) but for the safety of
          Our Person, the Honour of Our Crowne, and the good of
          the Kingdome; as if words directly contrary to these
          Actions of Hostility could satisfie Us, or any reason-
          able man, not blinded with selfe-opinion, or abused or
          misled by vaine and false Surmises or groundlesse
          Jealousies.

      This is followed by a detailed catalogue of Hotham's
      misdemeanors.

37   [July, 1642]
      THE PETITION OF The LORDS and COMMONS in PARLIAMENT,
      delivered to His MAJESTIE the 16. day of July: TOGETHER
      VVith HIS MAJESTIES ANSWER thereunto. (18 pp.)

      London: Barker, 1642

      Wing E 2174
      Thomason E. 107 (28)
      Hist. Reb., ii, 230-231 (petition); 232-237 (answer)

Wing records seven other editions: E 2171, E 2172, E 2173, E 2174A, E 2175, E 2176 (Oxford reprint; Madan 1014), E 2176A (Cambridge edition by Daniel).

The Parliament petition renews familiar demands, rejects familiar complaints, and adds one new requirement for accommodation: that the King recall his commissions of array on the ground of their illegality. Hyde, too, had doubts about the commissions, John Selden having spoken with the weight of his authority against them. In *Hist. Reb.*, ii, 202-203, he suggests a preferable expedient. Nevertheless, the King's answer retaliates with a catalogue of the illegal and arbitrary actions of Parliament, and denounces the ordinance of the militia as thoroughly illegal (also Selden's view). The circumstances of the King's unsuccessful attempt to secure the navy for his use are added to the list of complaints, among which the irritation of Hull is uppermost, where lately Sir John Hotham had seized a consignment of wine intended for the King's table. It concludes with a promise to forbear military action against Hull until July 27, by which date a full and positive answer is required of Parliament.

Hist. Reb., ii, 237-8, records the interesting aftermath of this answer. Parliament's messengers, the Earl of Holland, Sir Philip Stapleton, and Sir John Holland, persuaded some members of the Court that the answer was too sharp; others felt it was too mild. In this division of royalist opinion Hyde seems to have prevailed, for the King's response, which, of course, Hyde penned, condemns the "high dialect" of parliamentary messages, and refuses at the same time to soften his own answer.

There were other repercussions from this exchange, made on the very brink of civil war, of interest in this place. There are several London reprints of the Parliament petition purporting in their titles to carry the King's answer, but in fact reducing it to brief notes of his demands, or total omission, which indicates the desire to suppress royalist literature. One such is:

37A The Kings Majesties ANSWER OR, foure Propositions propounded to the Earle of Holland, Sir Philip Stapleton, and Sir John Holland. Which propositions was presented to both Houses of Parliament on Saturday last, being the 23. of Iuly, 1642. In the behalfe of all the Lords and Commons of England. Likewise the PARLIAMENTS Censure of the nine LORDS now resident in the North, July 20. 1642. Namely;

The Earle of Dover,	The Lord Andiver,
Earle of Devonshire,	Lord Savill,
Earle of Northampton,	Lord Capell,
Earle of Munmouth,	And
Earle of Conventry,	Lord Gray of Ruthin.

For their great Contempts to the Parliament, drawne up into two Heads, and assented to by both Houses of Parliament, July 20 1642.   (6 pp.)

London: T. Ryder, Iuly 25. 1642.

Wing C 2091
Thomason E. 108 (6)

A variation on this theme is:

37B PROPOSITIONS FOR PEACE. Presented to the Kings most excellent MAJESTIE, At Beverley in Yorkshire. By the Right Honourable the Earle of Holland of the LORDS House. Sir Phillip Stapleton, And Sir John Holland, of the COMMONS House. Whereunto is annexed His Majesties gracious Answer to the said Propositions. (6 pp.)

London: T. Faucet, Iuly 23, 1642

Wing P 3784
Thomason E. 108 (4)

In this instance the answer reads: "Also His Majesty having perused the aforesaid particulars, was graciously pleased to returne this Answer. That Hee would grant what in honour he could yeeld to the sequell being an expectation of Peace."
Resentment against what was taken to be an uncompromising answer is also evidenced in the commentaries upon the negotiations at York and Beverley. An interesting example of this response is:

37C SUNDRY OBSERVATIONS Of severall Passages and Proceedings IN THE NORTH, THERE Taken by a Subject well-affected to the Protestant Religion, His MAJESTIES Royall Honour and Greatnesse, and the Peace and Safety of this Kingdom; Sent unto a faithfull and intimate Friend of his in LONDON [etc.]   (6 pp.)

London: for F.C. July 29. 1642.

Wing S 6179
Thomason E. 108 (24)

This observer reports that there are ten types of person who mislead the King: Papists; rash noblemen; well-born gentlemen of decayed estates; delinquents; cavaliers; debtors; a sottish, drunken multitude; giddy gentlemen; preachers; and "Discontented and ambitious Lawyers, who against conscience and equity trouble themselves, and possesse the King with more quircks of Law, then this Age, or the safety of this Kingdom requires."

Another, and closer, observer of the scene reports more specifically in:

37D ADVERTISEMENTS FROM YORKE AND BEVERLY, July the 20th. 1642. (4 pp.)

London: Printed in the yeare, 1642

Wing A 627
Thomason E. 107 (30)

> Here are Mr. Hide, and Holborne, two Lawyers, that doe much mischiefe; the one makes himselfe as familiar with the King as if his fellow, hath been seen severall times to pull His Majesty by the Cloak, and when he talks with Him, to play with the Kings Bandstrings; the other will maintain the Legallitie of the Commission of Array, though he was of a quite contrary opinion when Ship-money was argued: but blame him not, the case is altered.

At this time Hyde was exempted from pardon by Parliament. In *Life* he tells the story of the King greeting him with the words "'Ned Hyde, when did you play with my bandstrings last?... Be not troubled at it, for I have worn no band-strings these twenty years'" (i, 133).
The pamphlet concludes:

> I have received just now Intelligence from so good a hand; as you may confidently report it for certaine, that His Majestie hath returned a most sharpe answer to the Parliaments petition, full of bitternesse, much after the Cavaliers and Mr. Hides daily expressions. It seems they have prevailed with His Majesty not to condiscend to a Peace.

38 [August, 1642]
HIS MAJESTIES Declaration TO All His Loving Subjects. Of the 12 of August 1642. (93 pp.)

York: Barker, 1642

Wing C 2248
Hist. Reb., ii, 277-281 n. (abridged)

There are numerous editions: Wing C 2241, a Cambridge
edition by Daniel (Thomason's copy of this, E. 115 (11),
is dated by him September 2); there is a second by Daniel,
unrecorded in Wing; Wing C 2242 and C 2243 (also Cambridge
editions by N.N.); Wing C 2244 (a Shrewsbury edition by
the official printer); C 2245 (Edinburgh, 1643); C 2249
(Oxford reprint by Lichfield, Madan 1025, which suggests
that it could have been issued as early as August 17).

When this tract was written the nation was, in effect,
in a state of war. On August 9 the Earl of Essex,
chosen by Parliament as its general, was declared traitor.
The following day a royal proclamation inhibited papists
from enlisting in the King's forces, and on August 12
the King announced that he would erect his standard at
Nottingham on the 22nd. This is, therefore, a retrospective account of the whole movement towards civil war, the
longest and most important of Hyde's tracts to date.

In conflating the MSS of Life and History, Clarendon
chose to omit this from the final *History*, perhaps because
of its length, but also probably because it is itself the
thesis of the first half of *Hist. Reb.* in miniature. Its
remarkable concinnity reveals Hyde's historiographical
genius: his mastery of the large theme and the detail
which illuminates it in perfect balance. His critique of
the Parliament faction does not concern itself only with
those of their actions which strike at constitutional
balance, or the letter of the law, or even with their
language, which is often the case in the briefer tracts,
but rather presents it as a cancerous evil at the center
of national life. It is this picture of a type of totali-
tarian regime which provides the unifying force of the
tract, and makes the King's position assume the dimension
of the defense of civilization itself as understood by
the nations of Christendom. One example may serve to
convey the flavor of his argument:

> How had the laws of hospitality and civility been
> violated, the freedom and liberty of conversation
> (the pleasure and delight of life) been invaded by
> them; the discourses at tables, whispers in gardens
> and walks, examined, and of persons under no accusa-
> tion; letters broken up, (his majesty's own to his
> dearest consort the Queen not spared,) read publicly,
> and commented upon, with such circumstances as made
> Christendom laugh at our follies and abhor our

correspondence? Was the constitution of the kingdom
to be preserved and monarchy itself to be upheld?
(*Hist. Reb.*, ii, 280 n.)

When describing the actions of the malignant faction
in Parliament his typical rhetorical pattern is to present the idealistic image of Parliament followed by
actions of bestial capriciousness. Again, a single
example may be instructive:

> Was the dignity, privilege and freedom of Parliaments
> (Parliaments, whose wisdom and gravity had prepared
> so many wholesome laws, and whose freedom distinguishes
> the condition of his majesty's subjects from those of
> any monarchy of Europe) precious to the people? ...
> Where was that freedom and privilege, when alderman
> Pennington and captain Venn brought down their myrmi-
> dons to assault and terrify the members of both
> Houses whose faces or opinion they liked not? (*Hist.
> Reb.*, ii, 279 n.)

As well as the familiar ingredients of royalist
apology, which are again rehearsed, occurs a somewhat
surprising treatment of the notorious Court of Star
Chamber and the High Commission Courts. It is their
universal notoriety which provides the rhetorical effect
when Hyde argues that however severe they might have been,
still they punished real offences, whereas Parliament
now with declarations, votes, and judgments punishes
actions not known to be crimes until they were punished.
The delay and expense involved in now obtaining a mere
parody of justice are much more grievous than in the
days of Star Chamber.

It is sometimes argued that a major defect in *Hist.
Reb.* is its blindness to the question of religious discontent. In this tract proportionately more attention is
given to religious discontent than in *Hist. Reb.* This is
achieved by emotional evocation of the blood of Protestant
martyrs (blood of several kinds figures throughout) set
against impending anarchy:

> if those desperate persons should prevail, when the
> principal men, to whose care and industry they had
> committed the managery of that part, refused com-
> munion with the Church of England as much as the
> Papists do; when such licence was given to Brownists,
> Anabaptists, sectaries, and whilst coachmen, felt-
> makers, and such mechanic persons, were allowed and
> entertained to preach, by those who thought them-
> selves the principal members of either House; when

such barbarous outrages in churches, and heathenish
irreverence and uproars, even in the time of divine
service and the administration of the blessed sacra-
ment, were practised without control; when the blessed
means of advancing religion, the preaching of the Word
of God, was turned into a licence of libelling, and
reviling both Church and State, and venting such seditious positions as by the law of the land were no
less than treason, and scarce a man in reputation and
credit with those grand reformers who was not notoriously guilty of this. (*Hist. Reb.*, ii, 278 n.)

The effect is, of course, not more sympathetic to ecclesiastical reform and religious zeal than *Hist. Reb.* as a
whole.

39   [August, 1642]
     HIS MAJESTIES ANSWER TO THE DECLARATION of both Houses of
     PARLIAMENT, Concerning the Commission of ARRAY: Of the
     first of July, 1642.   (62 pp.)

     Cambridge: Roger Daniel, 1642

     Wing C 2116
     Thomason E. 114 (20)

     Wing identifies two York editions by the official
printer: C 2113, C 2114, and an Oxford reprint, C 2115
(Madan 1013, by Lichfield, probably issued July 20).
Thomason annotated his copy to the effect that the pamphlet was first printed at York, reprinted at Cambridge
on August 15, and prohibited in London. A copy of this
edition in the Crawford Collection, however, carries the
dating in contemporary hand of August 10.
     The argument, extensively researched, was probably
prepared by Hyde in collaboration with other legal advisers
to the King. The bulk of the text consists in a point-by-
point rebuttal of the Parliament declaration and a work-
manlike exposition of precedents and legal niceties drawn
mainly from the statutes of Henry IV. Among the authori-
ties cited in support of the interpretation is Sir Edward
Cook (Coke).
     Rhetorical flourishes are restricted to the opening
and closing sections. In the former an appeal is made to
the peace of the kingdom in Elizabeth's time and in the
reign of the King's blessed father, now destroyed by
neglecting to consult the King's learned counsel before
declaring commissions of array. It concludes that what
Parliament's declaration really achieves is the

condemnation of its own ordinances which are "contrary to
the Law and Customes of the Realm."

The detailed argument of this answer is condensed by
Hyde in [40] below.

40 [August, 1642]
HIS MAJESTIES DECLARATION, In Answer to a DECLARATION of
the Lords and Commons assembled in Parliament; For the
raysing of all Power and Force, as well Trained Bands as
others, in severall Counties of this Kingdome, to lead
against all Traytours and their Adherents, &c.   (6 pp.)

Cambridge: Roger Daniel, 1642

Wing C 2208
Thomason E. 113 (19)

Wing C 2207 is the Oxford edition recorded in
Madan 1022. Madan remarks that the printing of it was
prohibited by Parliament. There is a York edition,
Wing C 2206, and another edition, Wing C 2208A, no place
of publication.

The King's declaration, almost certainly the work of
Hyde, is not included in the final *Hist. Reb.* It defends
Commissions of Array on the rather unsatisfactory ground
that since their institution in 5 Henry IV they have not
met with parliamentary complaint. We know, however, that
Hyde was not convinced of their legality (see [37] above).
It denounces the "inveterate rancour" of indefatigably
industrious parliamentarians, supported by "that rabble
of Brownists, and other Schismaticks declaredly ready to
appear at their call," and proceeds with a catalogue of
their acts of violence against the King and his loyal
servants. Familiar complaints such as the matter of Hull,
Ireland, and charges of Popish inclinations are swiftly
enumerated, along with a charge of growing significance:
the deliberate suppression of the King's answers and
declarations.

41 [August, 1642]
HIS MAJESTIES GRACIOUS MESSAGE To both Houses of Parlia-
ment, sent from Nottingham the 25. of August, 1642. By
the Earles of Southampton and Dorset, Sir Iohn Culpeper
Knight, Chancellour of the Exchequer, and Sir William
Uvedall, Knight.   (5 pp.)

London: Barker, 1642

Wing: not recorded.   It is Wing C 2333 plus one more page.
Perhaps it should be regarded as C 2333A.
Thomason E. 114 (29)
Hist. Reb., ii, 304-305

   Wing C 2332 is the York edition; the first London
edition giving the message only (4 pp.) is Wing C 2333.
(For Wing C 2334 and C 2335, which was, confusingly, in
the first edition of Wing, C 2334A, see [43] below.)
   The same material appears in:

41A The humble Answer OF THE Lords and Commons Assembled in
    Parliament, To the Message of the 25 of August received
    from His MAJESTY by the Earles of Southampton and Dorset,
    and Sir Iohn Culpepper, Knight, Chancellor of the Exchequer.
    Returned by the aforesaid Sir Iohn Culpepper, by order of
    both Houses, to be presented to his MAJESTY.   With a
    perfect Coppy of His MAJESTIES Message.

    London: J. Wright, August 30, 1642

    Wing E 1553

    There is also a report on the King's message:

41B TRVE AND IOYFVLL NEWS FROM HIS MAIESTIE, BEING A TRVE AND
    Exact Relation of His Majesties most Gratious Message
    [etc.]

    London: for F.L. & F.C., 1642

    Wing T 2505

       Nothing but the consideration that this message would
    be rejected could persuade the King to finally consent
    to it.   In the MS Life Clarendon writes, "The King was so
    exceedingly afflicted after he had given his consent that
    he brake out into tears" (*Hist. Reb.*, ii, 301 n.).   To
    provide another opportunity of presenting royalist actions
    as essentially defensive, and to gain time to recruit sol-
    diers were the motives for this manoeuvre, and they are
    reflected in the "softer and calmer style than his majesty
    had been accustomed to for some months" (ibid).   The in-
    adequacy of the royal forces can be inferred from the
    assurance that "nothing but Our christian and Pious care
    to Prevent the effusion of blood hath begot this motion,
    Our Provision of Men, Arms and Money being such as may
    secure Us from further Violence, till it shall please God
    to open the eyes of Our People."
       Clarendon remembers that the morning he prepared the
    message he was informed of the death of his son.   His

natural grief notwithstanding, he applied his energies to
persuading the King to "abolish that infectious sadness
in his own looks." He was prepared to persuade others
that this message was not a cause of gloom: "and to that
purpose he had always the message in his pocket, which he
read to many, who confessed that it was better than they
imagined" (*Hist. Reb.*, ii, 302 n.).

42   [Sept., 1642]
HIS MAJESTIES GRACIOUS MESSAGE To both Houses of Parlia-
ment, sent from Nottingham the 25. of August, 1642.
TOGETHER With the Answer of the Lords and Commons to the
said Message: AND HIS MAJESTIES REPLY to the same.
Septemb. 2. (6 pp.)

London: Barker, 1642

Wing: not recorded. It is Wing C 2333 plus two pages.
Thomason E. 116 (2)
Hist. Reb., ii, 307-308

       This is a reprint of [41] to which the King's brief
rejoinder is added. Thomason received his copy September 6.
       The messengers who carried [41] to the Parliament were
treated with unbending rigor and returned with a brief,
inhospitable reply. The King's rejoinder, again in accommodating tone, was carried this time by Falkland. He
returned in due course with another sharp parliamentary
response. Simultaneously Parliament issued a fierce, war-
like declaration which proposed that the costs so far
incurred be recovered from the estates of the "malignant
and disaffected party."

43   [Sept., 1642]
HIS MAJESTIES GRACIOUS MESSAGE To Both Houses of Parliament, sent from Nottingham, August 25. With the Answer of
the Lords and Commons to the said Message: And HIS MAJES-
TIES REPLY to the same. Sept. 2. TOGETHER With the Answer
and humble Petition of both Houses to His Majesties last
Message: And also His Majesties Message in Reply to the
said Answer, Sept. 11. 1642 (14 pp.)

London: Barker, MDCXLII

Wing C 2334
Thomason E. 116 (47)
Hist. Reb., ii, 310-11

This edition includes the materials of [41] and [42]
above. Wing records another edition for I. Wright,
September 17, as C 2334A in the old Wing, and C 2335 in
the revised edition. The King's message of September 11
is also reprinted in:

43A To the KINGS most Excellent Majesty, THE HVMBLE ANSWER OF
THE Lords and Commons Assembled in Parliament, To His
Majesties Last Message the 11. September, 1642. With a
true Coppy of the Message.

London: For Iohn Wright. 17 Septemb. 1642

Wing E 2371

and again in:

43B HIS MAIESTIES Last MESSAGE, Septemb. 12. 1642. Directed
to His Right Trusty and Wel-beloved, the Speaker of the
House of PEERES.

London: for J. Wright. 14. Septemb. 1642

Wing C 2371

This message, sent shortly before the King marched
westward from Nottingham, is said by Hyde to be "a farewell to his hopes of a treaty" (*Hist. Reb.*, ii, 310). It
is general and formulaic in its argument that the King
has reacted defensively since being forced to leave London.
In the exchanges since August 25 the King seems
largely to have gained his objectives. "The Parliament
vacillated between two courses. If they had desired to
prevent extremities, they should have replied to the
King's message in a more conciliatory tone; if they desired
an appeal to force, they should have prosecuted the war
with promptitude and vigour" (Lister, i, 203).

44 [Oct., 1642]
HIS MAIESTIES DECLARATION To all His loving Subjects,
UPON OCCASION OF HIS late Messages to both Houses of
Parliament, and their refusall, to treat with Him for the
Peace of the Kingdom. (22 pp.)

Oxford: Leonard Lichfield, 1642

Wing C 2257
Thomason E. 126 (6) (copy received November 2)
Madan 1045 (dates it about October 31)

There is a London edition, Wing C 2258, and Wing C 2259
is apparently another Lichfield edition, but Madan 1046
identifies this as "the first London counterfeit edition,
out of a series of at least 120, issued in 1642-4."

This is the parting shot in a series of exchanges
which starts with the message from Nottingham, August 25,
[41] above, and as such an attempt to extract the greatest
propaganda value from Parliament's maladroit replies. The
King's messages, [41] pp. 3-4, [42] pp. 7-8, [43] pp. 9-10,
with the relevant Parliament replies, are presented in
sequence with brief linking passages emphasizing the King's
pacific intentions, or the spirit of his replies ("Without
any bitternesse or reprehension of their neglect of Vs,
and the publique Peace"), or deploring the language of
Parliament. The final passage (pp. 14-22) is the new
declaration which again lays stress on the King's attempts
to avoid hostilities. It regrets the disorderly conduct
of royalist soldiers, while claiming the utmost care to
prevent it, and then points out that in his journey through
several counties the King has been careful not to oppress
even those who exercised the ordinance of the militia
against him. It then complains of outrages committed by
Parliament's soldiers, especially against churches in
Canterbury, Worcester, and Oxford. There is a catalogue
of familiar grievances: violation of the known laws, the
driving of members from Parliament, exercise of arbitrary
power, Pym's allegations, the matter of Ireland, and the
King's being driven from London. It observes that of the
five hundred members of the Commons only one hundred remain, and merely fifteen or sixteen of one hundred Peers
concur in their resolutions. It ends with a pledge to
support the families of men killed in the royal service.

45 [Oct., 1642]
HIS MAIESTIES DECLARATION To all His loving Subjects, Upon
occasion of a late Printed Paper, ENTITVLED, A Declaration
and Protestation of the Lords and Commons in Parliament
to this Kingdom, and the whole World, of the 22^{d} of
October. (9 pp.)

Oxford: Leonard Lichfield, 1642

Wing C 2255
Thomason E. 126 (30) (endorses his copy "Novemb. 9th")
Madan 1065 (dates it about Nov. 7)

Later editions add extra items: Wing C 2256 (Thomason
E. 128 (37), Madan 1066) contains the Proclamation to the
County of Kent; Wing C 2256A (Madan 1067), which was
published a month later, adds a Parliament petition of
Nov. 24 and the King's Answer, [48] below. See also
[46A] below.

This tract makes great play with the fact that the
Parliament Declaration and Protestation was issued the
day before the battle of Edgehill, the first full-scale
engagement of the war: "Wee were never so backward in
receiving, or so slow in answering the Petitions of either
or both Our Houses in Parliament, that there was need by
an Army to quicken Vs." In similarly ironic vein Hyde
comments on the Parliament's complaint that the King would
not trust their assurance that he could safely put himself
in their hands, when these hands were full of weapons to
destroy him. There is a lengthy refutation of Parliament's claim that the King refused to receive ⌐ petition
to be delivered to him by the Earl of Essex and others.
He asks whether the petition (which had not been published)
was framed to be delivered *after* a battle when the King
would no longer have power to decide whether or not he
should be deposed. Two other charges are refuted: of
encouraging papists to join his ranks, and of intending
to bring in foreign troops. It ends with a nervous glance
northward, expressing the hope that the Scots would not
engage in a rebellion against the King by being misled by
men who sought only the satisfaction of their private
ambitions.

46   [Nov., 1642]
HIS MAIESTIES DECLARATION To all His loving Subjects,
AFTER HIS LATE VICTORY against the Rebells on Sunday the
23 of October. (8 pp.)

Oxford: Leonard Lichfield, 1642

Wing C 2222
Madan 1057 (dates it about Nov. 5)

Thomason E. 242 (8) (Wing C 2223, Madan 1058) is the
London reprint, which carries in addition an account of
the battle of Edgehill and other engagements. Similarly
Wing C 2224 (Madan 1059).

This is reprinted, along with [44] and [45] above,
in a Cambridge edition of the same date:

46A HIS MAJESTIES Declarations to all His loving Subjects, I.
Upon occasion of His late Messages to both Houses of
Parliament, and their refusall, to treat with him for the
Peace of the Kingdome. II. Upon occasion of a late
Printed Paper, ENTITULED, A Declaration and Protestation
of the Lords and Commons in Parliament to this Kingdome,
and the whole World, of the 22$^\text{d}$ of October. III. After
His late victory against the Rebells on Sunday the 23 of
October.

Cambridge: Roger Daniel, 1642

Wing: not recorded. It is another edition of C 2290.

    Hyde watched the battle of Edgehill with the Prince
of Wales and the Duke of York in his care. The declaration opens by attributing "the preservation of Vs and Our
Children in the late bloudy Battel with the Rebells to
the mercy and goodnesse of Almighty God." It alleges
that there are more papists serving in the Parliament's
forces than in those which protect the King. This army
is not intended to subdue Parliament, but to protect him.

47 [Nov., 1642]
HIS MAJESTIES DECLARATION To all His Loving Subjects, OF
His true Intentions in advancing lately TO BRAINCEFORD.
(7 pp.)

Oxford: Leonard Lichfield, 1642

Wing C 2246
Madan 1083
Thomason E. 242 (25)
Hist. Reb., ii, 393 and 397-8 (a synopsis)

    Wing 2246 misleadingly comprehends two distinct edi-
tions: the genuine Oxford edition, Madan 1082, and a
counterfeit, which I cite here. Thomason E. 128 (35) is
another London edition with counterfeited Lichfield imprint, identified by Madan 1087, with the title:

THE ANSWER OF BOTH HOVSES OF PARLIAMENT To his MAJESTIES
Message of the 12. of November. WITH HIS MAIESTIES Reply
thereunto.
Wing E 1221

    This is a collection of several documents from the
aftermath of the Brentford affair. An earlier edition
which contains most of the important material from this
collection is:

47A THE HVMBLE PETITION Of the Lords and Commons now assem-
    bled in PARLIAMENT to His MAJESTY, WITH HIS MAIESTIES
    Answer thereunto. TOGETHER WITH HIS MAJESTIES Message
    on the 12. of November. (6 pp.)

    Oxford: Leonard Lichfield, 1642

    Wing E 1582B
    Madan 1075

        This contains the Parliament petition delivered at
    Colnbrook November 11, the Answer of the same day propos-
    ing Windsor as a meeting place, and the King's apologetic
    message of November 12.
        The first royal answer of November 11 is carried in:

47B To the Kings Most Excellent Majesty; The humble Petition
    of the Lords and Commons now assembled in Parliament
    Delivered at Colebrooke, 10. Nov. 1642 by the Earls of
    Pembroke and Northumberland, Lord Wainman, M. Perpoint,
    and Sir Jo. Hippesly. His Majesties Answer To the fore-
    said Petition, given to the Committee at Colebrooke,
    Nov. 11, 1642. (brs.)

    [s.n.]

    Wing E 2375
    Steele 2291

        The first royalist section of [47] is no doubt by
    Hyde, the answer to the petition. It professes abhorrence
    of the war--all victories will be bitter to the King be-
    cause of the destruction of his subjects. It proposes
    that the King reside at Windsor, if Parliament's forces
    are removed, in order to begin a treaty.
        Instead of waiting passively, Charles permitted an
    attack to be mounted against Brentford, thus directly
    threatening London, and destroying his hard-won credi-
    bility. This action, to Hyde's despair, dashed all hopes
    of a fair negotiated settlement, and put the King's apolo-
    gists to the unenviable task of retrieving the situation.
    Thus Falkland undertook an attempt to clear the King of
    charges of "Jesuiticall Counsells, and the personal
    Treachery to which some have presumed to impute it." It
    is an inelegant and somewhat strained account of the
    treatment of John White, a royalist emissary, which avoids
    the main issues.
        The last section is probably by Hyde. It is summarized
    by him in *Hist. Reb.*, ii, 397-8. This reply of November 18
    tries to convince readers that the King can have had no

intention of overawing the City, since he did not follow
up the military advantage gained at Brentford.   In fact
he had won none.   He offers to march away to remove all
misapprehension.

48   [Nov., 1642]
HIS MAIESTIES DECLARATION To all HIS Loving SVBJECTS, VPON
Occasion of a late Printed PAPER ENTITVLED, A Declaration
and Protestation of the Lords and Commons in Parliament
of this Kingdome, and the whole world of the 22^d of
OCTOBER.   The Kings Proclamation to His County of KENT;
With the Humble Petition of both Houses OF PARLIAMENT.
Presented to His Majestie on the 24th of November.   With
His Majesties Gracious Answer thereunto.   (8 pp.)

Oxford: Leonard Lichfield, 1642

Wing C 2256A
Madan 1067
Hist. Reb., ii, 401-402

The relevant passage is the Gracious Answer to the
petition of November 24.   The rest is a reprint of the
materials of [46] above.
Parliament's brief petition renews the demand that
the King return to London with his royal not his martial
attendance.   The answer is sharp, taking the petition as
an insult.   He sees no good reason why he should now
tamely surrender his crown when the rebel army has been
unable to snatch it from his head.   He complains that
explanations of the Brentford incident (like [47] above),
which he sent to his press in London, had been confiscated
from his messenger, and thus suppressed.

49   [Dec., 1642]
His Maiesties DECLARATION TO ALL HIS LOVING SVBJECTS,
UPON THE OCCASION OF THE ORDINANCE AND DECLARATION OF The
Lords and Commons, FOR The assessing of all such who have
not contributed sufficiently for the raising of Mony,
Plate, &c.   (6 pp.)

Oxford, December 8, Leonard Lichfield, 1642

Hist. Reb., ii, 424-429

Presumably this is the original Oxford edition of the
Declaration which Madan was unable to locate (see
Madan 1109).   The Declaration appears in two forms:

1. by itself, as in Wing C 2261 (Madan 1109) and Wing C 2262
   (Madan 1110) and Madan 1111, which are all London
   counterfeits. Madan also describes a rare fourth
   London counterfeit with the absurd misprint of
   "assissting" for "assessing" in the title (see
   vol. ii, xv);
2. appended to the London Ordinance, as in Wing E 1767
   (Madan 1106, and another described vol. ii, xv, a
   close London counterfeit), and Wing E 1768 (Madan 1108).

There appears to be another edition of the Declaration
alone, a copy of which is to be found in the Crawford
Collection, unnoticed in Wing:

49A His Majesties Declaration to all His loving Subjects upon
occasion of the Ordinance and Declaration of the Lords
and Commons, for assessing all such who have not contributed sufficiently for raising Money, Plate, &c. (8 pp.
unnumbered)

[s.n.]

Hyde represents the King as not unwilling to see the
parliamentary ordinances for raising money on the ground
that their patent illegality would sway much opinion to
the royal cause (*Hist. Reb.*, ii, 424). The Declaration
is suitably vigorous, Hyde sensing a fine propagandist
opportunity at hand. That the King's just rights are intimately linked with the preservation of property is very
strongly pressed. Thus the Parliament's action is no
better than plundering the populace. Several powerful
rhetorical devices are combined with specific argumenta-
tion. Thus rhetorical questions about liberty addressed
to the citizens of London go side by side with a discussion
of the proper relationship of parliamentary committees to
the two Houses, and of the illegality of committees publishing their proceedings. A catalogue of grievances is
seen from the perspective of posterity, and by contrast
the consciences of those who acquiesce are directly
challenged. Anabaptists, Brownists, and debauched persons
are even more heartily denounced than hitherto, and again
part of a speech by Pym (see [23] above) is compared with
the present reality, to ironic effect. The attack concludes with an appeal for freely rendered contribution to
the King's cause, and a command not to obey the Parliament
ordinance. (See also A LETTER From A SCHOLLER IN OXFORD-
SHIRE, [67] below, which adverts to a reply to this.)

50 [Dec., 1642]
THE DECLARATION OF THE LORDS AND Commons assembled in the
Parliament of England, to the Subjects of Scotland. WITH
HIS MAIESTIES Message to the Lords of His Privy Counsell
of SCOTLAND, upon that occasion. (10 pp.)

Oxford: Leonard Lichfield, 1642

Wing E 1471
Madan 1117
Hist. Reb., ii, 406-408

   Wing E 1472 is a York edition; Madan 1118 and 1119
identify two London counterfeits--the first of these is
also Thomason E. 244 (13).
   The King's message is a succinct account of the
royalist position. It expands the usual range of formulaic
complaints by putting the Council in mind of parliamentary
acts of both kingdoms to secure a pact of mutual non-
interference. It also emphatically discredits the English
Parliament in order to show that recent invitations to
the Scots to invade are illegal. It alleges that of five
hundred members of the Commons there are now no more than
eighty-five left, and of more than a hundred Peers, merely
fifteen or sixteen, "All which are so awed by the multitude of Anabaptists, Brownists and other Persons, desperate
and decayed in their Fortunes, in and about the City of
London, that in truth their Consultations have not the
freedom and Priviledge which belong to Parliaments."
   The message is reprinted more than a year later in a
collection of documents relating to the King's negotiations
with the Scotch.

51 [Dec., 1642]
THE PETITION Of the COMMITTEES FOR IRELAND TO His Majestie:
WITH HIS Majesties ANSWER Thereunto. (7 pp.)

Oxford: Leonard Lichfield, 1642

Madan 1124
Hist. Reb., ii, 492

   This is a counterfeit London reprint of Wing P 1789
(Madan 1123). Madan dates its publication December 15
and the counterfeit December 20, although the King's
answer was given on the first of the month.
   It is a sympathetic reply in general terms stressing
the King's continuing concern for the condition of Ireland
since the beginning of the rebellion, and alluding to his
attempts to alleviate it.

52   [Jan., 1643]
     THE HUMBLE PETITION OF The MAJOR, ALDERMEN, and COMMONS
     of the Citie of LONDON: AND His MAJESTIES Gracious ANSWER
     The fourth of January 1642.   (12 pp.)

     London: Barker, 1642 [1643]

     Wing H 3554
     Thomason E. 84 (14)
     Hist. Reb., ii, 433-35

     Madan 1163 is the original Oxford edition (Wing H 3555),
and 1164 a London counterfeit (Wing H 3556). There is also
another London counterfeit of the Oxford edition, unnoticed
in Madan:

52A THE HVMBLE PETITION OF THE MAIOR, ALDERMEN, and COMMONS
     of the City of London to His MAJESTIE. WITH HIS MAJESTIES
     Gratious Answer thereunto.

     Printed by His MAJESTIES Command AT OXFORD, Ianuary 5.
     By LEONARD LICHFIELD Printer to the Vniversitie.

     Other editions listed in Wing are H 3557 and H 3557A,
one by Humphrey Tuckey, the second by Henry Turkey.
     The King's reply was so sharp that instead of return-
ing it with the City petitioners, thus risking its suppression, he sent it directly by messenger of his own, and
its printing must have been immediate in the edition cited,
[52] above. This edition, in Gothic letter, and presumably
not counterfeit, explains the remark in Madan 1163 that
"It is astonishing that the King's Answer should have
leaked out so early as Jan. 5, considering its character."
     The City Petition Hyde regarded, with some justice, as
disingenuous in its "very specious and popular professions
of great piety and zeal to his service" (*Hist. Reb.*, ii,
432). The reply, written in the knowledge that a propor-
tion of the King's propaganda had been suppressed in
London, compresses the substance of earlier declarations
of the King's position, and adds, to fit the occasion,
the demands that the citizens arrest Lord Mayor Pennington
and three of his aldermen as an earnest of their professed
intent to live by the known laws of the land. Hyde hoped
by this to encourage London royalists sufficiently to
cause them to hamper the Lord Mayor's authority.
     The King's answer is again reprinted in a pamphlet
which reports the proceedings at the common-hall convened
for the purpose of hearing it publicly read by the royal
messenger, Captain Hearne (or Heron):

52B TVVO SPEECHES SPOKEN BY The Earl of Manchester, and JO:
    PYM Esq; AS A REPLY TO His MAIESTIES ANSVVER to the City
    of Londons Petition, sent from His MAJESTY By CAPTAIN
    HEARN, And read at a Common-Hall, on Friday the 13th of
    JANUARY, 1642. Also, a true Narration of the passages of
    that day. Ordered by the Commons in Parliament, That
    these Speeches be forthwith printed and published:
    H: Elsynge, Cler: Parl: D: Com.

    London: Peter Cole, 1643

    Wing M 402
    Thomason E. 85 (7)

        Thomason dates its publication as January 16. The
    King's answer is pp. 5-10. What is interesting in this
    case is the linking commentary which mentions that after
    the King's speech was read a group of malignants tried to
    set up a shout of approval, but with no support. After
    Pym's speech, however, popular enthusiasm was loud and
    prolonged. This must be the occasion which suggested to
    Hyde the grounds of his forgery, [66] below.

53 [Feb., 1643]
    THE HVMBLE DESIRES AND PROPOSITIONS OF THE LORDS and
    COMMONS in PARLIAMENT assembled: Tendered to His MAJESTY
    1. February, 1642. WITH HIS MAIESTIES Gratious Answer
    thereunto. (14 pp.)

    Oxford: Leonard Lichfield, 1642

    Wing E 1562
    Madan 1219
    Hist. Reb., ii, 444-5

        There is a genuine London edition by Barker, Wing E 1563
    (Thomason E. 88 (5); Madan 1222) and several counterfeits
    by Wright, Wing E 1561 (Madan 1220) and, not recorded in
    Wing, Madan 1221. For interesting comments on the bibliog-
    raphy of this item see Madan 1219.
        The propositions and reply constitute the first inti-
    mation of a move toward peace which continued in the next
    several months. But the beginning is not auspicious.
    Parliament's propositions were rejected and a counter set
    put forward. Despite the claim that the King will forbear
    expressions of bitterness, the answer is, in fact, bitter
    in tone and indicates the attempt at a balance between
    recrimination and accommodation, which the opening sen-
    tence makes evident:

If His Majesty had not given up all the Faculties
of His Soule to an earnest endeavour of a Peace and
Reconciliation with his People, or if He would suffer
Himselfe by any Provocation to be drawn to a sharpnesse
of Language, at a time when there seemes somewhat like
an Overture of Accomodation, He could not but resent
the heavy Charges upon Him in the Preamble of these
Propositions, and would not suffer Himselfe to be
reproached with protecting the Delinquents, by force,
from Iustice (His Majesties desire haveing alwayes
been, that all men should be tride by the knowne Law,
& having been refus'd it;) with raising an Army against
His Parliament....

NOTE: At the end of January, 1643, the Parliament sent commissioners to Oxford to propose a peace treaty. The negotiations had two distinct phases: argument over the procedure,
which involved determining the order in which the propositions and counter-propositions should be examined; and the
debate upon each of the issues determined. In the interval
between these phases Hyde was appointed Chancellor of the
Exchequer, having first refused an offer of the post of
Secretary of State. Thus he "was raised from the situation
of a secret agent, to that of an avowed and responsible servant of the Crown" (Lister, i, 215). Acting in consort with
the other members of the Privy Council, he helped to frame
the numerous royal replies to Parliamentary documents. A
considerable responsibility for writing the King's answers
seems to have fallen on Falkland. Many of the replies are
simply matter-of-fact, making it difficult and perhaps
unnecessary to identify specific authorship in each case.
In some few instances Hyde's characteristic style is dis-
cernable. For this reason a bibliography of the publications
of both parties while the treaty was in negotiation would
not be much to the purpose in hand. It would also be too
extensive for inclusion in this place. Fortunately, a summary collection of the treaty documents exists; see [56]
below. In the commentary on it the more notable aspects of
Hyde's contribution are remarked.

54 [Feb., 1643]
    THE DESIRE and ADVICE OF THE LORDS and COMMONS IN PARLIA-
    MENT TO His MAJESTY, THAT The next Assize and Generall
    Goale - delivery may not be Holden, &c. VVITH HIS MAIESTIES
    Gratious Answer thereunto February 21. 1642. (5 pp.)

Oxford: Leonard Lichfield, 1642 [1643]

Wing E 1522
Thomason E. 91 (26)
Madan 1253
Hist. Reb., ii, 525-526

The Parliament's advice that assizes and gaol-delivery
be suspended until the restoration of peace allowed Hyde
to score a nice point: that only the execution of justice
could alleviate the sufferings of the people, and that
therefore the King would continue to discharge his own
obligations in that regard. In *Hist. Reb.* he comments
that the King could in reality do very little to prevent
the disruption of justice, except to make it clear that
the Parliament was responsible for the "first avowed in-
terruption and suspension of the public justice that
happened, or that was known ever before in that kind"
(ii, 526).

55   [March, 1643]
HIS MAJESTIES ANSVVER TO A LATE PETITION presented unto
Him by the hands of M^r· ALEXANDER HENDERSON from the
Commissioners of the generall Assembly of the Church of
SCTOLAND.

Wing C 2097
Thomason E. 247 (16)
Steele, ii, 1785
Hist. Rep., ii, 510-516
This is pp. 7-14 of

TO THE KING'S MOST EXCELLENT MAIESTY. THE HVMBLE PETITION
OF THE COMMISSIONERS of the Generall ASSEMBLY of the Kirke
of Scotland, met at Edinborough Ianuary, 4. 1642. And
now lately presented to His Majesty, At OXFORD. WITH HIS
MAIESTIES Gratious Answer thereunto. March 16. 1642.

Oxford: Leonard Lichfield, March 20, 1642 [1643]

Wing C 4271
Thomason E. 247 (15)
Madan 1276

Madan is inclined to regard this as a London counterfeit of the genuine article, Madan 1275, and points to
the fact that Thomason received his copy only on March 31.
If Madan's supposition is in fact the case, Wing is in-
correct to make C 4271 the same as Madan 1075.

There had been a London edition of the petition only,
which is the first matter for complaint in the King's
reply. He found the petition, he complains, "to be dis-
persed throughout Our Kingdom, to the great danger of
Scandalling of Our well-affected Subjects, who may inter-
pret the bitternesse and sharpnesse of some Expressions
not to be so agreeable to that regard & Reverence which
is due to Our Person." The rest of the lengthy answer
is equally acerbic.

This is not surprising, for the petition requests
nothing less than the abolition of episcopacy in England,
and that the Church of England be remodelled after the
Scotch paradigm. There is also the unmentioned threat of
invasion. The authority of the commissioners is roundly
rejected. Their right to interpose themselves between
Parliament and King is also treated scornfully. This provides occasion for a rehearsal of the history of the
grievances in a manner typical of Hyde. As "good and
pious Preachers of the Gospell," their irenic impulses
might be used, so Hyde suggests, to compose distractions
in opinions among those of their countrymen who have been
disturbed by turbulent persons, and to "infuse into them
a true sense of Charity, Obedience, and Humility, the
great Principles of Christian Religion; That they may not
suffer themselves to be transported with things they doe
not understand."

56   [March-April, 1643]
     THE COLLECTION OF ALL THE PARTICULAR PAPERS that passed
     between HIS MAIESTIE, BOTH HOVSES, AND THE COMMITTEE,
     Concerning the late TREATY. (29 pp.)

     Oxford: Leonard Lichfield, 1643

     Wing C 2157
     Thomason E. 101 (3)
     Madan 1337
     Hist. Reb., iii, 1-9 (selections)

This is identified by Madan as a London counterfeit
of the original, Madan 1336, which he dates May 1. The
counterfeit he dates May 7.

The disorderly chronology of this omnibus collection
is reflected in the sequence of the King's replies which
Hyde presents in *Hist. Reb.* This consideration, together
with the fact that *Hist. Reb.* produces the variant readings of this edition, makes it probable that Hyde used
this collection, rather than the individual pamphlets,

whem compiling the seventh book of his *History* in Jersey,
October, 1647.

The final item of the series is worthy of note. Its
title is: His Maiesties Message to both Houses, Concerning
Disbanding of both Armies, and His Majesties Return to
both Houses of Parliament; Mentioned in HIS Majesties two
last Papers. April 12. 1643.

It is quoted in *Hist. Reb.*, iii, 8-9, and was
separately published in broadside:

56A His Maiesties Message to both Houses, concerning Disbanding of both Armies, and His Majesties returne to both
Houses of Parliament. OXFORD, 12. April, 1643.

Oxford, 1643

Wing C 2462
Thomason 669.f.7. (6)
Steele 2407
Madan 1319

It also appeared as a quarto pamphlet:

56B HIS MAJESTIES MESSAGE TO BOTH HOUSES, CONCERNING DISBANDING
OF both Armies, AND HIS MAJESTIES RETURNE TO BOTH Houses
of PARLIAMENT. OXFORD 12. April. 1643. (5 pp.)

Oxford: Leonard Lichfield, 1643

Wing C 2461
Madan 1318

There was also another broadside bearing the date April 13:

56C HIS MAJESTIES MOST GRACIOUS MESSAGE: Sent to both Houses
of Parliament, by Captain Henry Heron, the Thirteenth of
this Month of April, MDCXLIII.

Oxford: Leonard Lichfield, 1643

Wing C 2513
Thomason 669.f.7 (8)
Steele 2408
Madan 1320

The number of editions is some indication of the importance attached to this statement, which was meant to
demonstrate that the King did not reject a genuine offer
of peace. It is a firm rehearsal of the now familiar
position that nothing in the Parliament's overture was
sufficient to lead to a just compromise.

In [56] above is an appended paragraph, also by Hyde, which clarifies the royalist analysis, and which becomes the foundation of subsequent propaganda:

> To this gratious offer of His Majesties, by which his great Desire of Peace, and readnesse to disband His Army, and Returne to His Parliament (so He and His Parliament may be secured from Tumults and violence) are made visible to all the World, not so much as any answer hath yet been returned from both Houses, but upon the receipt thereof (as fearing perhaps least any continuance of the Treaty upon so reasonable an offer, might unavoydably produce a peace) The Committee of both Houses were immediately recall'd by new Orders; and that of the House of Commons commanded to hasten their returne in most strict and unusuall termes.

57   [April, 1643]
THE REASONS OF THE LORDS and COMMONS IN PARLIAMENT, Why they cannot agree to the Alteration and Addition in the Articles of CESSATION offered by HIS MAJESTY. WITH HIS MAIESTIES Gratious Answer thereunto.   April 4. 1643.
(25 pp.)

Oxford: Leonard Lichfield, 1643

Wing E 2214
Thomason E. 95 (1)
Madan 1309
Hist. Reb., ii, 523-24 (gives four reasons but not the
   answer)

Wing E 2215 (Thomason E. 247 (29); Madan 1310) is a London counterfeit.

The King's answer (pp. 9-25) responds exhaustively to each of six objections raised by the Lords and Commons, and apologizes for such enlargement, claiming that the language of Parliament makes this a necessary resort. It does not confine itself only to the six points, but frequently asserts the King's pacific intentions.   In *Hist. Reb.*, ii, 524, Hyde refers to the King's answer in order to explain why the King accepted a cessation on Parliament's terms, but does not quote it.

The pamphlet occurs in a volume which Thomason loaned to the King in the autumn of 1647, and which the King dropped accidentally in the mud. After the Restoration Thomason affected to regard this circumstance as a signal mark of honor. It is possible that this particular tract

was the one which Charles wished to consult at that time.
Thomason records on the fly-leaf the full particulars
which read in part,

> I sent it to his Mâtie who having done with it and
> having it with him when he was going towards the Isle
> of Wight let it fall in the durt, and then callinge
> for the two persons before mentioned (who attended
> him) delivered it to them with a charge, as they
> should answer it another day, that they should both
> speedily and safely return it to him, from whom they
> had received it, and withall to desire the partie to
> goe on and continue what had begun, which booke to-
> gether with his Mâtie signification to me by these
> worthy and faithfull gentln I received both speedily
> and safely.
>   Which volume hath the marke of honor upon it,
> which noe other volume in my collection hath.
> (Quoted in G.K. Fortescue, ed., *Catalogue of the
> Thomason Tracts,* London, 1908, vol. 1, pt. i, viii).

58   [May, 1643]
HIS MAJESTIES MESSAGE TO BOTH HOUSES Aprill 12. 1643.
CONCERNING DISBANDING of both Armies; AND HIS MAJESTIES
RETURNE TO BOTH Houses of PARLIAMENT. WITH HIS MAIESTIES
Message to both Houses of PARLIAMENT in Pursuance of the
same. OXFORD 19. May 1643. (6 pp.)

Oxford: Leonard Lichfield, 1643

Wing C 2458
Madan 1359
Hist. Reb., iii, 35-36

     The first part of this document is a reissue of [56A]
above. The second part is new material which was also
issued separately as

58A HIS MAIESTIES MESSAGE, Sent the twentieth of May, MDCXLIII.
    (brs.)

Oxford: Leonard Lichfield, 1643

Wing C 2438
Thomason 669.f.7 (16)
Steele 2427
Madan 1363

     Madan identifies it as a carelessly printed London
counterfeit, probably issued May 25. Since Hyde's MS
reproduces one of the false readings it is possible that

this is the edition he consulted when compiling book VII
in Jersey.
   Its purpose is to ensure that the public recognizes
that peace negotiations were broken off by Parliament.
It concludes with dire warnings of the consequences of
continuing hostilities, and points out that the royal
anxiety for peace is by no means a sign of martial weakness; on the contrary, the King's forces are now plenti-
fully supplied.

59   [May, 1643]
     THE KINGS MAJESTIES DECLARATION To all His loving Subjects
     of His Kingdome of SCOTLAND. WITH An Act of the Lords of
     His Majesties Privie Councell for the printing and pub-
     lishing thereof. (10 pp.)

     Edinburgh: Evan Tyler, 1643

     Wing C 2245
     Thomason E. 104 (24)

        This is by the official printer in Scotland. There
     is another by Barker at Shrewsbury (Wing C 2244), and one
     by Lichfield at Oxford (Wing C 2245A, Madan 1376). This
     later edition adds a letter from the Lord Chancellor of
     Scotland to the King.
        Vigorous denunciation of sedition and rebellion in
     England leads to a warning against the infectious poison
     working on Scottish affections. It complains about the
     rebels in England procuring agents in Scotland, and refers
     to one who wrote to Pym on January 9 assuring him of sup-
     port. That Scotland is the King's native country is much
     emphasized, and his subjects are asked to secure their
     peace and happiness against the claims of "Brownists and
     Anabaptists and other independent Sectaries." It con-
     cludes, "We cannot doubt Our good Subjects there, will so
     far hearken to the treason and malice of Our enemies, as
     to interrupt their own present peace and happinesse."

60   [June, 1643]
     HIS MAJESTIES DECLARATION To all His loving Subjects, IN
     ANSWER TO A DECLARATION of the LORDS and COMMONS upon the
     proceedings of the late TREATY OF PEACE AND severall
     Intercepted Letters, of His MAJESTY to the QUEENE, and
     of PRINCE RUPERT to the Earle of NORTH-HAMPTON. OXFORD,
     3. Iune 1643. (48 pp.)

Oxford: Leonard Lichfield, 1643

Wing C 2232
Thomason E. 104 (31)
Madan 1374

There is also a London counterfeit, Wing C 2233
(Madan 1375), actually the work of Royston, who was sent
for as a delinquent by the Commons (see Madan 1375).
Wing records a Shrewsbury edition by Barker, C 2231, and
a York edition, C 2233A.

This contains a detailed analysis of the proceedings
at Westminster, including such precise information as the
numbers of members voting on particular issues, the number
of sittings, etc. Its description of the strategy of the
aborted peace treaty is identical with that in *Hist. Reb.*,
and its account of the gradual effect of the King's replies, declarations, etc., in influencing public opinion
is consonant with the opinions Hyde offers from time to
time in *Hist. Reb.* Emphasis is laid on the claim that
Parliament, or what is left of it, has, in fact, covertly
made new laws, and has not observed the known laws of the
land. At the recent treaty it became apparent to many
(or, as Hyde characteristically phrases it, "to all the
world") that the King has made all reasonable concessions.
It objects again to the calumnious misconstructions of
the King's actions, extending even to malicious specula-
tion on his undeclared intentions: "After that from declaring of Law, they came to declaring of Thoughts, &
forgetting that The Hearts of Kings are inscrutable, presumed to dive into His."

The people to whom he refers are the most active
managers of the rebellion, and the account of their
actions, accompanied with a point-by-point rebuttal of
their arguments used in the recent treaty, is aimed at
the moderate faction in Parliament in an attempt to divide
them from the others. To this end he prophesies the
extremes to which the managers of rebellion are committed,
including democracy, the removal of distinctions in class
and quality, and the removal of the fundamental laws of
Church and State. The moderates will be persecuted by
extremists who will forget that they never opposed them.
This is a mature Hyde polemic in his high style. Madan
characterizes it as "gravely written."

61   [July, 1643]
     HIS MAJESTIES DECLARATION To all His loving Subjects,
     after His Victories over THE LORD FAIRFAX IN THE NORTH,
     AND, Sr WILLIAM WALLER IN THE WEST, AND THE TAKING OF
     BRISTOLL by His MAJESTIES FORCES.   (6 pp.)

     Oxford: Leonard Lichfield, 1643

     Wing C 2225
     Madan 1429
     Hist. Reb., iii, 118-120

        There are other official editions from York
     (Wing C 2226) and Shrewsbury (Wing C 2227).   The Decla-
     ration is dated July 30.
        This most important declaration, at the height of
     royalist military success, was regarded by Hyde as having
     been nearly decisive in bringing the war to a close.   To
     its general moderation and its offer of pardon to Parlia-
     ment opponents, Hyde attributes the initiative of the
     House of Lords, striving for accommodation, and the
     initial concurrence of the Commons.   For an account of
     these events, and reasons for the eventual rejection of
     peace, see *Hist. Reb.*, iii, 135-140.
        The declaration renews the King's assurances of pro-
     tection of the Protestant religion made in September,
     1642 (see *Hist. Reb.*, iii, 312-313) which were no doubt
     also penned by Hyde.   The declaration lays further empha-
     sis on matters of religion by condemning the intentions
     of the rebels to subvert established religion.   The happi-
     ness of the kingdom before the present distractions is
     also depicted in an appealing manner.   Ironically, although
     the declaration celebrates the King's now greater freedom
     to publish his intentions, the declaration seems to have
     been suppressed in London.

62   [Nov., 1643]
     A LETTER FROM THE LORDS AT OXFORD and other LORDS whose
     names are SUBSCRIBED, TO THE LORDS OF THE PRIVY-COVNCELL
     and the Conservators of the Peace of the Kingdom of
     SCOTLAND.   (5 pp.)

     Oxford: Leonard Lichfield, 1643 [1644]

     Wing E 2814
     Madan 1542
     Hist. Reb., iii, 287-288 n.

In *Hist. Reb*. Hyde states that this letter was sent at the end of November, 1643. This edition (probably the only one) is dated March 1, 1643, i.e., 1644.

Its purpose is to forestall an invasion by the Scots by means of discrediting the House of Lords at Westminster. This is said to be a rump, no more than twenty-five of its original complement continuing to sit, whereas fifty-two Lords of the Oxford Parliament, omitting recusants and minors, subscribe this document. The case of the Commons, it argues, is not dissimilar. Therefore the Scots should ignore the blandishments of the London Parliament and forbear military action. Nevertheless, as Hyde admits, it was much more likely to have an effect in England than in Scotland (*Hist. Reb.*, iii, 289 n.).

One of its most interesting features is the close resemblance of its opening sentence to that of *Hist. Reb.*: "If for no other reason, yet that posterity may know that we have done our duties, and not sat still while our brethren of Scotland were transported with a dangerous and fatal misunderstanding [etc.]."

Section B

Forgeries, Satires, and
Anonymous Political Tracts, 1642–1656

When the battle of officially sanctioned propaganda began to yield diminished results, Hyde's inventive pen turned to other means of persuasion, the variety of which is well illustrated below. He may properly be considered the innovator of these new types of polemic in the period, for which role he was apprenticed in the production of royalist apology described in Section A. The presses of London and Oxford were now well versed in the arts of counterfeit printing, and, later, with the exodus of royalists to the Netherlands and to France, presses there responded brilliantly to the exigencies of the English constitutional crisis and civil wars.

In the items recorded below, 63-74, may be seen a range of literary types. There are, so to speak, genuine forgeries, in which the fictional writer was meant to be mistaken (wholly, or to some degree) for his real-life counterpart, and thus dissension was to be sown, however briefly, in the opponent's ranks. Good examples of this method are [63], *A COMPLAINT*, [64], *TWO SPEECHES*, and [74], *A LETTER*, each of which seems, however briefly, to have achieved the desired effects in the enemy's counsels. Others, more satire than forgery, let slip their fictional masks quite quickly, even though they may continue to maintain the identity of the imaginary writer. Such are [65], *A LETTER*, [66], *A SPEECH*, [67], *A LETTER*, and [68], *A LETTER*. It is clear that in the forgery-satire category the old device of a letter (usually from the country) was highly popular.

A third type is that of the anonymous pamphlet usually written, by way of contrast, in a sober and serious vein, which comprises the rest, except for *The Difference and DISPARITY*, which for reasons given below is a problem. It may be a combination of the three types.

Whether any of these pamphlets (or their rebuttals) had the effect of converting opponents is to be doubted--not least because of the claims made in and for them of doing exactly that. They must, however, have amused and encouraged friends, and, it seems certain, enraged enemies.

Hyde was, of course, a diligent student of his opponents' literary mannerisms, and it is evident that he was eager to

continue this study in the years 1646 to 1648 when composing
the first part of the *History* and writing more royalist propaganda. (In fact, at the outset of his stay on Jersey these
two activities were one and the same.) A letter of April 7,
1647 to his friend Secretary Nicholas provides an amusing
insight into Hyde's habit of mind:

> I thank y^u for your freind Lilburne, and desire you to
> send me as many of his Bookes as you can, I learne much
> by them, and in earnest I finde a great benefitt by read-
> ing ill Bookes, for though they want Judgm^t. and Logique
> to prove what they promise, yet they bring good materialls
> to prove somewhat they doe not thinke off, and soe I
> gaine very much Law by reading M^r. Prynne, though nothing
> of it bee applicable to those purposes for wch. he produces
> it.

He then thanks Nicholas for the loan of a bundle of "Heresyes
and Frenzyes," including, it seems, Mr. Milton's "Opinions of
Wedlock (from whence a race of goodly conclusions will naturally flow)," although these are but a portion of the newly
propagated doctrines about to be pronounced orthodox by the
Assembly. There is also in this letter an interesting reference to Hyde's having caused a work by Nicholas (concerning
religion) to be translated into French.[1]

For some of the earlier forgeries I have included description and discussion of responses made by Parliament sympathizers, or irenicists, to show something of the venom they
caused. Sometimes the enraged responses suggest a delicious
self-indulgence, rather than genuine horror. When the war
was being waged in earnest, the penmen, Hyde among them,
increased the level of vituperation and scorn in their works,
but war leaves those engaged with little leisure or inclination to be persuaded by argument. In *A FULL ANSWER* [72] one
sees Hyde at an extremely crucial period revert to the method
of learned and forensic analysis, because once again, on the
edge of a fatal and fateful juncture of affairs, it was necessary to persuade enemies who might be wavering in their
courage to take a decisive step, to reconsider.

METHOD and ABBREVIATIONS: as in Section A.

1. Bodleian MS Clarendon 29, fol. 183. A portion of this
letter is printed in *State Papers* [155], ii, p. 363, and it
is noticed in *Calendar of Clarendon State Papers* [193], i,
p. 372, item 2488.

63   [Dec., 1642]
     A COMPLAINT TO THE House of Commons, AND Resolution taken
     up by the free Protestant Subjects of the Cities of London
     and Westminster, and the Counties adjacent. (22 pp.)

     Oxford: Leonard Lichfield, 1642

     Wing C 5620
     Thomason E. 244 (31)
     Madan 1148

         Thomason received his copy January 2. On the evidence
     of the *Journal of the House of Commons*, January 2, 1642/3,
     Madan considers this to be the printing of J. Wright in
     London, not Lichfield's, thus a counterfeit, and dates its
     publication as probably December 31. He quotes *Mercurius
     Aulicus*: "There came a Booke from London, being the com-
     plaint of London, Westminster and the parts adjoyning,
     which the King caused to be read unto him as He sate at
     supper: His Majestie not rising from the Table till the
     whole was finished."
         Madan has difficulty in establishing the order of
     editions. The following is the sequence he suggests:
     1149, a translation into Dutch; 1150, a second London
     counterfeit; 1151, probably a third London counterfeit;
     1152, a genuine Oxford reprint of about January 6; 1153,
     a second Oxford reprint of February or March. The several
     London editions were disseminated in the areas of St.
     Paul's, Westminster Abbey, and Westminster Hall. Parlia-
     ment moved to suppress it by ordering that it be burned,
     and by punishing the supposed printer, J. Wright.
         It is not difficult to appreciate the King's avid
     attention to this masterly Hyde forgery. The key to its
     success is the initial plausibility of the argument which
     establishes, as Madan remarks, the independence of the
     author's viewpoint. Its opening pages deal with notorious
     grievances prior to the outbreak of civil war, such as
     the soap monopoly, the Archbishop of Canterbury's tyranny
     ("equall to a Pope in England"), and the Court of Star
     Chamber. It is by no means clear that this is not an
     authentic complaint of London Protestants, being studded
     with invectives against papists, Jesuits, prelates, etc.
     Not until p. 6 does the author tip his hand by praising
     the "goodnesse of the King" evidenced in his willingness
     to accept the advice of his Parliament, and thus abolish-
     ing ship money, Star Chamber and the High Commissions, as
     well as passing an Act for Triennial Parliaments: "We
     blesse God we have such a King."

From this point on, with remarkable grasp of detail, the pamphlet is an indictment of Parliament's proceedings, and of the oppressive behavior of a number of London's aldermen. It calls for parliamentary justice to be brought down on them and their schemes. Remaining firmly in character throughout, the writer represents the interests of protestant citizens, wondering what will become of their liberties, and under this cover intruding those objections to the innovations of Parliament in matters civil and ecclesiastical which typify Hyde's political works in this period.

A postscript claims that this was written in some haste before its "authors" knew of the intentions of other counties, but urges them totally to oppose new ordinances and to abide by the laws of the land.

The effect of this pamphlet may be gauged not only by the number of editions, but also by the number and vehemence of objections to it. These are described and discussed below:

63A A COMPLAINT TO THE House of Commons, AND Resolution taken up by the free Protestant Subjects of the Cities of London and Westminster, and the Counties adjacent. (13 pp.)

Oxford: Leonard Lichfield, 1642

Wing C 5623
Thomason E. 245 (5)
Madan 1179

The title imitates the original, but the imprint is fictitious, and the whole is a satirical attack upon Hyde's forgery. It starts as if it were a parody of Hyde's work, imitating the opening sentence: "Loosers may speake by authority of a Proverb, and then we are sure we ought not to be silenced." This is not sustained as the pamphlet quickly becomes a complaint in earnest against anti-parliamentary pamphlets, prelates, papists, and malignants in general. It is marked by lively and uncouth diction, spelling, and syntax.

63B A IVST COMPLAINT, OR LOVD CRIE, OF ALL the vvell-affected Subiects in ENGLAND. AGAINST That false and scandalous Pamphlet, Intituled, A Complaint to the House of Commons, and Resolution taken up by the free Protestant Subiects of the Cities of LONDON and WESTMINSTER, and the Counties adjacent. In which Answer is given to all Obiections that doe arise, concerning the late Ordinance of Parliament, for the levying of the twentieth part of mens

estates, towards the maintainance of the Forces that are
raised by them, for the defence of the King and Parliament: And the Law sufficiently manifested and cleared.
(31 pp.)

London: "Printed in the yeare of our Lord 1642"

Wing J 1232
Thomason E. 245 (27)

In contrast to [63A] this is a head-on attack by a
parliamentary sympathizer. The just complainer addresses
the author of the original as "Thou spurious, ill-bred,
undocumented Brat, why wast thou not buried in the womb?,"
presumably reacting to Hyde's opinion that some Parliament
pamphlets should have been "strangled in the birth" and
"buried in oblivion." The just complainer continues in
this spirit with a point-by-point refutation.

63C AN ANSWER TO The late Scandalous and Libellous PAMPHLET,
ENTITULED, A COMPLAINT to the House of Commons; And
Resolution taken up by the free Protestant Subjects of
the Cities OF LONDON and WESTMINSTER, and the Counties
adjacent. Wherein 'tis proved, that the Lord MAJOR of
London doth not usurp his Office; but is a Legall Major,
and obedience ought to be given him. By PETER BLAND of
Grays-Inne, Gent. (14 pp.)

London: John Field, 1643

Wing B 3160
Thomason E. 244 (36)

It is addressed to the current Lord Mayor, Isaac
Pennington. The author of the scandalous pamphlet is
convicted of abominable lies, and the complaints he
expresses are systematically rebutted with the help of
appropriate legal arguments.

63D A VVhisper in the eare. OR A DISCOURSE BETWEEN THE KINGS
MAIESTY, AND THE HIGH COVRT OF PARLIAMENT. Concerning a
Pacification, and Conditions of PEACE. By a Scholler of
Oxford, and a Citizen of London. (7 pp.)

Oxford: Leonard Lichfield, 1642 [43]

Wing W 1676
Thomason E. 244 (43)
Madan 1171

This is a London counterfeit which Madan dates about
January 8, since Thomason received his copy January 9.

There was a good deal of moderate, accommodationist
literature penned in London, often with spurious Oxford
imprints, in December and January. In this instance a
motto enclosed in border ornament at the top of the title
page--"Blessed are the peace makers"--proclaims the
author's irenic intent. The citizen and the Oxford gentleman (his role as a scholar is not much emphasized) agree
in deploring acts of senseless destruction on the one
hand, such as damage done to the furnishing of Canterbury
Cathedral, and the behavior of royalist delinquents such
as John Digby, Earl of Bristol and the Earl of Newcastle.
Thus the citizen and the gentleman begin to come together
by agreeing in their respect for Parliament and their
belief in the King's peaceful intentions. They show that
the Parliament's positions and those of the King in his
published documents are not incompatible. Both save
their strongest language to condemn the scandalous pamphlet, *A COMPLAINT*. The citizen objects that

> the aforesaid pamplet is stuffed with intoller-
> able language, full of bitternesse and invectives
> against the Parliament, and their legall proceedings:
> therein that great Councell of the King and Kingdome
> is called a corporation of Projectors, and most un-
> justly taxed for doing nothing these two years past
> tending to the good of the Republique.

The gentleman is concerned with the punishment to be
inflicted on the perpetrators of the forgery:

> And as that scandalous Pamphlet is condemned to
> be burnt by the hand of the hangman, so may the
> malignant author, contriver, & publisher thereof be
> stigmatized and branded with the perpetual marke of
> infamy for defaming so renowned an Assembly in that
> false and infamous and libellous Pamphlet.

There is an interesting and inventive attack on *A Complaint* in *The Malignants Conventicle: OR, A learned Speech
spoken by M. VVEB* (see [66B]). The fictional speaker is a
royalist *agent provocateur* who rehearses the wickedness of
his fellow operators:

> So we drew up a most damnable abusive Booke amongst
> our selves, to scandalize the Parliament, I know you
> have all seen it, it is called the Cities Complaint
> to the House of Commons, &c. This Booke we got a
> foolish Printer that did not know what he did, to

> print, for it was such a most wicked, invective Pam-
> phlet, that had hee had either Conscience, Religion,
> Obedience, or humanity, if he knew what it was, he
> would not have meddled with it, nor indeed would I
> Gentlemen, had I any other hopes to rest on.

64 [Jan., 1643]
    TWO SPEECHES Made in the House of PEERS, On Munday the
    19 of December, For, and Against Accommodation. The one
    by the Earl of Pembroke, the other by the Lord Brooke.
    The latter Printed by Order of the House of COMMONS.
    Hen. Elsinge, Cler. Parl. D. Com.   (6 pp.)

    London: for Joh. Thompson, 1642 [1643]

    Wing P 1125
    Thomason E. 84 (35)

Thomason received his copy on January 10, 1643, which
was probably the day of publication. The *Thomason Catalogue* describes it as a satire, and there is no doubt an
element of satire running through this and the other forgeries described in this section. But, also in common
with the others, it was intended to deceive, and in this,
as Clarendon's entertaining account makes clear, wonder-
fully succeeded.

> After the king came to Oxford with his army, his
> majesty one day speaking with the lord Falkland very
> graciously concerning Mr. Hyde, said he had such a
> peculiar style, that he would know anything written
> by him, if it were brought to him by a stranger,
> amongst a multitude of writings by other men. The
> lord Falkland answered, he doubted his majesty could
> hardly do that, because he himself, who had so long
> conversation and friendship with him, was often de-
> ceived; and often met with things written by him, of
> which he could never have suspected him, upon a
> variety of arguments. To which the king replied,
> he would lay him an angel, that, let the argument be
> what it would, he should never bring him a sheet of
> paper (for he would not undertake to judge of less)
> of his writing, but he should discover it to be his.

Some days later the King read

> two speeches, the one made by the lord Pembroke for
> an accomodation, and the other by the lord Brooke
> against it; and for the carrying on the war with more

vigour, and utterly to root out the cavaliers, which
were the King's party.
   The king was very much pleased with reading the
speeches, and said, he did not think that Pembroke
could speak so long together; though every word he
said was so much his own, that nobody else could
make it. And so after he had pleased himself with
reading the speeches over again, and then passed to
other papers, the lord Falkland whispered in his ear,
(for there were other persons by), desiring him he
would pay him the angel. (*Life,* i, 136-137)

Clarendon then remarks that the King often called on
his services in this kind, and that he wishes he could
make a collection of the papers he had written at that
time.
   The target of this forgery, Lord Brooke, was not so
deceived, demanding of the House of Lords that the pamphlet
should be burned. But, because his "speech" was printed
in the same pamphlet, Pembroke refused his necessary
consent.
   Clarendon scarcely exaggerates his earlier literary
skill. The speeches are well crafted, contrasting in
style and appropriate to their supposed progenitors.
Also, the circumstances typically giving rise to a parliamentary order for printing are closely parodied. On the
final page the commendation by the House of Lord Brooke's
violent speech appears over the authorization of the Clerk.
   Ernest Sirluck regards it as a "brilliant forgery,"
and observes that "it has not been fully recognized how
prominent a feature such parodies were of the polemic of
the period" (Milton, *Complete Prose Works,* Yale University
Press, 1953-74, ii, 57-58 and ii, 801).

65   [Jan., 1643]
     A LETTER WITHOVT Any Superscription, Intercepted in the
     way to LONDON. Published, that the poore people of
     England may see the intentions of those whom they have
     followed   (7 pp.)

     [s.n.]   Printed in the Yeare, 1643

     Wing L 1757
     Thomason E. 86 (31)

        Thomason's copy is dated January 28, 1642.
        Although attribution to Hyde of this amusing forgery
     is not susceptible of conclusive demonstration, considera-
     tions of style and subject matter, and the similarity of

its form to that of *A LETTER WRITTEN Out of the Country*, [68] below, make for its inclusion here. The genre of a country letter to a townsman is a long-established vehicle of political satire which Hyde modifies, in this instance, by making his country correspondent a clandestine collaborator in the aims of Parliament's manipulators. A comparable device is also employed in *A LETTER FROM A TRUE AND LAWFULL MEMBER OF PARLIAMENT*, [74] below.

This fiction allows him to expose their designs by means of confidential advices, and at the same time to show their futility by reporting that the effectiveness of earlier deceptions is wearing thin. (Parliament's polemicists rapidly learned to turn the same trick: see *The Malignants Conventicle*, [66B] below). The people, on "whose weaknesse we have wrought to advance the wonderful things we have designed," now begin to see the truth of things. It is time, therefore, to resort to more stringent and blatant measures since people inquire into the legality of Parliament's actions. With the country informant's suggestions of new enterprises the exaggeration necessary to satire finds its full play. He asks whether it is now time to suppress the Prayer Book, and to disable from inheritance all children who are christened with the sign of the cross. It is now time also to declare the levelling intentions of Parliament, and, in a parody of enthusiastic language, he urges that the spirit must now be freed, and that any man with a gift be allowed to preach.

There are also mock definitions. "Malignants," as the term is used in parliamentary propaganda, are those who believe themselves bound by Acts of the former Parliament, not the Votes and Orders of this one. Parliament has "providently distinguished in the Kings case between his Person, and his Office, thereby enabling men without danger of the Law to conspire the death of the King in the behalfe of his office." This, and other devices, are treated in a congratulatory tone, but the ending reverts to the problem of keeping up pretences. So it is necessary to "lay out some new Baite for the people; and we conceive it will be better to perswade them that Peace is not good for them (which may be improved by many petty arguments) then to endeavour to make them beleeve that you endeavour to procure it."

66 [Jan., 1643]
A SPEECH MADE BY ALDERMAN GARROVVAY, AT A COMMON-HALL on Tuesday the 17. of IANUARY. UPON OCCASION OF A SPEECH

delivered there the Friday before, by Mr Pym, at the
reading of His MAJESTIES Answer to the late Petition.
(12 pp.)

[s.n.] 1642 [1643]

Wing G 280
Madan 1201
There is another edition under the title:

66A The Loyal Citizen Revived. A SPEECH MADE BY Alderman
Garroway, AT A COMMON-HALL, On Tuesday the 17. of
January, 1642. Upon occasion of a Speech delivered there
the Friday before, by Mr. Pym, at the reading of His
Majesties Answer to the late Petition. (4 pp.)

[s.n.]

Wing G 279

This lively and interesting forgery masquerades as a
speech by Sir Henry Garroway (Garway, or Garraway, the
latter form used in *DNB*), a former Lord Mayor of London
conspicuous for his loyalty to the King. Madan points
out that the title page omits all mention of London in
order that it might be supposed issued in that city. In
fact it is the work of Lichfield in Oxford.
The discourteous treatment afforded the King's messenger by the City men is contrasted to the prompt and civil
treatment of their messenger by the King. The King's
answer is then commended to the reader's favor:

Strangers are admitted to make bitter invective
Speeches against it and the King that sent it; While
no honest Citizen, who have only right to speake here,
durst speake his Conscience for fear of having his
Throat cut as he went home. Think (Gentlemen) what
an encouragement we have given His Majesty to treat
and correspond with us, whilest he is thus used.

Throughout it displays intimate knowledge of the
King's declarations, speeches, etc., and of recent
speeches by Pym. Following the "speech" there is an
elaborate account of subsequent proceedings, including
descriptions of how, during the speech, some hissed and
others cried "Hear him," and "we will not loose our
Priviledges." The author imaginatively devises remarks
passed by members of the public in the throng outside
the hall. For example, a butcher and a mariner declare
themselves persuaded by the King's arguments, and the
fictional Garraway carries the day. Madan (1201) regards

this as "an interesting and authentic narrative of the
subsequent proceedings of the day." Possible confirmation
of his view and, more significantly, of the effect of
Hyde's forgery may be found in:

66B The Malignants Conventicle: OR, A learned Speech spoken
by M. VVEB, a Citizen, to the rest of his Society, Which
did consist of

Citizen -	Priests,
Malignants,	Apprentices,
Papists,	Wenches.

At their common Tavern meeting-house in Lincolnes Inne-
fields. In which are many things very necessary to be
observed, and of so great concernment, that if you will
not believe, then take what followes: For now all is out.
(6 pp.)

London: Printed for Anti-Dam-mee, in Tell-troth Lane, at
the signe of the Holly-wand. 1643.

Wing W 1204 and M 322
Thomason E. 245 (24)

Thomason received his copy on January 28, 1643.
"M. Web's" speech rejoices in a number of clandestine
royalist activities in London, including the disruption
of a meeting at a common hall. This must refer to the
substance of [66] above. There is also an account of a
(foiled) mass rape-attempt by "Cavaliers" at Newark-on-
Trent. It concludes with the speaker admitting that he
has had a bad cause which fares accordingly. The title
page sports a lavish woodcut of wenches in a tavern.
There is a reprint of Hyde's Garroway forgery which
Madan (1201) mentions but does not describe, assuming it
to be a London counterfeit edition. Thomason regarded
it as Oxford work, and annotated his copy to that effect.
Its title is:

66C A SPEECH MADE BY Alderman Garroway, AT A COMMON-HALL, On
Tuesday the 17. of JANUARY. Upon occasion of a Speech
delivered there the Friday before, by M. Pym, at the
reading of His Majesties Answer to the late PETITION.
WJTH A LETTER from a Scholler in Oxfordshire [etc.]
(23 pp.)

[s.n.] MDCXLIII

Wing G 281
Thomason E. 245 (29)

Thomason dates his copy February 1. The second part
(*A LETTER from a Scholler* [etc.]) is discussed in [67]
below. The pagination runs 2-8, the "speech"; 7-18, the
"letter"; 19-22, relation of a victory.

An adversary able both to admire and deplore Hyde's
work wrote a reply:

66D A Briefe ANSVVER TO A Scandalous Pamphlet, ENTITULED A
Speech made at a Common Hall by Alderman Garroway. With
some few observations upon other Pamphlets of the like
nature, especially that, CALLED A Letter sent into Milk-
street. (6 pp.)

London: Francis Nicolson, Febr. 15 1643

Wing B 4542
Thomason E. 89 (18)

The brief answerer, whose claimed objective is to
clear Garroway's name, also understands very well Hyde's
methods: "the cunningest and most venomous serpent lurks
in the smoothest and greenest grasse." He compares
Hyde's method with that of the author of a *Letter sent
into Milk-street,* who has "a more acute and dangerous
stile" and therefore may be a pedantic University
scholar, a man of learning but no wisdom. He admires
the "craftie wit of the Author" of the Garroway scandal,
but cannot condone his conclusions, feeling that the King
should have continued to cooperate with Parliament. Of
royalist forgeries in general he observes:

I dare boldly averre, that bookes of this nature
have done more mischiefe since the beginning of these
distractions and troubles in this Kingdome, then any
one thing whatsoever, the people being more disturbed
in their minds, and staggered in their understandings
by such seditious untruths, then they could by any
other publike endevour, mans nature being desirous of
novelties, and apt to credit them, when they come
dressed like devells in Angells shapes, in the
painted outside of faire and specious language.

None of this was of much benefit to Sir Henry Garroway
who was dismissed from his several offices and on May 2,
1643 expelled from the court of aldermen. On November 5
he was arrested for refusal to contribute to Parliament's
coffers, and died in July 1646 in the parish of St. Mary
Magdalen, Milk street.

67 [Jan., 1643]
    A LETTER From A SCHOLLER IN OXFORD-SHIRE to his Vnkle a
    Merchant in Broad-street, upon occasion of a Book In-
    tituled, A Moderate and most Proper Reply to a Declaration
    Printed and Published under His Majesties Name, Decemb. 8.
    intended against an Ordinance of Parliament for Assessing,
    &c. Sent to the Presse by the Merchant, who confesseth
    himselfe converted by it. (21 pp.)

    [s.n.] 1642 [1643]

    Wing L 1436
    Madan 1166

       This is likely to be the first edition, and, as Madan
    establishes, printed in Oxford. He also draws attention
    to a rare Latin translation, the title of which he gives
    as:

67A EPISTOLA Studiosi Oxoniensis, Ad MERCATOREM LUNDINENSEM
    PATRUUM, STATUM Controversiae hodie-Anglicae strictim
    designans.

    [Amsterdam?]: M.DC.XLIII

       There is another edition, probably the second, in
    which the "Scholler's" letter is added to the reprinted
    materials of [66], i.e., [66C] above. The full title
    follows:

67B [Jan., 1643]
    A SPEECH MADE BY Alderman Garroway, AT A COMMON-HALL, On
    Tuesday the 17. of JANUARY. Upon occasion of a Speech
    delivered there the Friday before, by M. Pym, at the
    reading of His Majesties Answer to the late PETITION:
    WJTH A LETTER from a Scholler in Oxfordshire, to his Vnkle
    a Merchant in Broad-street, Upon occasion of a Book in-
    tituled, A moderate and most Proper Reply to a Declara-
    tion, Printed and Published under His Majesties Name,
    Decemb. 8. intended against an Ordinance of Parliament
    for Assessing, &c. Sent to the Presse by the Merchant,
    who confesseth himselfe converted by it. Also a true and
    briefe Relation of the great Victory obtained by Sir
    Ralph Hopton, neere Bodmin, in the County of Cornwall,
    Jan. 19. 1642. (23 pp.)

    [s.n.] MDCXLIII

    Wing G 281
    Thomason E. 245 (30)

The Garroway speech (Thomason E. 245 (29)) is pp. 2-8.
Pp. 7-18 (mispagination) are the Letter, and pp. 19-22,
the Relation of the Victory. Thomason received his copy
on February 1, and thought it to be Oxford work. Madan
is sure that it is London.

Hyde's fiction is elaborate. The scholar's uncle,
although kind and generous to him, credits Parliament's
position, and wishes the scholar to persuade his father
(a "Malignant") to pay one-twentieth of his estate before
the parliamentary assessors take it. He has sent to the
scholar a copy of the Ordinance and the King's reply (see
[49] above). The scholar, however, is satisfied by the
royal reply. The scholar's argument is that Parliament's
claims are weak; it can merely forbid publication of the
King's replies and plunder and imprison the printers of
them. If all the King's replies had been openly and
honestly published as required by the King, then "those
Paper-bullets (as hee calls them) would have killed this
War in the wombe, and the same People who have beene now
seduced into Rebellion, would have kept their Seducers
to their Loyalty, whether they would or no."

He objects to Parliament's declaring that a declaration
by the King was not from his pen, even though it was in
the royal hand and sealed with his signet. There follows
a detailed attack upon Parliament's proceeding by way of
ordinances rather than the known laws of the land, thus
echoing others of Hyde's recent works on the King's behalf. There is an account from the beginning of how the
war came about, which identifies one special cause: "All
this while (to prepare the people to suffer any wrong to
be offered the King) the Presses and the Pulpits (the two
seed-plots of this Warre) had swarmed daily with slanderous
Invectives against his Majestie: (besides Declarations of
a strange nature.)"

In a postscript the scholar puts himself in mind of
the fact that he is writing to his uncle, and thus apologizes for his "unusuall stile."

68   [Feb., 1643]
      A LETTER VVRITTEN Out of the Country TO Mr IOHN PYM
      Esquire, one of the Worthy Members of the House of
      COMMONS, February 1.   (5 pp.)

      [n.p.] W. Webb, M.DC.XLII

      Wing E 30
      Thomason E. 89 (5)
      Madan 1226

The letter is signed "R.E." Madan believes this to be
the work of an Oxford press, but not Lichfield's. Thomason also regards it as Oxford work. He received his copy
February 11. Is it more than coincidence that the printer's name is so similar to that of the pretended speech
maker in *The Malignants Conventicle*, [66B]?

This forgery is further evidence of Hyde's campaign
to discredit Pym. The ingenious fiction of the piece is
that a former confidant of Pym now finds it much more
difficult than formerly to dispense propaganda because it
is no longer believed by the royalist adherents: "their
sufferings hath prevailed above your Rhetorick." It then
develops into a critique of Parliamentary duplicity, and
as a defense of the King, written as if by one who has at
last seen the truth, the scales having fallen from his
eyes. Pym is represented as the leader of "Rebellion and
Lewdnesse," the maker of plausible lies at others' expense.
All this is the "faithfull advice of Your most affectionate
friend, and humble servant R.E."

A postscript advises that a recent title, *His Majesties Declaration and finall Resolution, concerning the
Honourable City of London*, has been detected by the King
as the forgery it is, and burned by the hangman: "pray be
more circumspect hereafter."

The *Letter* provoked an angry and knowing response:

68A An ANSVVER TO A LETTER Written out of the country, to
Master John Pym, Esquire, one of the worthy Members of
The House of Commons. (7 pp.)

London: Anno Dom. 1643.

Wing E 26
Thomason E. 246 (24)

"Though R.E. I am not acquainted with you, yet have I
often perused your Diabolicall forgeries, the bitternesse
of your complaints, the invective poison couched in your
speeches, and the treacherous calumnies written in your
Letters: wondring that a Papist dare be so saucie, to
invent such untruths against the State, knowing the Lawes
to condemne such Pharisees as treasonable."

69 [Nov., 1645]
TRANSCENDENT AND MVLTIPLIED REBELLION AND TREASON,
DISCOVERED, By the Lawes of the Land. (26 pp.)

[s.n.] 1645

Wing C 4428
Thomason E. 308 (29)
Madan 1823

Madan thinks this the work of Lichfield at Oxford.
He supposes it was printed on November 3, and Thomason
received his copy November 10. There is a copy in the
hand of Edgeman (Hydes's secretary and amanuensis at this
time) among MSS Clarendon in the Bodleian. It is also
reprinted in *Clarendon State Papers*.

The first section is an argument concerning the
source of the authority of the magistrate, which leads to
an analysis of the reasons for the war (pp. 1-8). The
next section is subtitled "SEVERAL TREASONS BY The Lawes
of the Land," which runs from p. 9 to p. 25. The several
treasons and definitions of rebellion are cited and
elaborated. There follows a rehearsal of affairs from
the beginning of the Long Parliament along familiar
lines, which concludes with a postscript.

This is hardly a forgery in the usual sense (or a
satire) in that no fictional author is presented, but
rather a serious, sober, and anonymous political tract.
Perhaps this is because the pamphlet is an adaptation in
(presumably) miniature form of what was to have been a
book in the *History of the Rebellion*. It was to have been
book V of *Hist. Reb.*, which, because it was never written,
Hyde referred to as the "great hiatus." In the original
MS (Bodleian MS Clarendon 112) pp. 262-243 were left
blank to accommodate this book. There is, however, no
gap in narrative between the end of the original book IV
and the original book VI. Because of the "great hiatus,"
the books were finally redistributed. An outline of the
projected contents of the unwritten book is preserved in
an MS of Hyde's own hand, described in *Calendar of
Clarendon State Papers*, i, 503. The pamphlet noticed
here does not deal with each of the intended topics. For
further information, see Macray's note, *Hist. Reb.*, ii,
292.

70 [April, 1648]
    The Royall Apologie: OR, AN ANSWER TO THE DECLARATION OF
    THE HOUSE OF COMMONS, the 11. of February, 1647. In which
    they express the Reasons for their Resolutions for making
    no more Adresses, nor receiving any from HIS MAJESTY.
    (46 pp.)

    Paris: 1648

Wing D 1447
Thomason E. 522 (21)
Madan 1978

  Madan believes it was not printed in Paris, or Oxford,
but rather in London.
  This is a problem piece. The British Library Catalogue attributes it to Sir Kenelm Digby, but this attribution must rest on Thomason's annotation of his copy.
I do not know of any other evidence in support of that
claim. In the Bodleian Library Catalogue it is attributed
to Clarendon. But if that were correct, one must ask why
Hyde should then compose *An Answer*, [71] below, and addi-
tionally *A Full Answer*, [72] below, both of which are
certainly by Hyde. *An Answer* looks like Hyde's first
response before either he consulted or collected his documents, and *A Full Answer* his response with documents to
hand. But *The Royall Apologie* predates both (according
to Thomason), and its author seems to have had such
material available, even if, as appears by the sequence
of the argument, it was unsorted. Whoever composed it
had many of Hyde's works as royal penman by his side, and
used some of his characteristic arguments, which may be
seen duplicated in *An Answer*. An example is the explanation of why the rebels in Ireland described themselves as
the King's (or Queen's) army, and as loyalists. At places
Hyde's characteristic vocabulary and the patterns of his
analysis are recognizable. Perhaps these alone are reasons enough to include this piece here. It is to be
observed, however, that by as early as 1643 Hyde's language as royal apologist had become widely current, con-
stituting a neat and accessible terminology with which
to castigate rebellion.
  It refers the reader, as does *An Answer*, to a collection of Parliament and royal documents (presumably Husbands' collections) printed in sequence, in order that
the reader may compare them and so judge for himself. In
the text Sir Kenelm Digby is mentioned, but not in such a
manner as to suggest that he was the author.
  It seems to me possible that this was composed by
someone in close sympathy with Hyde's attitudes, even
though the preamble, which is addressed to his fellow
countrymen, explicitly denies the kinds of argument which
Hyde might employ (such as the Law of the Land, proper
allegiance, loyalty, the judgment of God, etc.) and instead bases the apology on grounds of natural law.
  There were other responses to the Parliament declaration, anonymous with similar titles, which seems to be

the cause of some confusion. One such, *THE REGALL APOLOGY*
[etc.], is attributed to Hyde in a Bodleian copy. Madan,
however, knows it to be the work of Dr. George Bates, and
recognizes it as printed by Royston. Its method is logical, or mathematical, divided and subdivided by theme, and
without special reference to Hyde's pamphlets. It does,
however, cover the same ground, as do they all: the ground
dictated by the charges in Parliament's declaration.

71 [April, 1648]
    AN ANSWER TO A PAMPHLET, ENTIT'LED, A Declaration of the
    Commons of England in Parliament assembled, expressing
    their Reasons and Grounds of passing the late Resolutions
    touching no further Addresse or Application to be made to
    the KING. (13 pp.)

    [s.n.] 1648

    Wing C 4417
    Thomason E. 438 (3)

        The title page employs the same ornaments as [72]
    below, where they are visibly more worn. This, therefore,
    is probably the work of R. Royston in London. Thomason
    received his copy on May 3.
        Late March or early April seems to be the likely time
    of composition. The vote of no more addresses to the
    King was January 15, 1648, and the declaration to which
    this responds, an exhaustive retrospective account of
    Charles' misdemeanors since even before his accession,
    was not published until January 17. It would have taken
    a considerable time for a copy of this to reach Hyde in
    Jersey (possibly via royalist connections in France) and
    again a considerable time for the answer to reach Royston.
    The answer seems to have been written very shortly after
    Hyde read the declaration.
        The King, prisoner at Carisbrooke Castle in the Isle
    of Wight, rejected four proposals from the Parliament,
    and demanded a personal treaty. This was no doubt an
    attempt to gain time by prevarication while emergent
    royalist military strength gathered head. The severity
    of the Parliament response is evidence of a growing sym-
    pathy for republicanism both in Parliament and in the
    army.
        Clearly Hyde was struck by the urgency of the new
    note of finality in the Parliament response, and so felt
    obliged to lay aside his *Hist. Reb.* on which he had been
    working single-mindedly for the past two years in his

island haven of Jersey, and resume the role of royal
apologist.

The authorial voice in this case uses the first person: "I (lying under Persecution, for my Conscience, and
Love to Regall Authority) have not the means, in everything, to make full Probations." What follows is a plain
man's refutation by common sense of the Parliament's
irrational and sometimes frivolous charges.

No doubt this was written very quickly with no time
taken to order and consult the relevant state papers.

72   [April, 1648]
A FULL ANSWER TO AN INFAMOUS AND TRAYTEROUS PAMPHLET,
ENTITULED, A Declaration of the Commons of England in
Parliament assembled, expressing their Reasons and
Grounds of passing the late Resolution touching no fur-
ther Adresse or Application to be made to the KING.
(172 pp.)

[n.p.] R. Royston, 1648

Wing C 4423
Thomason E. 455 (5)

Thomason's copy is dated July 28. Hyde must have
begun its composition immediately following *AN ANSWER*,
[71] above. It is to this work that Clarendon refers in
Life when he states that no sooner had he received the
Parliament declaration

> than he prepared a very large and full answer to it;
> in which he made the malice and the treason of that
> libellous declaration to appear; and his majesty's
> innocence in all the particulars charged upon him,
> with such pathetical applications and insinuations,
> as were most like to work upon the affections of the
> people: all which was transmitted (by the care of
> Mr. Secretary Nicholas, who resided in Caen in Nor-
> mandy, and held constant correspondence with the
> chancellor) to a trusty hand in London; who caused it
> to be well printed and divulged, and found means to
> send it to the king: who, after he had read it, said
> he durst swear it was writ by the chancellor, if it
> were not that there was more divinity in it than he
> expected from him, which made him believe he had con-
> ferred with Dr. Steward. But some months after,
> being informed by secretary Nicholas, he sent the
> chancellor thanks for it; and expressed upon all

occasions, that he was much pleased with that vindication. (i, 210; see also *Hist. Reb.*, iv, 286 n.)

This is an orderly, systematic refutation which con-
trasts with the style of *AN ANSWER*. The Parliament's
allegations are laid out numerically (27 in all), responded
to in the same sequence, and given a conclusion. The
tone is much more aloof and magisterial, avoiding the
first person, and in a scholarly fashion providing marginal notes to sources such as Husbands' collections. Hyde
relies on his former series of apologies for the royal
cause, believing them sufficient to dispel the calumnies
of Parliament's declaration.

The "divinity" which Charles noted is evident even in
the title page which cites a text from Micah. For the
most part the citations of Scripture are employed as cues
for those passages which provide "pathetical applications
and insinuations" to work on people's affections. There
is a heavy vein of prophetic foreboding as if he is aware
that here is a last chance to avoid a destructive course
of action. If people now sin, they do so wilfully, having
received knowledge of the truth so that "there remaineth
no more Sacrifice for Sins, but a certain fearful looking
for a Judgement, and a fiery Indignation, which shall
devour the Adversaries." There is also some inducement
to Army or Parliament to make the King's restoration their
own work, for which they will be gratefully rewarded.

This is the longest and most comprehensive of Hyde's
apologies, excepting, of course, the *History*; a sort of
summary view. It achieves a stately, sometimes barbed
tone, with an element of stridency occasionally to be
heard.

The *FULL ANSWER* was thought important enough to merit
a Latin translation:

72A PLENVM RESPONSVM AD FAMOSVM ET PRODITORIVM LIBELLVM,
Inscriptum, (Declaratio Communium Angliae congregatorum
in Parlamento, explicans rationes, propter quas nuper
statuerint non ampliùs agere cum REGE,)˙ [MICAE III, vers
XI] Impressum pro R. Royston. 1648. Ex Anglico in
Latinum fideliter translatum. (148 pp.)

Wing C 4424A and H 3867

The title given two Wing numbers is one and the same.
H 3867 is erroneously ascribed to Edward Hyde, the divine.

73   [?]

The Difference and DISPARITY Between The Estates and Con-
ditions OF GEORGE Duke of Buckingham, AND ROBERT Earl of
ESSEX.   By Sir Henry WOTTON Knight; And dedicated to the
Earl of PORTLAND.

Pp. 37-70 of:

Reliquiae Wottonianae.   OR A COLLECTION Of LIVES,
LETTERS, POEMS; With CHARACTERS OF Sundry PERSONAGES:
And other Incomparable PIECES of Language and Art.   By
the curious PENSIL of the Ever Memorable Sr Henry Wotton
K^t, Late, Provost of Eton Colledg.

London: Thomas Maxey for R. Marriot, G. Bedel, and
T. Garthwait, 1651.

Wing W 3648
Thomason E. 1254

        This is a curious and puzzling piece.   It was first
printed in this edition, where it follows directly upon a
Parallel between the two royal favorites actually composed by Wotton.   It is in plain contradiction to the
arguments of Wotton's *Parallel*, finding no grounds on
which to argue the similarity of Buckingham and Essex.
Why was it inserted into this commemorative volume?
        It appears to be an almost academic exercise in Plu-
tarchian character writing, but is suffused with dark and
cryptic comments upon the present times compared with the
days of Queen Elizabeth, and thus seems to refer to the
troubles of the 1640's.   The reign of Elizabeth is, for
example, characterized as a time when subjects were humbly
obedient, even though she often consulted with them.
When they had grievances they reverently conveyed them to
her notice, leaving the solution to her princely discretion.   When he speaks of an indefinite later period he
seems to be picturing conditions like those of the 1640's
as seen from a royalist perspective:

        'Twas a busie querulous froward time, so much
    degenerated from the purity of the former, that the
    people under pretences of Reformation, with some
    petulant discourses of Liberty (which their great
    Imposters scattered among them, like false glasses to
    multiply their fears) began Abditos Principis sensus,
    & quid occultius parat exquirere: extended their
    enquiries even to the chamber and private actions of

the King himself, forgetting that truth of the Poet,
Nusquam Libertas gratior extat, quam sub Rege pio:
'Twas strange to see how men afflicted themselves to
find out calamities and mischiefs whil'st they borrowed the name of some great persons to scandalize
the State they lived in. A generall disorder throughout the whole body of the commonwealth, nay the vital
part perishing, the Laws violated by the Judges,
Religion prophaned by the Prelats, Heresies crept
into the Church and countenanced: and yet all this
shall be quickly rectified without so much as being
beholding to the King, or consulting with the Clergy.

That the intention of the piece is to condemn the
developments of the Civil War seems to me unmistakable in
a comment on the opprobrium incurred by Buckingham as a
consequence of the wild rages of the people which branded
him enemy to King and country, "which certainly in the
next age will be conceived marvellous strange Objections;
the one being a strong argument of his Worth, the other a
piece of Reward." There is an ominous sense of future
outrages and, indeed, it ends on such a note, suggesting
to the reader that this argument may be continued, and
that the author dare not tell more.

As a Plutarchian character comparison it is highly
successful. There is a wit, economy, and penetration
which is not to be found in Wotton's more superficial
venture. Was it originally written as such and later
altered in order to reflect upon the 1640's, or was the
whole elaborate work from the outset intended to be a
critique of the rebellion? Internal and external evidence
seems to me inconclusive.

Wotton died in 1639, and his *Parallel* was first
printed separately in 1641. A MS of the *Parallel* in
Bodleian MS 4° Rawlinson 550 attributes the parallel to
Clarendon, but this must be erroneous. MS Clarendon 127
endorses a copy of the Parallel "for Mr Hide" and in the
same MS a copy of the *Difference and Disparity* is also
endorsed "for Mr Hyd," which suggests that Hyde had a
copy made for him, being unable to come by a printed version of the former. These works are bound with material
dating from about 1636, but that fact does not necessarily
indicate a date of composition. Indeed, the watermark
of the paper on which it is written indicates that this
MS copy of the *Difference and Disparity* (not in Hyde's
hand) cannot be earlier than 1639. The executors of
Hyde's estate, who ordered his papers, thought this piece
written in his younger days, and may, therefore, have
disposed it accordingly.

I suggest, tentatively enough, that it was written
(or at least revised) after Hyde was declared a delinquent
excepted from possible pardon (1642), and perhaps later
than *The King's Cabinet opened* (1645). It seems likely
to have been a product of his Jersey period when he composed forgeries in a variety of styles.

The Reliquiae was republished in 1654, 1672, and
1685. In the 1672 edition the authorship is acknowledged
to be Clarendon's for the first time. It is reprinted
again in *An Appendix,* 1724, where it is said to have been
the product of his youth.

74   [June?, 1656]
A LETTER FROM A TRUE AND LAWFULL MEMBER OF PARLIAMENT,
AND One faithfully engaged with it, from the beginning of
the War to the end. To one of the Lords of his Highness
Councell, upon occasion of the last Declaration, shewing
the Reasons of their proceedings for securing the Peace
of the Commonwealth, published on the 31th of October 1655.
(67 pp.)

[s.n.] 1656

Wing C 4424
Thomason E. 884 (2) (E. 883 (2) in the *Catalogue*)

The Thomason *Catalogue* is inaccurate in this case in
giving the date of the letter as October 31, 1655 and its
number as E. 883 (2). Thomason's copy is endorsed July 21,
[1656]. Thomason 883 (2) is in fact *The Horn of the He-
goat broken*, a satire on Quakers.

An unsuccessful royalist insurrection in 1655 provided Cromwell with the necessary provocation to deal
with royalist sympathizers in a punitive fashion. The
provisions of this policy were announced in the declaration of October 31, and included decimation of the estates
of known sympathizers. Charles II was then resident in
Köln, where he received a copy of the declaration

> and the chancellor was commanded by the king to write
> some discourse upon it, to awaken the people, and
> shew them their concernment in it; which he did by
> way of "a Letter to a Friend;" which was likewise
> sent into England, and there printed; and when Crom-
> well called his next parliament, it was made great
> use of to inflame the people, and make them sensible
> of the destruction that attended them; and was thought
> to produce many good effects. (*Life*, i, 263)

This is a forgery in that the fictional author was
meant to be identifiable--probably Sir Henry Vane, Jr.
He writes as one disillusioned by the threatening and
arbitrary nature of the new tyranny, despite his confessed
complicity in the whole course of rebellion to date. He
is a zealous and strident puritan who is now brought to
this confessional mode: "truly I had no more desire to
alter the fundamental Government of Church and State,
than you have to restore it." He now sees that the
nation is unworthy of the name of a nation, having shrunk
to a Protector and Council, a *gentem impudentem* which
cares neither for man nor God.

A *LETTER* takes care, in the more orthodox manner, to
repudiate point by point Cromwell's declaration, mixing
scornful and derisive comments with information and
royalist propaganda.

Section C

Works by and about
Clarendon, 1660–1811

1660 is an obvious watershed in the career of Clarendon, as
it is in the political history of his country. Although he
had held the title Chancellor for some time, he was now invested with the real power of this supreme office. His activities as anonymous pamphleteer and forger came to a halt
(unless [88] is genuine), but he continued to play a role as
a royal penman, enunciating the policies he devised on behalf
of, and in the name of, his royal master. The equivalent
role prior to 1660, delineated in Section B of this bibliography, had been necessarily clandestine. In 1660 he became a
highly prominent public figure in his own right, so much so
that his name was to sanction policies for which he himself
had little or no enthusiasm, such as the agglomeration of
punitive measures known to posterity as the Clarendon Code.
His position had, therefore, undergone a profound sea change.

There is no doubt that he continued to write royal
speeches, and some other public documents, some if not all
of which are recorded below, with a number of translations
into Dutch. His energy was directed much more directly than
hitherto to managing the interests of the Crown in an over-
enthusiastically royalist Parliament. They consisted as much
in attempted restraint of allies who grew, as a consequence,
more factious and frustrated, as in attacks upon republican
sympathies. He became, also for the first time, a dispenser
of political favor, a wielder of power. For these reasons
both the acuteness of his wit and the loftiness of his impartiality which characterize his best writings are much
diminished.

The memoirs of Sir Philip Warwick [105], published in
1701, speak of the "elegancie and ironie" of Clarendon's
earlier period, when he and Sir Philip were comrades in the
royalist cause. Enunciating the policies of an established
government created a different and more restrictive milieu,
and while some sparks of a former acerbity shine through in
the speeches written in the 1660-1667 period, there is
generally a more subdued and stately tone. He was also a
Chancellor in different orbit: that of the University of
Oxford. I have recorded one encomium of him in this capacity,

[82], but omitted others, verse and prose, which greeted his
Lord Chancellorship.

Affairs of state commanded much of the time of the Chancellor, but he nevertheless remained loyal to his avocations
as bibliophile and collector of portraits. In fact, as Aubrey
tells Pepys, many suppliants for political favor and office
recognized that to bestow on him portraits of the most eminent
men in English affairs was a way to find his ear. Evelyn himself tells us that he dedicated to Lord Clarendon his

> INSTRUCTIONS Concerning Erecting of a LIBRARY: Presented
> to My LORD The PRESIDENT De MESME. BY GABRIEL NAUDEVS,
> P. And now Interpreted BY Jo. EVELYN, Esquire. (London,
> 1661)

Ashamed of the work of the printers, he attempted to withdraw
as many copies as possible from possible circulation (see
[214]).

Certainly Clarendon, on his own initiative and following
his own highly developed inclinations, put together, with the
approbation and assistance of such aesthetes and bibliophiles
as Evelyn, a remarkable library and gallery of portraits,
housing them in a noble edifice constructed of the stones of
old St. Paul's which came to be known as "Dunkirk House." In
1756 the library was put up for sale [146], and in 1764 his
manuscripts came under the auctioneer's hammer [151]. The
fate of his portrait gallery is not that easily accounted for,
and does not concern this section.

Throughout this period, his political philosophy in its
various manifestations is evident enough. It received full
treatment from his pen when, after 1667, he entered into his
final, powerless exile. Once again the spirit of controversy
moved him to defend the memory of Falkland [97] and the Anglican Church. His scholarly mind exercised itself in a wide
variety of topics while he vigilantly defended his family,
especially his daughter, from accusations of apostasy.

1811 saw the last product of his final period, *Religion
and Policy* [161], which date is therefore made the terminus
of this section. During this period, 1660-1811, in his lifetime, and increasingly afterwards, he himself becomes the
subject of many writers. Their attitudes range from suppli-
cation (e.g., [77]), to encomium, to vituperation [91], to
political partisanship, to measured estimation of his historiographical reputation [112] and of his prose style [144]. In
these and similar works, we see the assimilation of Clarendon
into the mainstream of English culture—but not uncontested.

There are also many collections of parts of his writings
motivated by historical and antiquarian interest, and some
concern for establishing his *oeuvres*. In the following

bibliographical sketch the reader may trace the transmission
of Clarendon's influence, a fascinating chapter of politico-
cultural history. This influence remained controversial, and
the controversy was periodically freshened by gusts of party
animus right through the nineteenth century.

Titles collected in this section fall into three broadly
defined categories:

1. parliamentary speeches and state papers;
2. other works by Clarendon from his flight in 1667 to his
   death in 1674;
3. works wholly or in part concerning his reputation as a
   politician and author.

Arrangement of entries is chronological by date of publication, rather than categorical, in the interest of clarity.
It is conceivable that entries could be arranged in terms of
categories such as "state papers," "familiar letters," "controversy," "memoirs," etc., but exact demarcation would prove
to be a considerable difficulty. Nevertheless, two categories
have been set aside for separate consideration:

1. the editions of *Hist. Reb.* and *The Life* in Section D;
2. the controversy concerning the genuineness of *The History
   of the Rebellion* in Section E.

In order to preserve continuity, and hence the sense of cultural transmission, individual items set aside for comment in
these two sections are noticed by short title and date of
publication in Section C.

Not every passing reference to Clarendon in the period
designated is here recorded. Whatever seemed, in my judgment,
a substantial treatment is recorded. Incidental remarks,
however interesting in themselves, are ignored. Thus, for
example, Pepys' remarks which sometimes provide a very lively
picture of the Chancellor in action are omitted. Similarly,
many references in the poetry, such as that by Dryden, Johnson,
and Pope, and in their turn, contemporary commentaries upon
these poets, are left out. Dryden's "To My Lord Chancellor
Presented on New-years-day" (1662) is the most important and
challenging of these. In the Commentary on this poem, vol. i,
pp. 241-247 of *The Works of John Dryden* (University of
California Press, 1956), the editors observe that the poem's
difficulty is a subtle compliment to Clarendon's understanding
and to his reputation as a wit. Joseph Warton in *An Essay on
the Writings and Genius of Pope* (1782) comments on the character of Clarendon in glowing terms in his notes to Pope's
"Sixth Epistle of the First Book of Horace Imitated." But
notes of this kind I have considered to be non-essential to
the argument or purpose of the work in question. Thus, by

rough rule of thumb, I have tried to make each entry falling
into category 3 above answer to the criterion that the use of
Clarendon's work, or criticism of his conduct, or writing, in
that work be an important part of the work's argument or
purpose.

Satirical poetry concerning Clarendon, particularly frequent in 1667, is also omitted for reasons briefly outlined
in a note following [90], not, in this case, because it would
fail to conform to this criterion, but because it should be
part of a separate study, and because poems on affairs of
state in any given period might be more instructively gathered
as a genre than abstracted and subdivided to illustrate the
careers of their ostensible subjects.

The bibliography of Clarendon's writing from 1660 until
his death, pen in hand, is itself complicated. The major
causes of this are twofold. First, the bulk of his work was
published posthumously, and, second, following the publication
of *The History of the Rebellion* in 1702-04, such was the fame
of the author that publishers competed with each other to
sell collections and snippets of his writings in a bewildering
variety of combinations. Controversy over the authenticity
of *Hist. Reb*. was not of a scholarly or disinterested kind,
but directed and sharpened by party spirit. Thus, many passages borrowed from authorized publications, or (as in the
case of Borlase's *The Reduction of Ireland* [100]) prior to
authorized publication, appeared often in mangled or abridged
form. Anthony à Wood is probably the first to attempt more
than a desultory bibliography of Clarendon. He experienced
difficulty in ascription, and remarks of one publication, *The
Natural History of the Passions,* that many doubted he was the
author of it, thinking it a "sharking trick of a bookseller
to set his name to it for sale sake" (*Athenae Oxonienses*,
ed. Philip Bliss, 1817, iii, 1024).

To add to the difficulty, Clarendon's two most important
works, so far as modern readers are concerned, are in a sense
indistinguishable from each other. Or rather, *Hist. Reb*. and
Life are like Siamese twins, sharing a considerable portion
of common body. That Clarendon himself intended the sacrifice of the latter to the former by process of conflation is
clear. We now have a definitive *Hist. Reb*., but this frequently attempted goal was not achieved until Macray's edition
of 1888. No definitive edition of the *Life*, with restored
passages, has yet been made. Those who have studied the
relevant MSS will not be too severe in their judgment on the
efforts of a line of dedicated editors.

As a public man, even in his enforced retirement from
affairs, Clarendon composed works with some tincture of state
papers about them. Even quasi-philosophical essays on such

subjects as Education, Youth, Age, and time-honored themes
like the active versus contemplative life, and contemplations
on the Psalms, are strongly colored with the political considerations of his times. The eighteenth-century readership
was eager for every instance of his political acumen which
could be uncovered. Nevertheless, much remained hidden, most
notably *Religion and Policy*. There are also portraits--one
long enough to qualify as a biography--in Bodleian MS
Clarendon 122 which have never been adequately published, but
were doomed to the obscurity of an appendix to the three-
volume collection of *State Papers* [155].

The variety of combinations in which Clarendon's works
were published in these years is bewildering. In order to
ease comprehension, the main works, or groups of works which
recur between 1660 and 1811, are listed below.

1. Parliamentary speeches, 1660-1667
2. Second thoughts, or the case of a limited toleration
   stated
3. Defenses against charges of treason
4. Animadversions upon a book, intituled, Fanaticism
   fanatically imputed to the Catholic Church by
   Dr. Stillingfleet
5. Two letters written by the Right Honourable Edward earl
   of Clarendon ... to His Royal Highness the Duke of York:
   the other to the Dutchess occasioned by her embracing
   the Roman Catholic religion
6. The history of the rebellion and civil wars in Ireland
7. The history of the rebellion and civil wars in England
   [*The History*]
8. The life of Edward earl of Clarendon and The continuation
   of the life [both *The Life*]
9. A brief view and survey of the dangerous and pernicious
   errors to church and state in Mr. Hobbes's book, entitled
   Leviathan
10. Contemplations upon the Psalms of David
11. Essays moral and entertaining
12. Religion and policy and the countenance and assistance
    each should give to the other
13. Letters and state papers

Works written in an earlier period are often republished.
These include his early parliamentary speeches, *The Difference
and Disparity, A Full Answer*, etc.

I have not included the important state document, *The
Declaration of Breda*, which made known the terms upon which
Charles II was prepared to return to England, although to a
large extent it is Clarendon's work.

75   KING CHARLES HIS SPEECH to the Six Eminent Persons who
     lately arrived at Brussels, to Treat with His MAJESTY
     touching His Restoration to the Royal Throne and Dignity
     of his Father.

     ANWERP [sic]: 1660

     Wing C 3608
     Steele 3164

         This is a politic denial of rumors concerning the
     possible use of foreign forces to effect a restoration.
     The King's piety is stressed, no doubt to counteract per-
     sistent suspicion of his inclination toward popery.
         A copy in the Bodleian is annotated "supposed to be
     fictitious."

76   [May, 1660]
     TWO LETTERS FROM HIS MAJESTY THE ONE To the SPEAKER of
     the COMMONS Assembled in Parliament. The other to His
     EXCELLENCIE The Lord Generall MONCK. With His Majesties
     Declaration inclosed. TOGETHER With the Resolve of the
     House thereupon. (13 pp.)

     London: Edward Husbands and Tho. Newcomb, 1660

     Wing C 3624
     Thomason E. 1075 (1)

         The letters, dated Breda, April 14, were read in the
     Commons on May 1. They are couched in typically Clarendonian
     rhetoric suitable to the formal occasion and consonant
     with his sentiments in the final book of *Hist. Reb.* where
     he attributes the recall of the King by his kingdom to
     the working of Providence. It is interesting that the
     letter to Monck praises him as a blessed instrument of
     Providence. In *Hist. Reb.* this view of Monck is developed
     in a wholly unflattering manner, so that he is made to
     appear an unwitting and unwilling agent of designs beyond
     his comprehension.

77   L'ESTRANGE, Roger
     [June, 1660]
     L'ESTRANGE HIS APOLOGY: WITH A Short View, of some Late
     and Remarkable Transactions, Leading to the happy Settle-
     ment of these Nations under the Government of our Lawfull
     and Gracious SOVERAIGN CHARLS the II. whom GOD Preserve.
     By R.L.S.

London: Henry Brome, 1660

Wing L 1200
Thomason E. 187 (1)

    This is a long, dishevelled, and rambling vindication
of L'Estrange's extraordinary conduct from the outbreak
of the Civil War. Following a 16-pp. Preface is the main
Apology, in turn followed by sections with subtitles such
as "A Seasonable Word," "No Fool to the Old Fool," etc.,
the whole paginated (preface excepted) 1-157 from which
pp. 5-38 have been omitted, as L'Estrange informs us, on
second thoughts. Second thinking elsewhere is little in
evidence, for the writing is shrill, aggrieved, self-
righteous, and abusive by turns. From this work, which
appeared according to Thomason's dating on June 6, he
distilled:

77A To The Right Honorable, EDVVARD EARL OF CLARENDEN, Lord
    High CHANCELLOR OF ENGLAND: The Humble APOLOGY OF ROGER
    L'ESTRANGE Verbera, sed Audi. (6 pp.)

London: Henry Brome, MDCLXI

    It is dated by L'Estrange December 3, 1661, and in
fact appeared in 1662. It is not recorded in Wing.
    L'Estrange was well known to Clarendon, who had em-
ployed him in the royalist cause during the early 1650's,
although he held a low opinion of L'Estrange's competence
and coherence as appears in *Hist. Reb.* descriptions of
L'Estrange's luxuriant fancy and his style of public
speaking "very much his own, and being not very clear to
be understood" (iv, 334-5).
    An associate of Prince Rupert and George Digby, 2nd
Earl of Bristol, and cast in a similar mould, he had had
a romantic war involving, among other exploits, his be-
trayal to the Cromwellians and a long sojourn in Newgate
under sentence of death, whence he escaped in 1648 with
the connivance of the governor.
    It was his return from Europe in August 1653, thanks
to the terms of an act of indemnity, which tarnished his
reputation for pure royalist ardor. Dispersal of the
prejudice against him so that he might claim some of the
dues of his loyalty and sufferings is the aim of the
apology. On his return to England, L'Estrange was strictly
examined, and eventually freed from all impositions and
penalties, so his detractors alleged, by the payment of
bribes, taking the Covenant, and accepting some six hundred
pounds of Cromwell's money for future service. There is

also the farcical story of Cromwell's unexpected visit
to a musical practice at which L'Estrange was exercising
his considerable musical talent, which gained him the
title "Noll's fiddler."

In this apology, he briefly rehearses his activities,
stressing his loyalty in all respects, and confutes the
charges of treachery brought against him by the Presbyterian minister Edward Bagshaw, with whom a brief but
furious controversy ensued.

In 1662 he dedicated to Clarendon "A Memento directed
to all those that truly reverence the Memory of King
Charles the Martyr [etc.]," and in 1663 he obtained his
reward as Licenser, in effect political censor, of the
press. His career thereafter is well known.

78   His Majesties Most Gracious SPEECH, Together with the Lord
     Chancellors, TO THE TWO HOUSES OF PARLIAMENT; On Thursday
     the 13 of September, 1660.   (23 pp.)

     London: Bill and Barker, 1660

     Wing C 3169
     Thomason E. 1075 (14) (14) is the item number in E. 1075.
     The Thomason *Catalogue* employs an earlier numbering now
     cancelled. Thus, as in this and the following entries
     77-80, 14 = 16 (*Catalogue*), 20 = 22, 23 = 25, 26 = 28.)

         Wing C 3169A is an Edinburgh reprint.
         The Chancellor's speech, intended to allay anxiety
     about royal policy, lays stress upon the disbanding of
     the army, and the Act of Indemnity.

79   [Oct., 1660]
     HIS MAJESTIE'S Declaration To all His Loving Subjects of
     His Kingdom of England and Dominion of Wales CONCERNING
     Ecclesicastical Affairs.   (18 pp.)

     London: Bill and Barker, 1660

     Wing C 2997
     Thomason E. 1075 (20)

         The spirit of this declaration is in keeping with
     promises made at Breda for the ease of tender consciences.
     It is an elegant address and characterized by Clarendon's
     Erastianism.   Thus it argues against penal laws for dif-
     ferences in opinion.   As the civil government has changed
     somewhat, so may the ecclesiastical, so long as essentials

are not altered. There is praise for the wisdom of former times when ecclesiastical power readily subordinated itself to the civil. The King is now represented as having benefitted by his conversations with learned Protestants in France, the Low Countries, and Germany, and as ready to enact liberal legislation toward a settlement.

80 [Nov., 1660]
His Majestie's GRACIOUS DECLARATION For the settlement of His Kingdome OF IRELAND, AND Satisfaction of the severall Interests of Adventurers, Souldiers, and other His Subjects there. (35 pp.)

London: Bill, 1660

Wing C 3013
Thomason E. 1075 (23)

Wing C 3014 is a Dublin edition.
The miraculous working of Providence in bringing King and kingdom together is the topic. Dated November 30, 1660.

81 His Majestie's GRACIOUS SPEECH, Together with the Lord CHANCELLOR'S, To both Houses of PARLIAMENT; on Saturday the 29th day of December, 1660. Being the day of their Dissolution. As also, that of the SPEAKER of the Honorable House of COMMONS, at the same time. (29 pp.)

London: John Bill, 1660 [1661]

Wing C 3074
Thomason E. 1075 (26)

Wing C 3074A is an Edinburgh edition.
Much of the Chancellor's speech is given to praising the good accord of Parliament and King and to admiring the miracle of God's blessing on England.

82 WHITEHALL, Robert
VIRO, FAVORE REGIO, ET MERITIS, SUIS HONORATISSIMO, AMPLISSIMOQUE DOMINO, EDVARDO HIDE, Equiti Aurato, summo Angliae & optato Oxoniae Cancellerio, necnon Serenissimo Regi CAROLO 11.do a secretionibus Conciliis, & c. CARMEN GRATULATORIUM. (brs.)

[s.n.]

Wing W 1879
Thomason 669.f.26 (27)

    Robert Whitehall, Fellow of Merton College, was an
habitual composer of such verses. This is a Latin acros-
tic in which the initial letters of each line form ver-
tically "EDUARDUS HIDE CANCELLARJUS." An English translation occupies the right-hand column.
    Madan refers to it, but gives it no number, supposing
it to be London, not Oxford, printing. He adjudges it
the work of Royston.

83 His Majesties GRACIOUS SPEECH to THE LORDS & COMMONS,
    Together with the Lord CHANCELLOR'S At the opening of the
    PARLIAMENT, On the 8th day of May, 1661.

London: Bill and Barker, 1661

Wing C 3071

    Wing C 3072 is an Edinburgh edition.
    This is an interesting instance of the political
moderation Clarendon attempted to foster. He warns the
royalist assembly of the dangers of excessive zeal in
matters of religion and law: "If the good old known tryed
Laws be for the present too heavy for their necks, which
have been so many years without any Yoke at all, make a
temporary provision of an easier and lighter yoke."
    There is a Dutch version:

83A AENSPRAECK Van den KONINGH VAN ENGELANDT. Aen de Herren
    van het Opper ende van het Lager-Huys. EN DE ORATIE van
    de Heere Cancelier aen den voorsz twee Huysen. Beyde
    gedaen den 8/18 Mey 1661. Wanneer de openinge van het
    Parlament geschiede.

[s.n.]

84 THE SPEECHES OF Sir Edward Turner K^{t}, BEFORE KING, LORDS
    & COMMONS ASSEMBLED IN PARLIAMENT, when he was presented
    SPEAKER of the Honorable House of Commons, On Friday the
    Tenth of May, 1661. TOGETHER With the LORD CHANCELLORS
    Speeches in Answer thereunto.

London: Bill and Barker, 1661

Wing T 3365

    Wing T 3366 is an Edinburgh edition.
    The speeches of Clarendon are largely ceremonial.

85 His Majesties Most Gracious SPEECH, Together with the
    LORD CHANCELLORS, To the Two HOUSES of PARLIAMENT, AT
    THEIR Prorogation, On Monday the Nineteenth of May, 1662.

    London: Bill and Barker, 1662

    Wing C 3170

        Wing C 3171 is an Edinburgh edition.
        Clarendon imperiously instructs Members of Parliament
    in the answers they should give to complaints about the
    supply which Parliament has voted to the King. The happy
    reign of Queen Elizabeth is invoked with the caveat that
    much greater sums of money are now required to do the
    necessary work of government than was then the case.
    Bacon and Machiavelli are both highly praised.

86 His Majesties DECLARATION TO All His loving SUBJECTS,
    December 26. 1662. Published by the Advice of His Privy
    Council. (14 pp.)

    London: Bill and Barker, 1662

    Wing C 2988

        Other editions are Edinburgh, 1663 (Wing C 2988A),
    Edinburgh, 1663 (Wing C 2988B), and Dublin, 1662
    (Wing C 2988C).
        This is almost certainly the work of Clarendon, and
    is intended to reassure a populace alarmed by the Decla-
    ration of Indulgence (December 6, 1662). It asserts that
    the King has no intention of ruling by military force,
    and that the clause concerning tender consciences in the
    Declaration of Breda is not a lie. It also denies that
    the King is indulgent of Papists in a manner likely to
    harm the Protestant religion. Published December 26, 1662.

87 DIALOGUS OFTE TSAMEN-SPRAKE Tusschen sijn Exellentie den
    Heer CANCHELLIER van Engelant, ENDE Den ADVOCAET's Landts
    van Hollandt, Over de tegenwoordige gelegentheydt vande
    uytgewerckte TRACTATEN. (24 pp.)

    t'ENCH-HVYSEN: Gedrucht voor Ysbrant Hyde-Wittenzoon,
    Anno 1662

        A presentation in dialogue form of a prelude to
    articles of a treaty of friendship, 1663.

88 SECOND THOUGHTS; OR THE CASE OF A Limited Toleration,
    Stated according to the present Exigence in CHURCH and
    STATE.   Nihil Violentum Durat.   (10 pp.)

    [s.n.]

    Wing C 4425

        Authority for attributing this work to Clarendon seems
    to derive from the British Library Catalogue, which gives
    two editions [1660?] and [1689?], and the Bodleian Cata-
    logue.   This is repeated in other bibliographies such as
    the *New Cambridge Bibliography* and the *National Union
    Catalog*, the latter giving 1660 and [1663] as possible
    dates.   The date of publication must be between late 1662
    and early 1663 because of its immediate relevance to the
    Declaration of Indulgence (published December 6, 1662).
    Clarendon's position was consistent in favoring toleration
    of recusancy--the reasons for which he later developed in
    detail in *Religion and Policy* [161].   Others, however,
    who seemed to share this position saw it as a first step
    to the introduction of Popery.   Perhaps for this reason,
    knowing the designs of Sir Henry Bennet (later Lord
    Arlington) who framed it, Clarendon strongly opposed the
    bill when it was before the Lords.   This circumstance may
    help to explain the title *Second Thoughts* and its
    anonymity.
        The argument of the tract is that it would be wholly
    impractical to attempt to root out dissenters, and that
    to continue in their persecution would encourage the
    spirit of civil war.   If left to themselves the sects,
    known collectively as Puritans, would fall out according
    to their differing tenets.   The argument resolves itself
    in Hobbesian terms: men act out of interest, and the art
    of government lies in harnessing those interests, for
    true conscience can never be known to man.   It includes
    the further consideration that English power depends upon
    the navy, and because many seamen are nonconformist, it
    would be against national interest to persecute them.
    It does not, however, recommend that those of heterodox
    beliefs be allowed the full rights of the orthodox
    citizen.
        However the argument coincides with Clarendon's views,
    the style seems quite unlike that of any of his works,
    and raises doubt about the validity of the attribution.

89 HIS MAJESTIES Gracious SPEECH TO BOTH HOVSES OF PARLIA-
    MENT, Together with the LORD CHANCELLOR'S Delivered In
    Christ Church Hall in OXFORD, The 10th of October, 1665.
    (19 pp.)

    Oxford: Lichfield for Bill and Barker, 1665

    Wing C 3052
    Madan 2678

        Other editions are Wing C 3053, C 3053A (York), and
    C 3054 (Edinburgh).
        Clarendon's speech concerns the Dutch War. He re-
    views British naval policy since the Restoration, remark-
    ing its cost and the proportion the King had contributed
    to meeting it. The progress of the war is considered,
    concluding in a request for fresh supplies since the
    Dutch are already refitted for battle.

90 NEWS from DVNKIRK-HOVSE: Or CLARENDON's Farewell to
    England. In his seditious Address to the Right Honourable
    the House of Peers, Decemb. 3. 1667. VVhich was after-
    wards, according to the Sentence and Judgement of both
    Houses of Parliament, burnt by the hand of the Common
    Hangman, in the presence of the two Sheriffs with a great
    and signal Applause of the People, December 12. 1667.
    (brs.)

    [s.n.]

    Wing N 955

        This is in fact Clarendon's "Humble Petition and
    Address" [93].

NOTE: It is not possible in a work of this scope to notice
    all the allusions to Clarendon in the satirical verse of
    the period. For a bibliography of collections in which
    such poems appear, see CASE, Arthur E. A BIBLIOGRAPHY OF
    ENGLISH POETICAL MISCELLANIES 1521-1750. Oxford: University
    Press for the Bibliographical Society, 1935 (for 1929).

    For several such poems, with commentary, see LORD, George
    de F. (ed.). Poems on Affairs of State AUGUSTAN SATIRICAL
    VERSE, 1660-1714 (Vol. i, 1660-1678). New Haven & London:
    Yale University Press, 1963.

    Two poems which do not appear in the above collection are:

91   A HUE AND CRIE AFTER The Earl of CLARENDON.   (brs.)

   [n.p.]: Printed in the Year of Clarendon's Confusion,
   1667

   Wing H 3289

       This is a more than usually bloodthirsty attack:
           With Stab of Dagger; anyway; so th' World
           Be rid of him; so he to Hell be hurld.

   The second is:

92   [WITHER, George?]
   VOX & Lacrimae Anglorum: OR, The True English - mens
   COMPLAINTS, To their Representatives in PARLIAMENT.
   Humbly tendred to their serious Consideration at their
   next sitting, February the 6th 1667/8.

   [n.p.]: 1668

   Wing W 3208

       This is 16 pp. of roughly rhymed couplets, in which
   Clarendon is made largely responsible for all ills in the
   kingdom:

           Till he himself to Justice doth resigne,
           Let all men call him, Cursed Clarendine

93   To the Right Honourable, the Lords Spiritual and Temporal,
   in Parliament Assembled: THE HVMBLE PETITION AND ADDRESS
   OF Edward Earl of Clarendon.   (brs.)

   [s.n.] [1667]

   Wing C 4427

       This is the first of several messages in self-defense
   against articles of impeachment. It was no doubt composed before he had received a detailed list of charges,
   and therefore seeks to answer the two most damaging reflections on his conduct and character, namely the size
   of the fortune he had amassed, and the imputation that he
   had been sole manager of affairs from 1660 until "August
   last" (1667), and was, therefore, the cause of all national
   misfortunes in that period.
       The answer is sober and detailed. The counsels he
   urged and the monies he received are itemized and systematically defended. He represents himself as having been
   opposed to the (Second Dutch) war, for the misconduct of

which he had been popularly blamed. He professes to have accepted nothing from foreign kings and princes, with the one interesting exception of "the Books of the *Louvre* Print, sent me by the Chancellour of *France*, by that Kings direction."

It closes with the expressed intention of returning to make full defense in person.

Anthony Wood records its fate:

> This was by command of the parliament burnt by the hands of the common hangman before the gate of Gresham college, then the place of exchange, 12 Dec. 1667. This being by him sent to the house by way of excuse and apology for himself, was esteemed by the members thereof such a vile imposture, that they throw'd it from them with scorn, and commanded it to be burnt.

It has been frequently reprinted in collections of State Tracts, and in Somers tracts, the Harleian miscellany, and other collections including Clarendon's work. The address was published in a Dutch translation:

93A Ootmoedige PETITIE ende ADDRESSE Van EDUARD, Graef van Clarendon, gewesene Cancelier van ENGELANDT. AEN De recht eerwaerdige, de Geestelijcke ende Wereltlijcke Lords, in't Parlement vergadert.

[s.n.]

In the British Library Catalogue this is mistakenly dated 1662.

94 Den vluchtenden GROOTEN CANCELIER van ENGELANDT, EDVARD HYDE, Grave van Clarendon.

Duynkercken: 1668

A somewhat sympathetic account of the circumstances of Clarendon's fall, of the charges against him, and his letter to the Lords.

95 DE PROCEDUREN Gehouden in ENGELANDT, Tegens den Graef van Clarendon, Gewesen CANCELIER In beyde Huysen des PARLE-MENTS.

[Amsterdam?]: 1668

A brief account of Clarendon's fall.

96   [FRENCH, Nicholas]
     A NARRATIVE OF THE EARL of CLARENDON'S Settlement and
     Sale of IRELAND. Whereby the Just English Adventurer is
     much prejudiced, the Ancient Proprietor destroyed, and
     Publick Faith violated; to the great discredit of the
     English Church and Government, (if not recalled and made
     void) as being against the principles of Christianity,
     and true Protestancy. Written in a Letter by a Gentleman
     in the Country, to a Nobleman at Court. (38 pp.)

     Louvain: MDCLXVIII

     Wing F 2179

         The letter writer writes as an Englishman deploring
     the way Englishmen have oppressed the Irish. He represents
     Irish Catholics as having been instrumental in restoring
     Charles II, but they are now punished for their service
     more than they were under Cromwell. The letter is signed
     F.N. Little specific is said of Clarendon; his name is
     used as a symbol of English policy.
         The pamphlet is reprinted from the original 1668
     edition in Vol. 1, pp. 75-123 of:

96A FRENCH, Nicholas
     THE HISTORICAL WORKS OF THE RIGHT REV. NICHOLAS FRENCH,
     D.D. BISHOP OF FERNS, &c &c.

     Dublin: James Duffy, 1846

97   ANIMADVERSIONS Upon a Book, Intituled, FANATICISM
     FANATICALLY Imputed to the Catholic Church, By D^r. STILL-
     INGFLEET, And the Imputation Refuted and Retorted by
     S.C. By a Person of Honour.

     London: R. Royston, 1673

     Wing C 4414

         The second and third editions are 1674, Wing C 4415,
     and 1685, Wing C 4416.
         This late work of Clarendon's pen is a most interest-
     ing piece in that it declares his early philosophical
     inclinations, and reveals much about his mind in the con-
     ditions of enforced exile. At its core is the still
     urgent desire to preserve the reputation of Falkland,
     immortalized in *Hist*. *Reb*. and elsewhere. The range of
     the skirmish attests also to his abiding concern for the
     health of the Church of England. Although it is not an
     important document in intellectual or political history,

it possesses the inherent interest of a great man's
reminiscence over the deplorable alteration in mores
since his youth. For this reason--and because it is not
elsewhere considered--I take the liberty of presenting
here a fairly extensive commentary.

Cressy (Hugh Paulin, later "Serenus" in religion)
died in the same year as Clarendon, and had been his contemporary at Oxford. Like Clarendon, he was intimately
connected with Falkland, and owed to him his nomination
to a canonry of Windsor, which he never took up. By
1646, he had recanted his Protestantism, and was subsequently to move in English Roman Catholic circles at the
Paris court of Henrietta Maria. In 1660 he returned to
England as one of Catherine of Braganza's chaplains, and
so became an important focus of English recusant sentiment. Wood describes his *Exomolegesus* as the "golden
calf" to which English Catholics bowed, thinking it had
overthrown Chillingworth and Falkland's *Discourse of
Infallibility*. Given these circumstances the reasons
for Clarendon's hostility are plain. Nevertheless, he
writes in this controversy as an old friend, with a view
to demonstrating that laymen too could defend the Anglican
position as well as clergy.

The author, in exile, read the attack on Stillingfleet
rather later than most men interested in such matters,
but decided to give answer immediately, as he put it, to
the pride, bitterness, and virulence of Cressy. He
starts with reference to the "never enough admired"
Advancement of Learning (which, as a young man, Clarendon
had partly transcribed into his commonplace book,
Bodleian MS Clarendon 127), and asks what Bacon would
think now that the disease of ignorance is grown to epi-
demic proportions. And now the spirit of Martin Marprelate
stirs again--but in a modern style, full of "vain and
comical expressions." If this habit be not suppressed,
it threatens a general corruption of manners and the
purity and integrity of the language, along with modesty,
good humor, and the modest conversation of the nation.

> Thom. Nash was well known as an author in those
> days, as Martin, who with Pamphlets of the same kind,
> and size, with the same pert Buffoonry, and with more
> salt and cleanliness, rendred that libellous, and
> seditious crew so contemptible, ridiculous and odious,
> that in a short time they vanished and were no more
> heard of.

In those days, he observes, serious charges were
answered by serious divines, and scurrilous prose by

mocking writers. The two veins should not be mingled,
for grave writers must beware of dishonoring their cause
with ironical writing. Therefore, Clarendon will not in
this matter descend to ill words.

As in *Religion and Policy* [161] he argues that Roman
Catholicism itself is not the matter in dispute, but
rather the conflicting claims on English Roman Catholics
of the laws of their king, and the demands of their Pope.
If they were to renounce the latter, then all their
beliefs would be no more important than errors in grammar.

He also refers to the Lushington sermon [113] and corrects Cressy's erroneous interpretation of it. He goes
on to controvert in orthodox fashion each of Cressy's
arguments, calling on that same breadth of learning deployed also in *Religion and Policy*.

Clarendon's defense of Stillingfleet was repaid when
he in his turn defended the religious orthodoxy of
Clarendon's daughter. In 1686 he wrote a refutation of
papers purporting to be professions of conversion to
Roman Catholicism by Charles II and Anne Hyde.

98 [CRESSY, Serenus]
AN EPISTLE APOLOGETICAL OF S.C. To a Person of Honour:
Touching his VINDICATION OF Dr. STILLINGFLEET. (138 pp.)

[n.p.]: MDCLXXIV

Wing C 6893 (The entry is mistaken in giving *The epistle*
[etc.] rather than the above title.)

    This replies to *Animadversions* [97]. It is said to
be written "Permissu Superiorum" from his cell on
March 21. He is concerned, among other matters, to
exonerate himself from the charge of having dishonored
the memory of Falkland by describing him as Socinian.

99 [HICKES, George]
A Letter sent from beyond the Seas to one of the chief
ministers of the non-confirming party.

[n.p.]: 1674

Wing H 1855

    This is not Clarendon's work. It is listed here
because it has been attributed to him, usually on the
strength of contemporary notations in several copies.
One such, owned by Rawlinson and now in the Bodleian,
bears a note to the effect that it was written at "Roan,"

and prepared for the second edition by Dr. Hickes. In
fact George Hickes is the real author.

100 BORLASE, Edmund
     THE REDUCTION OF IRELAND To the CROWN of ENGLAND.
     With the GOVERNOURS since the Conquest by King HENRY II.
     Anno MCLXXII. With some Passages in their Government.
     A Brief Account of the Rebellion Anno Dom. MDCXLI. Also,
     The Original of the Universitie of DUBLIN, And the
     COLLEDGE of Physicians.

     London: Andr. Clarke for Robert Clavel, 1675

     Wing B 3771

        Here is to be found the first use (unacknowledged)
     of Clarendon's MS on Irish affairs. See [102], *The
     History of the Execrable Irish Rebellion.*

101 A BRIEF VIEW and SURVEY OF THE Dangerous and pernicious
     ERRORS TO CHURCH and STATE, In Mr. HOBBES'S BOOK,
     Entitled LEVIATHAN. By EDWARD Earl of Clarendon.

     [Oxford]: At the Theater, 1676

     Wing C 4420
     Madan 3110

        There is a second impression, Wing C 4421, Madan 3111.
        This is a finely printed quarto volume with several
     of the headpieces and engraved capitals in the style of
     other Oxford editions of Clarendon, and with an engraved
     allegorical frontispiece. It was a long time getting
     into print, no doubt because of the restraints imposed
     on the author by the terms of his exile. The manuscript
     was completed in early 1670, and the imprimatur of
     Oxford's Vice-Chancellor was granted July 1, 1676. Madan
     records that it was printed by August 6 of that year.
     The Epistle Dedicatory, to the King, is dated May 10,
     1673, Moulins. Its contents reveal the intention of
     the work. It reminds Charles II of the author's long
     and unbroken service since the reign of his father, and
     challenges Hobbes' view that a banished man is not a
     true subject during his banishment.
        The remainder of the book controverts in orthodox
     style, point by point, and at length, each of Hobbes'
     arguments and conclusions.
        This long-neglected work has in recent times attract-
     ed some scholarly attention.

102   BORLASE, Edmund
      THE HISTORY Of the EXECRABLE Irish Rebellion Trac'd from
      many preceding ACTS, TO THE Grand Eruption The 23. of
      October, 1641.   And thence pursued to the Act of Settle-
      ment MDCLXII.

      London: Robert Clavel, MDCLXXX

      Wing B 3768

         In 1675 Borlase had published *The Reduction of Ire-
      land to the Crown of England* [100], which contained a
      brief account of the rebellion in that country.   This
      was lifted from Clarendon's hitherto unpublished MS of
      Irish affairs, later published under the title *The
      History of the Civil Wars in Ireland* [119].   Borlase
      interpolated passages to make the account sort with his
      own views.   This edition, above, is the same work but
      expurgated by L'Estrange in the exercise of his official
      powers as censor.
         In his preface to the reader Borlase writes, "It was
      my happiness (I must acknowledge) to meet with a Manu-
      script, whence I was supplied with much of the latter
      part of this History."

103   TWO LETTERS Written by the Right Honourable EDWARD Earl
      of CLARENDON, late Lord High Chancellour of ENGLAND:
      One to his Royal Highness the Duke of YORK: The other
      to the DUTCHESS, Occasioned by Her embracing the Roman
      Catholic Religion.   (brs.)

      [s.n.]

      Wing C 4429

         Most bibliographies hazarding a guess at the date of
      publication choose 1680.   One copy in the Thomas Fisher
      Rare Books Library, Toronto, is annotated "about 1670.
      She died March 1671" (not in contemporary hand).   This
      is a reasonable date for the composition, but not the
      date of publication.   Anthony Wood, *Athenae Oxonienses,*
      is probably close to the mark in thinking 1681-82 as the
      date, and London the place of publication.
         It was written before Clarendon moved from Montpellier
      in about May, 1670.   His daughter died, aged 34, on
      March 31, 1671, but she had earlier proclaimed her alle-
      giance to the Roman faith, and in the letter to her, he
      adverts to much earlier rumors to the same effect heard
      in Paris.   The conversion of his daughter was, of course,

a supreme embarrassment, outdoing that caused by her initial liaison with the Duke. The letter to her is, in effect, a reprimand seasoned by the frustration he feels in not being able to talk with his daughter on controversial matters concerning the Roman and Anglican churches. Some of these are briefly rehearsed, and the letter closes with the plea that she communicate all doubts with him before taking hasty action.

The letter to the Duke is written in the assumption that he is ignorant of his wife's conversion, although there are hints that he fears the Duke is also (as indeed he was) a secret Roman Catholic. Clarendon remarks that the Duke is well aware that he never wished Roman Catholics to be prosecuted with severity.

The letters are reprinted in *State Tracts* (1693), *The Harleian Miscellany* (1744 and 1808), and *Clarendon State Papers* [155] iii, Supp., xxxxviii-xl.

The letter from Clarendon to the Duchess, his daughter, is also printed in a miscellany, typical of its period, entitled:

103A THE POETICAL WORKS Of the Honourable Sir Charles Sedley Baronet, AND HIS SPEECHES in PARLIAMENT, WITH Large Additions never before made Publick. Published from the Original MS. by Capt. AYLOFFE, a near Relation of the Authors. With a New MISCELANY of Poems by several of the most Eminent Hands. And a Compleat Collection of all the Remarkable Speeches in both Houses of Parliament: Discovering the Principles of all Parties and Factions; the Conduct of Our Chief Ministers, the Management of Publick Affairs, and the Maxims of the Government, from the year 1641, to the Happy Union of Great Britain: By several Lords and Commoners. VIZ.

The Duke of Albermarle,	Algernon Sidney Esq;
Earl of Clarendon,	Mr. Waller,
Earl of Bristol,	Sir Frances Seymor,
Lord Wharton,	Mr. Pym,
Earl of Pembrook,	Richard Cromwell,
Lord Hollis,	Mr. Strode,
Lord Brook,	Sir William Parkins,
Earl of Essex,	Sir William Scroggs,
Earl of Argile,	Sir J_____ P_____,
Lord Melvil,	
Lord Haversham,	
Lord Belhaven, &c.	

And several other Lords and Commoners.

London: Sam. Briscoe, 1707

104 FANSHAW, Sir Richard
     Original LETTERS Of his Excellency Sir Richard Fanshaw,
     During his EMBASSIES IN SPAIN and PORTUGAL: Which,
     together with divers Letters and Answers FROM The Chief
     Ministers of State of England, Spain and Portugal, con-
     tain the whole Negotiations of the Treaty of Peace
     between those three CROWNS.

     London: Abel Roper, 1701

          This was reprinted with a more explicit title page:

104A ORIGINAL LETTERS AND NEGOTIATIONS Of his EXCELLENCY Sir
     RICHARD FANSHAW, The Earl of SANDWICH, The Earl of
     SUNDERLAND, AND Sir WILLIAM GODOLPHIN. WITH The several
     LETTERS and ANSWERS of the Lord Chancellor Hyde, the Lord
     Arlington, Mr. Secretary Coventry, Sir Joseph Williamson,
     Sir Philip Warwick, Sir George Downing, and other chief
     Ministers of State. WHEREIN Divers Matters of Importance
     between the three Crowns of ENGLAND, SPAIN, and PORTUGAL,
     from the Year 1663 to 1678, are set in a clearer Light
     than is any where else extant. (2 vols.)

     London: John Wilford, MDCCXXIV

          The several state papers of Clarendon are in vol. i.

105 WARWICK, Sir Philip
     MEMOIRES Of the reigne of King CHARLES I. WITH A CON-
     TINUATION TO THE Happy Restauration OF King CHARLES II.

     London: R. Chiswell, 1701

          This contains the following interesting character of
     Clarendon:

               His natural parts were very forward and sound;
          his learning was very good and competent; and he had
          the felicity both of tongue and pen; which made him
          willingly hearkened unto, and much approved; and
          having spent much of his studies in the Law, this
          made his discourse and writings the more significant;
          and his language and stile were very suitable to
          business, if not a little too redundant. So as it
          was supposed, tho' there was alwaies a concurrence
          of the other's two judgements [Culpepper and Falk-
          land]; that it was his pen, that was made most use
          of. Hence it was, that his Majesties Propositions,
          Messages, Replyes, and Declarations were so well
          answering unto the rules of the House, and the

subject matters treated of, and found so much better
acceptance with the world, than those of the House
of Commons. Which for a time was very advantageous
to his Majestie's service.... But I remember a wise
Lord ... would complain, that their wit and elegancy,
as it was very delightful, so it would not long last
usefull: since contests betwixt a King and his Houses
of Parliament could not be separated from ill consequences ... and would beget a frowardness in men to
see such things treated of with elegancy and ironie,
than any delight or complacence; and therefore he
was wont to say "Our good Pen will harm Us."

106   The History of the Rebellion [etc.]

      See Section D: *THE HISTORY OF THE REBELLION* AND *THE LIFE*

107   [ANON.]
      A VIEW OF THE REIGN OF King CHARLES the First. WHEREIN
      The True Causes of The Civil War Are Impartially Delin-
      eated, By Strokes borrow'd from Lord Clarendon, Sir
      Philip Warwick, H.L'Estrange, and other most Authentick
      and Approved Historians. In ANSWER To the LIBELS lately
      Publish'd against a Sermon Preach'd by the Reverend
      WHITE KENNETT, D.D. Archdeacon of Huntingdon, &c.
      (28 pp.)

      London: A. and J. Churchill, 1704

         The pamphlet rebuts aspersions that the sermons of
      White Kennett are seditious. He is represented as wish-
      ing to reconcile differences, while his detractors
      operate under pretense of vindicating the royal martyr.
      Thus quotations from Clarendon are chosen to demonstrate
      that reciprocal provocations of Parliament and the King
      resulted in civil war. Some of the excerpts concern the
      mismanagement of government by Charles I prior to the
      calling of the Long Parliament. The authenticity of his
      account is praised.

108   [ANON.]
      An Antidote against Rebellion: OR, THE PRINCIPLES OF THE
      MODERN POLITICIAN, Examin'd and Compar'd WITH THE
      Description of the Last Age By the Right Honourable the
      Earl of CLARENDON. To which is added A LETTER to the
      Nonjuring Party. AND A POSTSCRIPT to Mr. SACHEVEREL On
      his Late SERMON Preach'd at the Assizes at Oxford. (50 pp.)

London: A. Baldwin, 1704

A tract for the times, with copious quotation from
Clarendon applied to the political exigencies of 1704.
It warns the reader of the dangers of Jacobitism in terms
similar to those in which Clarendon describes the Pres-
byterians of the 1640's. It is in effect an attack on
Sacheverell and Charles Leslie.

It is interesting to note that the author describes
himself as a "Trimmer," by which he means an adherent of
neither High nor Low Church parties. He praises the
lofty impartiality of Clarendon, and imitates it with
considerable success.

109   [ANON.]
The Occasional Letter. Number 1. Concerning several
Particulars in the New Association: The Occasional Bill;
a MS History, &c. With An Examination of some Proceed-
ings in the late Reign by some Passages in the Lord
Clarendons History. With a Postscript Relating to Sir
Humphrey Mackworths Book intitled, Peace at Home: Or his
defence of the Occasional Bill.

London: MDCCIV

Passages from *The History of the Rebellion* are cited
in support of the position of the Bishops.

110   THE CHARACTERS OF Robert Earl of Essex, FAVOURITE To
Queen Elizabeth, AND George D. of Buckingham, FAVOURITE
To K. James 1. and K. Ch. 1. With a Comparison. By the
Right Honourable EDWARD Lake Earl of CLARENDON. (36 pp.)

London: A Baldwin, 1706

This is a reprint of *The Difference and DISPARITY*
[73], the only addition being a page of recommendation
of the literary skills of Clarendon.

111   [OLDMIXON, John]
THE LIVES OF ALL THE LORDS Chancellors [etc.]

See Section E: OLDMIXON AND THE GENUINENESS OF *THE
HISTORY OF THE REBELLION*

112 OZELL, J.

Mr. Le CLERC'S ACCOUNT OF THE Earl of CLARENDON'S
HISTORY OF THE CIVIL WARS. Done from the French Printed
at Amsterdam. By J. O. PART I.

London: Bernard Lintott, 1710

This is an expansive essay with copious quotation
from *The History of the Rebellion* and synopses of the
arguments of the *Hist. Reb.*, books 1-8.

Le Clerc was a leading figure in Dutch Arminian
circles, and therefore inclined to sympathy with Clarendon's views. He provides a brief biographical notice of
Clarendon to fill a gap he noticed in the first edition
of the *Hist. Reb.*, which has merely a preface with
reference to the politics of 1704.

This is the first real critique of the *Hist. Reb.*
It suggests that Clarendon is rather too zealous on the
King's behalf. In its comments on the genre and arrangement of the *Hist. Reb.*, it is judicious and perceptive,
comparing it with other accounts of the period, in the
course of which it develops an impressive theory of what
makes for good history, good style, and good form. It
also suggests that since Clarendon professes to write
for posterity marginal dates of events should be provided.

There is a second edition:

112A Mr. Le CLERC'S ACCOUNT OF THE Earl of Clarendon's HISTORY
OF THE CIVIL WARS. Done from the French Printed at
Amsterdam. By J.O. The Second Edition Corrected.

London: Bernard Lintott, 1710

The first part is the same as that in the first edition. Part two is added with a separate title page:

Mr. LE CLERC'S ACCOUNT OF THE Earl of Clarendon's HISTORY
OF THE CIVIL WARS. Done from the French, Printed at
Amsterdam. By J.O. The Second and Last PART.

London: Bernard Lintott, 1710

The Advertisement is signed J. Ozell. This second
part provides synopses of the remaining books of
Hist. Reb., 9-16.

113   [LUSHINGTON, Thomas]
      [1710?]
      The Resurrection of our Saviour rescued from the Sol-
      diers Calumnies. IN A SERMON Preach'd at St. MARY's in
      Oxon. Together with the Author's RECANTATION. Formerly
      published under the feign'd Name of Robert Jones, D.D.
      and now first printed with a Preface discovering the real
      Name of the Author, and the true Reasons which drew upon
      him the Censure of the University, By the Right Honour-
      able EDWARD Earl of CLARENDON.

      London: T. Warner [n.d.]

         The British Library Catalogue gives [1741?] as the
      publication date. This is improbable. There is another
      edition, noticed below, genuinely of 1741, but this in
      the style of its printing and layout looks considerably
      earlier: perhaps about 1710.
         The later edition is:

113A The Resurrection of our Saviour vindicated, and the
      Soldiers Calumnies against it fully answer'd. IN A
      SERMON Preach'd at St. Mary's in Oxford By Mr. LUSHINGTON.
      Formerly printed under the feigned name of ROBERT JONES,
      D.D. And now publish'd, with a PREFACE Discovering the
      true Reasons which drew upon him The CENSURE of the
      UNIVERSITY. By the RIGHT HONOURABLE Edward Earl of
      Clarendon.

      London: T. Davies, MDCCXLI

         This is an offshoot of the Cressy controversy [97,
      98]. The use of Clarendon's name in the title is almost
      certainly an attempt to attract sales, for his part of
      it is confined to excerpts from his confutation of
      Cressy [97]. In brief, Clarendon argues that the reason
      Lushington's witty and dramatic sermon drew censure was
      not so much its extravagant invention, but rather its
      political reference to the activities of the Parliament.
      Cressy's purpose was clearly to denigrate the seriousness
      and piety of his former Oxford acquaintance, Clarendon
      included, by giving an example of outrageous and blasphe-
      mous (Protestant) preaching. Clarendon's preface reminds
      the reader that he is one of the few surviving auditors
      of the actual sermon (Cressy is the only other who comes
      to mind!) which was delivered as long ago as 1624 or
      1625.
         Lushington, sometime tutor of Sir Thomas Browne at
      Lincoln College, was a Laudian and suspected of

Socinianism. The sermon was first printed in 1659 under the name Robert Jones. It appears again in 1708 in vol. ii of *The Phenix*.

114 [OLDMIXON, John]
The Secret History of Europe [etc.]

See Section E

115 FELTON, Dr. Henry
A DISSERTATION On Reading the CLASSICS, And Forming a JUST STYLE. Written in the Year 1709, And addressed to the RIGHT HONOURABLE, JOHN Lord ROOS, The Present Marquis of GRANBY.

London: Jonah Bowyer, 1713

Although this is to some extent a party work in praise of the Tory bishops--Atterbury, Aldrich, Small-ridge, etc.--it is also an interesting excursion into literary stylistics. It is a small book which neverthe-less manages a compendious treatment of style in all literary genres from classical to modern times, touching on taste, eloquence, the relationship of words to thoughts, etc. Felton offers Clarendon to his patron as an especially inspiring example:

> I dare not attempt my Lord Clarendon's Commendation: To give his just Character, requireth a Happiness of Expression, a Clearness of Judgement, and Majesty of Style equal to his own: Or to say all in a Word, that peculiar Felicity in designing Characters, in which he hath succeeded beyond example. Your Lord-ship will want no Sollicitations to read the noblest, the most impartial Historian this Nation hath produced.

This is an adroit reworking of Livy's praise of Cicero: that it would take a second Cicero to praise him adequately.

He continues to praise in this vein, selecting for final commendation the noble "Negligence of Phrase which maketh his Words wait every where upon his Subject."

It was a successful work, running to five editions, and considerably expanded.

116   THE PETITION AND ADDRESS Of the Right Honourable EDWARD,
      Late Earl of Clarendon, TO THE House of Lords; Upon his
      withdrawing out of this Kingdom, towards the Close of
      the Year 1667.   In Answer to the Charge of the then
      House of Commons against his Lordship.   Together with
      The said Accusation at Large.   (18 pp.)

      London: John Morphew, 1715

          This is Clarendon's full and detailed defense
      against the seventeen specific charges.   Compare the
      shorter first defense, *The Humble Petition* [93].

117   [ANON.]
      Clarendon against Lesley; OR, THE DIFFERENCE between TWO
      RESTORATIONS: THE ONE, Legally Effected, of CHARLES the
      Second, THE OTHER, Illegally Attempted by a Popish
      Pretender.

      London: R. Burleigh, 1715

          In parallel columns under topic headings such as
      "Legitimacy," the cases of Charles II and the Pretender
      are posed.   Clarendon's authority is invoked to demon-
      strate that Charles never took Papist money, nor himself
      became a Catholic.   References to Leslie are slight.
      The conclusion rests upon the authority of *The History
      of the Rebellion*.

118   THE Lord Clarendon's HISTORY OF THE Grand Rebellion
      COMPLEATED.   CONTAINING, I. The Heads of the Great Men
      on both Sides, whose Characters he gives, (being 85 in
      Number) Drawn from Original Paintings of Vandike,
      A. More, Dobson, Cor. Johnson, and other Eminent Painters.
      And Engraven by Mr. Vertue, Mr. Vandergutcht, Mr. Sturt,
      &c.   II. The Tracts, Speeches, Letters, Memorials, &c.
      mention'd in the said History, are here at large, and
      refer'd to the Page therein.   With his Lordship's Life.
      III. Three Maps, viz. 1. South Britain (with the Tract
      of King Charles the Second's miraculous Escape from
      Worcester.) 2. North Britain. 3. Ireland. IV. Two
      Tables, one of the Heads, and who Painted and Engrav'd
      them.   The other, of all the Battles that was fought;
      both referring to the Pages in the aforesaid History.

      London: John Nicholson, MDCCXV

There was a second edition, 1717, and a third, Dublin, 1720. See *History of the Rebellion* [106G]. It is intended as a companion to the three-volume octavo Oxford editions of the *Hist. Reb.* *The Church Quarterly Review* [169] assesses the quality of the maps and portraits.

119 THE HISTORY OF THE REBELLION and CIVIL WARS IN IRELAND, WITH The true State and Condition of that Kingdom before the Year 1640; and the most material Passages and Actions which since that Time have contributed to the Calamities it hath undergone. Written by the Right Honourable EDWARD Earl of CLARENDON, Late Lord High Chancellor of England, Privy Counsellor in the Reigns of King CHARLES the First and the Second.

Dublin: Patrick Dugan, 1719-20

The advertisement, which claims that this edition is more correct than that of London (see below), also carries the attestation of William King, Archbishop of Dublin, to the authenticity of this work, it having been compared with two manuscripts in his library. The work was written at Cologne, with the assistance of Ormonde and his memoirs, and came into the Archbishop's possession via Baxter, Ormonde's steward, in 1686.

The running title of the work is AN HISTORICAL VIEW OF THE Affairs of IRELAND. This, however, is misleading, for it is really a defense of the activities of Ormonde in the period following 1642. The title of the work mimics that of the *Hist. Reb.*, but its similarity is limited to its vindication of Charles I's policy in Ireland, as conducted by Ormonde, and its claim to the same historical impartiality. Its method is also broadly comparable in that it looks on the pre-1640 period as a happy era destroyed by rebellion. The root of the troubles is Roman Catholic ambition, but the focus is on Ormonde and his actions.

Another edition, similarly entitled, is:

119A London: H.P. for J. Wilford and T. Jauncy, MDCCXX

And a second London edition, also similarly entitled, is:

119B London: for J. Wilford MDCCXXI

The preface speaks of Borlase's acquisition of this material, but can offer no explanation of how he came by it. See [100] above.

120 BULSTRODE, Sir Richard
     MEMOIRS AND REFLECTIONS UPON THE REIGN and GOVERNMENT OF
     King CHARLES the 1st. AND K. CHARLES the 11d. Containing
     an ACCOUNT of several remarkable Facts not mentioned by
     other Historians of those Times: Wherein the Character
     of the ROYAL MARTYR, and of King CHARLES II. are Vindi-
     cated from Fanatical Aspersions. Written by Sir RICHARD
     BULSTRODE, Resident at Brussels to the Court of Spain,
     from King CHARLES II. and Envoy from King JAMES II. till
     the Revolution 1688. Now First Published from his
     Original MANUSCRIPT.

     London: Charles Rivington, 1721

         Nath. Mist, the printer, claims to have acquired
     these memoirs from Sir Richard, son of Sir Richard
     Bulstrode, in Paris "last year." It is also stated that
     a second son, Whitlock Bulstrode, published a book of
     essays in 1715 wherein is a character of his father.
         The point to be made here is that some of Clarendon's
     most famous characters, especially one of Cromwell, are
     here reproduced, without acknowledgment, in some of
     their most striking phrases and passages. How Bulstrode
     came by them--whether perhaps from Clarendon's MS, or
     from the 1702-04 edition of *Hist. Reb.* or otherwise--is
     unknown. He died in 1711. It may be also that his son,
     Sir Richard, incorporated some of Clarendon's work. In
     any event, the similarities of phrasing are surely not
     coincidental.

121 [BARWICK, Peter]
     VITA Johannis Barwick, S.T.P. ECCLESIAE Christi & S.
     Mariae Dunelmensis primùm, S. Pauli postea Londinensis
     DECANI, ET Collegii Sancti JOHANNIS EVANGELISTAE apud
     Cantabrigienses aliquando SOCII: A PETRO BARWICK, M.D.
     Ejusdem etiam Collegii olim ALUMNO, CONSCRIPTA; Et in
     istius Collegii Bibliothecâ asservata: IN QUA Non pauca
     Arcana Studia pro REGNO BRITTANNICO, motibus intenstinis
     collapso in pristinum statum restituendo difficillimis
     temporibus fideliter impensa, tandemque feliciter
     praestitia & consummata, in lucem proferuntur. Adjicitur
     APPENDIX EPISTOLARUM tam ab ipso Rege CAROLO II. quam à
     suo CANCELLARIO exulantibus, aliarumq; Chartarum ad
     eandem Historiam pertinentium. Omnia ab ipsis Auto-
     graphis nunc primùm edita.

     London: Gulielmi Bowyer, MDCCXXI

The letters from Charles to Clarendon, and from him
to various parties start at August, 1655. There is also
an interesting table of numerical cyphers, much used at
that time, and of a rather unsophisticated kind. In
this cypher Hyde = 589, Barwick = 572 (most are of proper
names), and "victory" = 623.
    It appeared in an English translation in 1724, and
again, abridged, in 1903.

122 AN APPENDIX TO THE HISTORY OF THE Grand Rebellion.
     Consisting of some Valuable PIECES, written by The
     Right Honourable EDWARD Earl of CLARENDON. AND Recom-
     mended to the Perusal of those who have read his former
     Volumes; as illustrating several PASSAGES therein. To
     which is prefix'd A new and particular Account of his
     Lordship's LIFE; from good Authorities, as well as living
     Information. Together with A large and full Vindication
     of his CHARACTER.

     London: John Wilford, MDCCXYIV [sic]

       The Preface reviews Clarendon's literary career with
     laudatory comments on several works, including *The Dif-
     ference and Disparity* [73], which is said to be the work
     of a young man before he had "enter'd the Stage of
     Business." The other contents are an anonymous biography
     of Clarendon; the letter from Oliver Long to Sir William
     Coventry, 1668, recounting the attempted murder of
     Clarendon at Evreux; A declaration of the Commons to
     which the next item *A Full Answer* [72] responds; *The
     Difference and Disparity*; Some Observations and Reflec-
     tions, which are excerpts of letters in 1659; Speeches
     in Parliament after 1660; Clarendon's *Humble Petition and
     Address* [93]; the Loyal Dedication to *A Brief View and
     Survey* [101]; the letter to the Duke of York and the
     letter to the Duchess [103]. The first volume of *A
     Collection of Several Valuable Pieces* [128], 1727, re-
     prints most of this material.

123 BURNET, Gilbert
     Bishop BURNET'S HISTORY OF His Own Time. (2 vols.)

     London: Thomas Ward, 1724

       Although criticizing Clarendon's "too magisterial
     manner," Burnet is on the whole well disposed toward him.

Much of his account, he tells us, is obtained from
Clarendon's eldest son. The major section is as follows:

> He was a good Chancellor, only a little too rough,
> but very impartial in the administration of justice.
> He never seemed to understand forreign affairs well:
> And yet he meddled too much in them. He had too much
> levity in his wit, and did not always observe the
> decorum of his post. He was high, and was apt to
> reject those who addressed themselves to him with too
> much contempt. He had such a regard to the King,
> that when places were disposed of, even otherwise
> than as he advised, yet he would justify what the
> King did, and disparage the pretensions of others,
> not without much scorn; which created him many ene-
> mies. He was indefatigable in business, tho' the
> gout did often disable him from waiting on the King:
> Yet, during his credit, the King came constantly to
> him when he was laid up by it.

Burnet tells the story he had from Lady Ranelegh of
the last advice Clarendon's father told him moments
before his fatal attack of apoplexy: "that he should
never sacrifice the laws and liberties of his countrey
to his own interests, or to the will of a Prince." He
then considers how Clarendon responded to the admonition,
and concludes that one of the reasons Charles II hated
him was because Clarendon refused to obtain for him more
independence from Parliament than was wise for a king,
and on the other hand took care to restore to monarchy
those necessary things extorted by the Long Parliament.
Burnet defends his integrity against aspersions at
the time of his trial. All he ever received as a per-
quisite were books of the Louvre impression, a gift of
the French king.
Burnet's *History* was published simultaneously in
Dublin, also a two-volume edition.

124   [OLDMIXON, John]
       THE Critical History of ENGLAND

       See Section E

125   [GREY, Zachary]
       A DEFENCE OF OUR ANTIENT and MODERN HISTORIANS

       See Section E

126   [OLDMIXON, John]
      A REVIEW OF Dr. Zachary Grey's DEFENCE OF OUR ANCIENT
      and MODERN HISTORIANS

      See Section E

127   [OLDMIXON, John]
      CLARENDON and WHITLOCK COMPAR'D

      See Section E

128   A COLLECTION OF SEVERAL valuable Pieces, Of the Right
      Honourable EDWARD Earl of CLARENDON.   (2 vols.)

      London: J. Wilford, MDCCXXVII

          This seems to be an expanded version of AN APPENDIX,
      1724 [122], also published by Wilford. Volume ii is
      The History of the Rebellion and Civil Wars in Ireland.

129   A COLLECTION OF SEVERAL TRACTS Of the RIGHT HONOURABLE
      Earl of CLARENDON, AUTHOR of the HISTORY of the REBELLION
      AND CIVIL WARS in ENGLAND. Published from his LORDSHIP'S
      Original Manuscripts.

      London: T. Woodward and J. Peele, MDCCXXVII

          There is a variant title page of what is perhaps
      another issue rather than another separate edition:

129A A COLLECTION OF SEVERAL TRACTS Of the RIGHT HONOURABLE
      EDWARD, Earl of CLARENDON, AUTHOR of The HISTORY of the
      REBELLION and CIVIL WARS in ENGLAND. Published from his
      LORDSHIP's Original Manuscripts.

          In this version there is added, "The EDITOR to the
      Reader," before the table of contents. It remarks that
      the papers were procured from Frances Keightley before
      her recent death. The special characteristics of the
      contents, such as the Vindication, Moral Essays, Divine
      Essays, and Prayers are summarized. The MSS now with
      the publisher may be consulted by anyone who doubts
      their authenticity.
          The Vindication, 88 pp. in length, is dated July 24,
      1688 at Montpellier. Following this are the seventeen
      articles of treason which the vindication answers

exhaustively. The *Contemplations,* dated from Dec. 26,
1647 at Jersey, to February 27, 1670 Montpelier [sic]
are included, prefixed by a letter to his children. The
whole of this section seems to have been completed
18/28 February, 1670/1.

130   [OLDMIXON, John]
      THE HISTORY OF ENGLAND

      See Section E

131   CLARKE, John
      AN ESSAY UPON STUDY

      See Section E

132   ATTERBURY, Francis
      "I have lately seen an Extract of some Passages...."
      [Vindication]

      See Section E

133   OLDMIXON, John
      Mr. OLDMIXON'S REPLY

      See Section E

134   [ANON.]
      Mr. OLDMIXON'S REPLY ... Examin'd

      See Section E

135   [ANON.]
      THE CLARENDON FAMILY VINDICATED

      See Section E

136   GRANVILLE, George, Lord Lansdowne
      THE GENUINE WORKS IN VERSE AND PROSE Of the Right
      Honourable GEORGE GRANVILLE, LORD LANSDOWNE. (2 vols.)

      London: J. Tonson and L. Gilliver, MDCCXXXII

Volume i contains "A Vindication of Sir Richard Granville, General in the West for King Charles the First, from the Misrepresentations of the Earl of Clarendon and the reverend Mr. Archdeacon Echard."

Clarendon's depiction of Granville in *The History of the Rebellion* is utterly damning. The case for the defense made here by his great-nephew is that he was a scapegoat for the mistakes of the civilian Council dominated by Clarendon. Granville bore a heavy grudge on account of Clarendon's treatment of him at the end of the Civil War, which he sought to make good by means of charges brought against the future Chancellor in 1654. Of these Granville wrote a *Defence Against all Aspersions of Malignant Persons*. It was of no avail, for his accusations were based on hearsay derived from military quarters, always disaffected to the policies of Hyde.

Granville's *Works* were republished in three volumes in 1736.

137 ATTERBURY, Francis
Bishop ATTERBURY'S VINDICATION

See Section E

138 [ANON.]
THE LIVES OF THE English Bishops

See Section E

139 [DAVYS, John?]
CLARENDON AND WHITLOCK Farther compar'd

See Section E

140 BURTON, John
THE GENUINENESS OF Ld Clarendon's History

See Section E

141 A COMPLEAT COLLECTION OF TRACTS, BY THAT EMINENT STATES-MAN The RIGHT HONOURABLE EDWARD, Earl of CLARENDON. CONTAINING, A VINDICATION of himself from the Impeachment of the House of COMMONS, in Regard to the sale of DUNKIRK.

ESSAYS MORAL and ENTERTAINING on the various Faculties
and Passions of the Human Mind. REFLECTIONS upon War
and Peace. A TREATISE upon EDUCATION. DISCOURSES upon
the Psalms of DAVID, with an Historical Application of
them to the Times of the CIVIL WAR.

London: C. Davis, S. Austen, S. Baker, Lockyer Davis,
MDCCXLVII

Following the vindication, dated July 24, 1668, there
are twenty-five essays with Baconian titles, several of
which were composed in Jersey, 1647, and the remainder
in his second exile, 1669-72. They reflect the pious
and stoical cast of Clarendon's mind, stressing the
spiritual, and even more so, temperamental qualities
exhibited by Clarendon himself in his adversity. Most
are brief, but lack the arresting aphoristic quality of
the Baconian originals. The longest--44 and 33 pp. re-
spectively--are "Against the multiplying Controversies"
and "On an Active and Contemplative Life," which was
published separately in 1765 [153].
There are two Dialogues, also printed separately in
1764 [152] and 1765 [154].
The final section contains *Contemplations and Reflections upon the Psalms of David*, again a work which was
begun in the first exile, and resumed in the second.
The whole is a reprint of the 1727 edition *A Collection of Several Tracts* [128] and was again reprinted in
The Miscellaneous Works, 1751 [143]. The essays were
reprinted in *Essays moral and entertaining*, 1815 [199],
and, with omissions, in *British Prose Writers*, vol. i,
1819-21. A list of the titles of the essays and dialogues may be found in *The New Cambridge Bibliography of
English Literature*.
One essay, "Of Sacrilege," is incorrectly dated
Jersey 1641. It should be 1647.

142 [TOWGOOD, Michaijah]
     AN ESSAY TOWARD ATTAINING A TRUE IDEA OF THE CHARACTER
     and REIGN OF K. CHARLES the First

     See Section E

143 THE MISCELLANEOUS WORKS OF THE RIGHT HONOURABLE EDWARD
     Earl of Clarendon, Lord High Chancellor of ENGLAND,
     AUTHOR of the History of the REBELLION and CIVIL-WARS

in England. BEING A COLLECTION of Several Valuable
Tracts, written by that Eminent Statesman. Published
from His LORDSHIP'S Original MSS.

London: Samuel Paterson, MDCCLI

It is described as the second edition and is a reprint of the 1727 *Tracts* and the 1747 *Compleat Collection*
[141].

144   [JOHNSON, Samuel]
      THE RAMBLER. VOLUME SECOND.

London: J. Payne, MDCCLII

This is Number 122, Saturday, May 18, 1751, pp. 725-
730.
Johnson is appraising Clarendon's place among the
English historians. He remarks the supposed ease of
writing history, with its emphasis upon narrative, and
the actual difficulty of it evidenced in the fact that
so few have succeeded. English culture, in comparison
with those of neighbour nations, is deficient in this art.
Raleigh is praised for his skill, but more so is Clarendon, despite his style marked by a "rude inartificial
Majesty." Best of all is Knolles in his *History of the
Turks,* but it is likely to be forgotten because of lack
of interest in his subject.

145   [BOYLE, John, Earl of Orrery]
      REMARKS ON THE LIFE and WRITINGS OF Dr. JONATHAN SWIFT,
      Dean of St. PATRICK'S, Dublin, In a Series of LETTERS
      FROM JOHN Earl of ORRERY To his SON, the Honourable
      HAMILTON BOYLE.

London: A. Millar, MDCCLII

Remarks on Clarendon's style occur in a letter
critical of many well-reputed styles of the period, for
the purpose of praising Swift's in comparison. Clarendon's periods are too long, his parentheses too numerous,
and his inaccuracies conspicuous.

146   Bibliotheca Clarendoniana: A CATALOGUE OF THE VALUABLE
      and CURIOUS LIBRARY OF THE RIGHT HONOURABLE EDWARD Earl
      of CLARENDON, Lord High Chancellor of England, and
      Author of The History of the GRAND REBELLION. Containing

a great Number of rare and choice Books in the Latin,
English, French, Italian and Spanish Languages. Many of
the Books are on ROYAL PAPER, and in MOROCCO and other
Elegant Bindings, and all in very neat Condition. [Two
columns of titles.] Which will begin to be sold cheap,
for ready Money only, (the Prices printed in the Catalogue,) on Thursday Aug. 26, 1756, and continue on Sale
to the End of October next, By THOMAS WILCOX, Bookseller,
Opposite the New Church in the Strand.

1086 titles are listed.

147   THE HISTORY OF THE REBELLION and CIVIL WARS IN IRELAND,
      WITH The true State and Condition of that Kingdom before
      the Year 1640; and the most material Passages and
      Actions, which since that Time have contributed to the
      Calamities it hath undergone: BEING A SUPPLEMENT to the
      History of the Grand Rebellion. Both written by the
      Right Honourable EDWARD, Earl of CLARENDON.

      London: J. Woodyer, MDCCLVI

      This is called the third edition. It contains Arch-
      bishop William King's testimony that the work was written
      at Cologne, and "An ACCOUNT of Dr. Borlase's History of
      the execrable Irish Rebellion, taken from Dr. Nalson's
      Preface to the Second Volume of his Collections; wherein
      may be seen the Partiality and Disingenuity of Dr. Bor-
      lase, and his unfair Dealing with a Copy of my Lord
      Clarendon's Manuscript, which is now faithfully and
      intirely publish'd." Borlase is accused both of plagiar-
      ism and of distorting Clarendon's MS to fit his own
      thesis.
         The running title is "A VINDICATION of James, Duke
      of Ormond." There is an appendix containing an account
      of massacres and murders in Ireland since 1641.

148   WALPOLE, Horace
      A CATALOGUE OF THE ROYAL AND NOBLE AUTHORS OF ENGLAND,
      With LISTS of their WORKS. (2 vols.)

      Strawberry-Hill, MDCCLVII

      Walpole sets out to steer a middle course between
      the excessive condemnation and excessive praise of
      Clarendon which has marked judgments of his work hither-
      to. But this involves a reversal of standard attitudes
      which praise his work as a historian, while condemning

his record as a politician. Walpole's own political
bias is clear enough when he praises Clarendon for having
resisted an "infatuated" nation's demand for absolutism.

> His designing or blinded cotemporaries heaped the
> most unjust abuse upon him: The subsequent age, when
> the partizans of prerogative were at least the loud-
> est, if not the most numerous, smit with a work that
> deified their Martyr, have been unbounded in their
> encomiums.

Clarendon's political services to the nation are
most marked in the Restoration period: "A corrupted court
and a blinded populace were less the causes of the Chancellor's fall, than an ungrateful King, who could not
pardon his Lordship's having refused to accept for him
the slavery of his country."
Again, it is Clarendon's "cotemporaries" who come in
for the harshest criticism, having

> removed the only Man, who, if He could, would have
> corrected his Master's evil government. One reads
> with indignation that buffooneries too low and insipid
> for Bartholomew-fair were practiced in a court called
> *polite*, to make a silly man of wit laugh himself into
> disgracing the only honest Minister he had. Bucking-
> ham, Shaftesbury, Lauderdale, Arlington, and such
> abominable Men were the exchange which the Nation
> made for my Lord Clarendon!

As a statesman, therefore, Clarendon's memory is
venerable. "As an Historian he seems more exceptionable.
His majesty and eloquence, his power of painting characters, his knowledge of his subject, rank him in the
first class of writers--yet he hath both great and little
faults." Among the latter are his stories of ghosts and
omens.
In terms of the structure and bias of *The History of
the Rebellion,* it may be that the character of Falkland
takes too great a share.

> One loves indeed the heart that believed till He
> made his friend the Hero of his Epic. His capital
> fault is, his whole work being a laboured justifi-
> cation of King Charles. No Man ever delivered so
> much truth with so little sincerity. If He relates
> faults, some palliating epithet always slides in;
> and He has the art of breaking his darkest shades
> with gleams of light that take off all impression
> of horrour. -- One may pronounce on my Lord

Clarendon in his double capacity as statesman and
Historian, that He acted for liberty, but wrote for
prerogative.

There follows a brief bibliography of Clarendon's
works.

149   THE HISTORY OF THE REIGN OF King CHARLES the Second,
      FROM THE RESTORATION To the End of the YEAR 1667.
      WRITTEN BY EDWARD Earl of CLARENDON, LORD HIGH-CHANCELLOR
      of ENGLAND. αυεκτατου.
      (2 vols.)

      [London]: M. Cooper [n.d.] [1757?]

      The British Library Catalogue suggests 1757 as the
date of publication. In the copy owned by that library
is the following MS note:

> This is the Edition of Lord Clarendon's Life
> printed by Dr Shebbeare the sale of which was re-
> strained by an Injunction of the Court of Chancery
> obtained by the Dutchess of Queensbury in conse-
> quence whereof the whole impression (except a very
> few Copies) was destroyed. The Tory Introduction
> was never printed in any other form.

Also in this copy the Greek in the t.p. is corrected to
"αὐέκδοτου," apparently in the sense of "unpublished."
The meaning of the uncorrected word is not at all apparent, nor is it clear how a misprint, if such it is,
would take this form.

      Shebbeare attempted to recover his losses from Francis
Gwyn, the publisher, who had been involved with him in
this venture. In the following year Shebbeare was sen-
tenced to stand in the pillory, was fined, and was given
three years in prison for the offenses caused by his
political writings. Later in his career he became a
target of Whig scorn on account of his progress from
pillory to pension. He and Samuel Johnson were described
by Wilkes in 1776 as "state hirelings."

      His introduction is an able defense of Clarendon,
and an appreciation of his talents. The continuation of
the *Life*, which is here printed under the title "Reflections," Shebbeare says was given in MS to Francis Gwyn,
the politician (1648?-1734), the special friend of
Laurence Hyde, by Henry Hyde. This Gwyn was sometime
secretary of war to Queen Anne.

150 THE LIFE OF EDWARD EARL OF CLARENDON [etc.]

See Section D: *THE HISTORY OF THE REBELLION* AND *THE LIFE*

151 A CATALOGUE OF A COLLECTION OF MANUSCRIPTS Of the GREAT
     EARL OF CLARENDON, LORD HIGH CHANCELLOR of ENGLAND, in
     the Reign of King CHARLES II. Consisting of a great
     Number of Original Treatises wrote by him on various
     Subjects. Original Letters and Negotiations between
     him and many of the Sovereign Princes and States of
     Europe, English Ambassadors and Residents abroad. Some
     original Letters of King CHARLES I. King CHARLES II.
     King JAMES II. and other Princes. A great Number of
     Letters, &c. between Lord CLARENDON and others when
     abroad with King CHARLES II. during the Usurpation; and
     their Emissaries in England. Of secret Intelligence
     from them, and of CROMWELL'S Transactions, &c. And a
     very large Number of Papers, relating to the PUBLICK
     AFFAIRS of these Kingdoms and the Plantations, with
     Foreign States. Collected by EDWARD Earl of CLARENDON,
     Lord High Chancellor; his Son HENRY Earl of CLARENDON,
     Lord Lieut. of Ireland; and his Grandson EDWARD Earl of
     CLARENDON, sometime Governor of New York, New Jersey, &c.
     Very few of which were ever published. Together with a
     Manuscript of the History of the Rebellion; being the
     first Draught of it, in Lord CLARENDON'S Hand-Writing.
     Which will be sold by AUCTION, (By Order of the Executors
     of JOSEPH RADCLIFFE, Esq; of the Inner Temple, deceased)
     By SAMUEL BAKER, Bookseller, in York Street, Covent-
     Garden. On Monday the 9th of April, and the following
     Day: beginning each Day at Twelve o'Clock. The Manu-
     scripts may be viewed on Monday the 2d. (26 pp.)

     [London: 1764]

     A note explains that Radcliffe (d. 1760) was an execu-
tor to Edward Earl of Clarendon (the first Clarendon's
grandson), sometime governor of New York, etc., and was a
godson of Lady Frances Keightley, who was an aunt to
Queen Anne.

152 A DIALOGUE CONCERNING EDUCATION. By the right honourable
     EDWARD, Earl of CLARENDON, Lord high Chancellor of
     ENGLAND.

     Glasgow: Robert Urie, MDCCLXIV

The publisher claims this was procured from Frances Keightley, Clarendon's daughter. This is true inasmuch as the text of *A Collection of Several Tracts*, 1727 [129], in which it first appeared, was printed from the MSS in her possession. There is a promise that more of these tracts will soon appear.

Clarendon originally conceived this dialogue as following from *A Dialogue on the Want of Respect due to Age* [154]. The five characters who debate that topic are joined here by a bishop whom the Alderman invites to attend them. Education of the young is clearly a matter of concern to Clarendon because he saw the new generation as having been severed from its cultural roots by the destructive effects of civil war, and thus deporting itself in an insolent manner. The purpose of the dialogue is to develop sound moral bearings for the observance of posterity.

153   AN ESSAY ON An Active and CONTEMPLATIVE LIFE: AND, Why the one should be preferred before the other.

Glasgow: Robert Urie, MDCCLXV

This essay, which, like the others printed singly, first appeared in *A Collection of Several Tracts,* 1727 [129], is the longest and arguably the best of his work in the genre. Although he greatly admired Bacon, Clarendon does not adopt his essay style. As the title suggests, the model taken here is Cicero. The similarity is not superficial, nor a matter of prose style alone, nor again of the expansive and discursive form, but rather a fundamental likeness in philosophy which the author shares with him. Practical experience of the greatest affairs, dedicated opposition to tyranny at personal risk, this active life sustained by deeply ingrained habits of contemplation, and life-long devotion to reading the best books, form together Clarendon's prescription for the complete man, of which Cicero is regarded as an exemplar. He was no doubt keenly aware of the parallels which might be drawn between his life history and that of his mentor.

Interestingly, the essay opens with a witty sneer at the amount of time wasted, especially among the Italians, in considering this fashionable and artificial topic: it is rather like arguing whether one should undertake a journey on a black or a bay horse.

What follows is both an illustrated argument for the
necessary interdependence of the active life and the
habits of intellectual and spiritual reflection, and, at
the same time, a sustained attack upon extreme forms the
contemplative urge has devised, especially monasticism.
This second element is developed into a critique of Roman
Catholicism along similar lines to *Religion and Policy*
[161].

Clarendon's own personal and political philosophy,
once formed, remained remarkably stable. Its major ingredients are given admirable expression here. An
example is his commitment to the fundamental rightness
of Jacobean ecclesiastical polity. The Church should be

> reduced within that Inclosure in which our Saviour
> left it, to be directed and instructed by learned
> and pious Bishops, in Subjection to and under the
> Government of those Christian Kings who are appointed
> by him to reign over us.

Finally he moves to consider what makes a good historian, with comments on ancient and modern practitioners.

> It is not a Collection of Records, or an Admission
> to the View and Perusal of the most secret Letters
> and Acts of State, (though they are great and neces-
> sary Contributions) which can enable a Man to write
> a History, if there be an Absence of that Genius
> and Spirit and Soul of an Historian, which is con-
> tracted by the Knowledge and Course and Method of
> Business, and by Conversation and Familiarity in the
> Inside of Courts, and the most active and eminent
> Persons in the Government; all which yields an admir-
> able Light, though a man writes of Times, and Things
> which were transacted for the most Part before he
> was born.

154   A DIALOGUE ON The want of Respect due to Age. By the
right honourable, EDWARD Earl of CLARENDON Lord High
Chancellor of England.

Glasgow: Robert Urie, MDCCLXV

This first appeared in *A Collection of Several
Tracts,* 1727 [129].

Five characters--an old courtier, an old lawyer, an
old soldier, an old country gentleman, and an old alder-
man--at a dinner provided by the latter, discuss this
Ciceronian topic. A part consists of censure on the

influences now swaying an unruly younger generation.
These largely derive from France and the French academies.
Later the characteristics of old age are enumerated, in
contrast to the vigor and folly of youth. Good statecraft is the larger context in which the proper relationship of youth to age may be defined.

155 STATE PAPERS COLLECTED BY EDWARD HYDE, EARL OF CLARENDON.
     COMMENCING FROM THE YEAR MDCXXI. CONTAINING THE MATERIALS
     FROM WHICH HIS HISTORY OF THE GREAT REBELLION WAS COM-
     POSED, AND THE AUTHORITIES ON WHICH THE TRUTH OF HIS
     RELATION IS FOUNDED. (3 vols.)

155A VOLUME THE FISRT [sic]

     Oxford: Clarendon Printing-House, MDCCLXVII

155B STATE PAPERS COLLECTED BY EDWARD, EARL OF CLARENDON
     VOLUME THE SECOND

     Oxford: Clarendon Printing-House, MDCCLXXIII

155C STATE PAPERS COLLECTED BY EDWARD, EARL OF CLARENDON
     VOLUME THE THIRD

     Oxford: Clarendon Printing-House, MDCCLXXXVI

     The preface to vol. ii is by Richard Scrope of
Magdalen, which gives some account of the provenance of
the papers. Dr. John Douglas, Canon of Windsor, is
said to have been particularly active in collecting "all
the detached and scattered Parts of the Original Collection." The shortened title of this volume is explained:
many of the papers here presented have no relationship to
the *Hist. Reb.* or the recently published *Life* (1759).
     The preface to vol. iii is by Thomas Monkhouse of
Queen's College. It opens with an explanation of his
delay in bringing it to publication. Scrope had found
the labor excessive, and having made some headway, returned the unpublished papers in 1775 to Monkhouse, who
assumed the duties of editor. As this volume was preparing for the press, it came to light that there were
many more Clarendon letters which had been detached from
the main body of MSS. It took until 1780 to complete
the arrangement, then another batch of letters in the
possession of Mr. Godschall surfaced. These covered a
wider time-span than anticipated, thus a further delay
in incorporating them resulted. The problems of selection

were now overwhelming. Thus Monkhouse found his task
"disagreeable at the best, but rendered completely so,
by a Concurrence of perplexing Circumstances, that have
greatly prolonged and increased his Labours."

156 DODD, William
A COMMENTARY ON THE BOOKS OF THE Old and New Testament.
IN WHICH ARE INSERTED THE NOTES AND COLLECTIONS OF John
Lock, The Right Honourable Edward Earl of Clarendon,
Daniel Waterland and Other Learned Persons with Practical
Improvements. (3 vols.)

London: MDCCLXX

The Preface comments that the Clarendon contribution
comes from "a curious MS written in Lord Clarendon's own
hand, containing his lordship's remarks on the sacred
books." These are his *Contemplations on the Psalms of
David,* also printed in [129] and [141]. Dodd was the
ill-fated friend of Samuel Johnson, hanged for forgery.

157 THE SECRET HISTORY OF THE COURT AND REIGN OF CHARLES THE
SECOND, BY A MEMBER OF HIS PRIVY COUNCIL: TO WHICH ARE
ADDED INTRODUCTORY SKETCHES OF THE PRECEDING PERIOD FROM
THE ACCESSION OF JAMES I. WITH NOTES, AND A SUPPLEMENT
CONTINUING THE NARRATIVE IN A SUMMARY MANNER TO THE
REVOLUTION: BY THE EDITOR. IN TWO VOLUMES.

London: T. Gillet and J. Bew, 1792

A fine introduction explains the advantages of secret
history and supposes that the authenticity of this will
shine clearly through. It is said to be an excellent
example of secret history, but even this author [Claren-
don] attempts to soften the most odious features in the
character of a king he could not but censure and despise.
There are no special thanks due to him (we are told) for
a truth he selfishly intended to withhold. It is, therefore, a Whig way of using Clarendon's history [i.e.,
Life].

The *Life* is freely altered, with interpolations to
suit the editorial viewpoint, and is thus correctly
described in the Bodleian catalogue as a modernized and
altered version of the *Continuation*. There is also copious commentary. The edition is the work of Charles
McCormick.

158 CHARACTERS OF EMINENT MEN IN THE REIGNS OF CHARLES I.
     and II. Including the Rebellion, FROM THE WORKS OF LORD
     CHANCELLOR CLARENDON.

     London: R. Faulder, MDCCXCIII

        The reason for publishing this selection of Clarendon
     is to warn against the causes and effects of revolutions
     such as that currently laying waste France, and specific-
     ally to

          guard against the visionary projects of those who in
          their endeavours to reform the English constitution,
          would endanger those substantial blessings which
          were secured to us, not by the fury of the times of
          Charles the first; but at the peaceable and glorious
          revolution of 1688.

        It is a well-made, compact selection of characters
     with linking narrative. The editor is E. T[urner].

159 MEMOIRS OF KING CHARLES I. AND THE LOYALISTS WHO SUF-
     FERED IN HIS CAUSE; CHIEFLY EXTRACTED FROM LORD CLAREN-
     DON'S HISTORY OF THE REBELLION. ILLUSTRATED WITH THEIR
     PORTRAITS, FROM VANDYKE, &c.

     London: I. Herbert, 1795

        Royalist hagiography. There is another edition
     which differs in a few particulars such as the position-
     ing of engravings and other ornamental effects, but the
     text, drawn from the *Hist. Reb.*, is the same.

160 PALM, G.F.
     Interessante Scenen aus der Geschichte der Menschheit.

     Hannover: 1799

        Vol. ii (Zweites Bändchen), pp. 1-33, is a chapter
     entitled "Karls des Zweiten Schicksale nach der Schlacht
     bei Worcester, bis zu seiner Throngelangung. (Aus dem
     Memoires des Grafen Clarendon.)." It is his account in
     the *Hist. Reb.* plus an explanatory, scene-setting intro-
     duction and conclusion.

161 RELIGION AND POLICY AND THE COUNTENANCE AND ASSISTANCE
EACH SHOULD GIVE TO THE OTHER. WITH A SURVEY OF THE
POWER AND JURISDICTION OF THE POPE IN THE DOMINIONS OF
OTHER PRINCES. (2 vols.)

Oxford: Clarendon Press, 1811

A brief preliminary notice establishes the authenticity of the work by reference to the 407-pp. MS dated
at the end, Moulins, 12 Feb., 1673/4 and noting the
names of the trustees of the Clarendon MSS.

It is essentially a history of, and argument against,
papal supremacy. Although the work is scholarly, detailed, and documented, its concern is not purely aca-   -
demic. Clarendon's daughter had declared her allegiance
to Rome (see *Two Letters* [103]), the Duke of York, her
husband, was suspected of having done the same, and
rumors persisted throughout his reign of Charles II's
similar inclination.

Clarendon's Erastian position is clear: kings were
ordained for the protection of the Christian religion,
not popes. Catholic subjects of a Protestant monarch
should renounce claims on them of papal authority and
supremacy, which would not contravene the articles of
their faith. If this were to be done, by clergy and
laity alike, Catholics could be admitted to the full
rights and political privileges of their nations, and
penal laws against them dropped.

This is the topical direction of the argument. Its
foundation is a painstakingly scholarly history of the
Roman Catholic Church.

The format of this edition was intended to match
that of the 1807 edition of the *Hist. Reb.* [106 N].
Carter, p. 365, records that 1016 copies were printed
at a price of 26 s. In 1826 510 were left. In 1862
459 were pulped.

Section D

The History of the Rebellion
and *The Life*

THE HISTORY OF THE REBELLION

Begun in 1646, taken up at irregular intervals and completed
in 1672, it was, as the author had anticipated, not for publication in his lifetime. In the long years of eclipse following the Glorious Revolution, the Tory party at its "head-
quarters," Christ Chruch, Oxford, undertook the editorial work
necessary to produce an edition of the *History* which was
"intended to provide a standard for the new Tory party"
(Bennett, G.V., *The Tory Crisis in Church and State 1688-1730*,
Oxford: Clarendon Press, 1975, pp. 30-31). Because of the
extraordinarily complex conflation of MSS and the near ille-
gibility of Clarendon's hand, it was no easy matter to arrive
at an accurate text, and before Macray's edition of 1888 none
was achieved. There were also, of course, many delicate political considerations.

     With the accession of Anne in 1702, the time had arrived
for publication. The introduction of the first of the Occasional Conformity bills in that year, and its attendant Tory
expectations, created a suitable, if controversial, atmosphere
in which to begin one of the most interesting publishing ven-
tures of the eighteenth century.

     In the interest of clarity, the following list is presented
separately from the chronological list of Clarendon's works,
etc. in Section C. One conclusion to be drawn simply from the
number and variety of editions is that there was an almost
insatiable appetite for the *History*, at least initially. This
was greatly stimulated by controversy, especially concerning
its authenticity, which was initiated by Oldmixon (see Section E). So valuable was Clarendon to the Oxford press that
in 1703 the Queen approved a grant of fourteen years copyright
on the work to the University (dating from June 24 of that
year) which later became a singular instance of perpetual
copyright. This also forbade the importation, abridgement,
buying, uttering, vending, or distributing of the *History* in
England and abroad. From the proceeds of the first edition,
the Clarendon Press was founded.

149

106 THE HISTORY OF THE REBELLION and CIVIL WARS IN ENGLAND,
     Begun in the Year 1641. With the precedent Passages,
     and Actions, that contributed thereunto, and the happy
     End, and Conclusion thereof by the KING's blessed
     RESTORATION, and RETURN upon the 29th of May, in the
     Year 1660. Written by the Right Honourable EDWARD Earl
     of CLARENDON, Late Lord High Chancellour of England,
     Privy Counsellour in the Reigns of King CHARLES the
     First and the Second.

     Oxford: Printed at the Theater, MDCCII (vol. i),
     MDCIII (vol. ii), MDCCIV (vol. iii)

          As it is no easy task to determine exactly what
     Clarendon intended to include of the several MSS he
     conflated to create the *History*, and as he himself seems
     to have authorized the exercise of editorial discretion,
     all editions are substantially inaccurate before Macray's,
     which is open to question in only a few relatively minor
     matters. Although the difficulties inherent in the
     arrangement of the MSS are important factors in the
     failure to present an accurate text, there are others
     suggested by Harry Carter, *A History of the Oxford Uni-
     versity Press* (Clarendon Press, 1975), vol. i, pp. 230-
     231. A fair copy was made for the printers in 1699 by
     William Wogan and an amanuensis named Low who transcribed
     a copy of the original MSS by William Shaw, Clarendon's
     secretary, which itself contained alterations in the
     hand of the author. Shaw's copy has vanished. The fair
     copy made by Wogan and Low, which was undertaken at the
     behest of Thomas Sprat, modernized Clarendon's spelling,
     and in some places clarified his involved syntax.
     Several characters were softened--notably one of Arundel,
     whose grandson became a benefactor of the University--in
     order to avoid giving offense to living descendants, but
     in general no really significant alteration was made.
     The Wogan and Low copy was corrected in places by
     Laurence Hyde.
          This edition has been described as the great landmark
     in Aldrich's management of the Oxford University Press
     (Nicolas Barker, *The Oxford University Press and the
     Spread of Learning 1478-1978* [Oxford: Clarendon Press,
     1978], p. 27). Henry Aldrich (Dean of Christ Church
     from 1689, died 1710) was involved not only in the edi-
     torial decisions and revisions, but also in the design.
     He "drew the designs for the headpieces and initials
     which made the folio one of the handsomest books hitherto
     produced in England" (Barker, p. 28; see also Carter,

p. 149, on the discovery of Aldrich's designs for the
engravings).

The visual effect of this edition is imposing indeed.
Vols. i & ii have full portraits of Clarendon (vol. i
by R. White, vol. ii by Michael Burghers) after a portrait
by Lely. Each of the sixteen books has an engraved head-
piece, initial capitals, and endpiece, executed by
Burghers from Aldrich's designs. These are allegorical
in style, and in some instances, obscure. Barker, p. 27,
remarks that "His taste for allegory was not shared by
Whig detractors of the University, who were apt to detect
treason in what they could not understand." One of the
finest capitals--W--opens vol. ii (book VI of the *History*): death, a skeletal reaper, approaches a flourishing
palm tree, on the far side of which a swain sits, head on
knees. This book opens, of course, with Charles signal-
ling civil war by erecting his standard, which was blown
down that night, at Nottingham. The upright palm is a
kingly symbol especially associated with Charles I.
Book V's (vol. i) initial A is on a scene of Adam and
Eve at dalliance in the Garden, but the subject matter
concerns Charles' reception in York. The headpieces are
solemn or triumphant by turns, depending upon the moods
of the books they represent.

The Preface to vol. i (probably by Laurence Hyde,
though Carter, p. 234, casts doubt on this assumption)
is a vindication of Clarendon's reputation and an antici-
pation of the beneficial effects of this publication.
Vol. ii has a preliminary dedication to Queen Anne,
which commends the work as a faithful counsellor to her,
since its author in his person faithfully served two
kings. It attacks republican sentiments. Carter,
p. 235, thinks the dedications to vols. ii and iii may
be ascribed to Laurence Hyde unaided, because they lack
the "prevailing magnanimity" of the vol. i preface.
This is followed by the Queen's grant of fourteen years
copyright to the University.

Vol. iii has a second dedication to the Queen and an
even fiercer attack on republicans who asperse the true
sons of the Church with the name of Jacobites. It is
outraged by alleged celebrations of the horrid 30th January (date of Charles I's death) with scandalous mirth
in some quarters. The copyright grant is reprinted.
The *Church Quarterly* reviewer [169] of Macray's 1888
edition remarks

It is a common belief in that ancient seat of
learning that the perpetual and sole copyright of

reprinting Clarendon's *History* in any shape whatever
is for ever vested in the University. The Copyright
Act was not passed until 8 Anne, and, though the
book has been so frequently reprinted within the
period since elapsed that the benefit of the Act is
secured to each successive edition, there is, of
course, nothing to prevent a man from reprinting
one of the earlier editions whose copyright has
expired.

The same reviewer has interesting and sometimes whimsical
remarks on the engravings. The edition, he concludes,
"is a marvel of beautiful printing."

In some sets, all three volumes are dated 1704, and
it is not unusual to find the second and third volumes
dated 1704. Perhaps these should be regarded as separate
editions. However, a useful clarification of the circumstances is provided by Carter, p. 235, part of which
follows.

> The first edition of the *History* is made up of
> several printings not easy to distinguish. Only of
> the third volume are all copies alike: all those
> dated 1704 were printed before Michaelmas in that
> year. Of Volume ii, there were three printings from
> different type settings, of 1704, 1704-05, and 1707,
> all dated 1704. Volume i, first printed in 1702,
> was printed again in 1703, 1704 and 1707. A new edi-
> tion of all three volumes in folio format was printed
> at the Theatre in 1707 for John Baskett, the London
> Stationer, who paid for it and sold it. Since it is
> indistinguishable, except by its date, from the Uni-
> versity's edition of 1702-04, sets of three volumes
> are sometimes a mixture of the two.
>
> Books warehoused after printing in those days
> were all folded sheets and might remain such for a
> long time before being bound. Sheets printed at
> different times might be put together to make
> volumes: it is not an infallible guide to the date
> of Volume i of Clarendon that it includes the Queen's
> privilege for the work granted a year after it was
> first printed, or that the engraving of the frontis-
> piece or title-page device has a late date. These
> things can at most indicate the earliest date for
> the binding.

There is no doubt that the *History* was the most valuable Oxford book of its period, even though the value
may often have accrued to London booksellers and, of

course, to the notorious vice-Chancellor who diverted
some of the profits to his own use.

NOTE: For the subsequent editions listed below, I give the
place of publication, the publisher when it differs from
the above, the editor where relevant, and the date, but
forbear listing variants in the title pages.

It is clear that many sets of the volumes of the
History made up of elements of discrete editions have been
assembled and described as "editions." One example is the
collection of 8° volumes of the *History* listed in the
National Union Catalog as an edition of Oxford, 1707-1720.
The use of the word "edition" for the reasons Carter ex-
pounds is unavoidably imprecise.

It is also common in many library catalogues to add to
the count of volumes in an edition of the *History* materials
which are in fact separate and supplementary, but which
appear from their titles to be integral, such as *Continuation of the History*, which is, in fact, the *Life*, or *The
Lord Clarendon's History of the Grand Rebellion Compleated*.
In this bibliography such works are regarded as separate
entities, and noticed in Section C.

There is a version of the *History* "Faithfully abridg'd,"
London: John Nutt, 1703, which is not a genuine *History*,
and therefore omitted from this list.

106A   1705-06   Oxford   3 vols.   8°

Each volume has two parts. Vol. i is 1705, vols. ii
and iii, 1706. This edition was bought *en bloc* by a
London stationer, Thomas Bennett, who had a part in distributing the first edition (Barker, p. 28). The *Church
Quarterly* reviewer (see [106] above) remarks that this
edition is

interesting from its having become the subject of
interleaving upon the most gigantic scale known in
the history of literature. In 1795, a well-known
antiquary, Mr. A. Sutherland, began a collection of
prints, portraits, water-colour drawings, engravings
of medals, &c., to illustrate Clarendon and Burnet.
After forty-two years' labour, and an estimated ex-
penditure of 20,000 l., his widow presented the
Collection, bound in sixty-one elephant folio
volumes, and enriched with over nineteen thousand
illustrations of various kinds, to the Bodleian
Library, where it at present remains.

106B   1704-09   La Haye   6 vols.   8°

    A French translation, which might have been regarded
as a violation of Oxford's privileges (*Church Quarterly*
review).

106C   1707   Oxford   3 vols.   folio

    Lowndes, *The Bibliographer's Manual of English*
Literature (London: Bell [1857?]), 4 vols., says that
only six copies of this were printed--which seems im-
probable judging by the number of American libraries
alone which record it.   Indeed, Carter, p. 451, citing
Press records, gives vol. i, 700 & 250 L.P.; vol. ii,
700 & 217 L.P.; vol. iii, 700 & 203 L.P.

106D   1707   Oxford   3 vols. in 6   8°

    A copy in the Bodleian contains MS notes by White
Kennett.

106E   1709   Oxford   3 vols. in 6   8°

    The existence of this edition is recorded only by
Lowndes.   I have not seen a copy.

106F   1712   Oxford   3 vols. in 6   8°

    John Baskett took all 1,500 copies of this edition,
paying £100 in advance to the University, and 4 s. in
the pound for the use of the University's Letters
(Carter, p. 306).

106G   1717   Oxford   3 vols. in 6   8°

    The *Church Quarterly* reviewer remarks that this edi-
tion is accompanied by a number of plates which are not
Oxford work, but rather the work of J. Nicholson who
provides with this edition a companion volume containing
"a few unimportant tracts" etc.   This volume is the
second edition of *The Lord Clarendon's History of the*
Grand Rebellion Compleated (1717) [118].
    Carter, p. 477, records the order for John Baskett
to print 1,650 copies, 150 of which were intended for
the University.

106H   1719   Dublin: John Hyde and Robert Owen   3 vols.   folio

    Lowndes, following Wood's *Athenae* (1817 ed.) calls this a "spurious edition."

106I   1720-21   Oxford: At the Theater   3 vols. in 6   8°

    The Bodleian copy of vol. i, part i, is dated 1721.

106J   1731   Oxford   3 vols. in 6   8°

    Wood, *Athenae*, in a note by Bliss, describes this as "the master's edition; as it was printed for masters of arts only." According to Carter, p. 306, it was the 150 copies on large paper done for the University by Mount and Page in London which gives it this title. Elsewhere (p. 509) he refers to 100 copies, which were printed in 1732-33 from the type of the 1731 edition.

106K   1732   Oxford   3 vols. in 1   folio

    This is printed in double columns with portraits. Carter, p. 306, thinks it might have been done at the Bible Press--the only secular work to have enjoyed this distinction.

106L   1732   Oxford   3 vols. in 6   8°

106M   1798   Basil   12 vols. in 6   8°

    The *Life* (*Continuation*, etc.) is included in the same edition [150].

106N   1807   Oxford   3 vols. in 6   8°

    Advertised as a new edition.

106 O   1816   Oxford   3 vols. in 6   4°

    This also contains the *Historical view of the affairs of Ireland*, which had appeared earlier as *The history of the rebellion and civil wars in Ireland*   [119].

106P   1819   Oxford   3 vols. in 6   8°

    Also contains the Irish materials.

106Q   1826   Oxford   8 vols.   8°

    Advertised as a new edition with a new collation of the original MSS and suppressed passages, plus the notes of Bishop Warburton. This edition was prepared by

Dr. Bulkeley Bandinel as an attempt to correct the mis-
readings of previous editions. While preparing it,
according to the *Church Quarterly* reviewer, he heard
from the Dean of Worcester of a copy in the college
library containing Warburton's MS notes. These Bandinel
saw, transcribed, and here reproduced.

106R   1827   Boston

A reprint by Wells and Lilly of the 1826 Oxford
edition [106Q].

106S   1839   Oxford   7 vols.   12°

106T   1839   Oxford   1 vol.   8°

106U   1840   Oxford   2 vols.   8°

106V   1843   Oxford   8°

This edition occurs in both single and two-volume
formats. It contains the *Life* (*Continuation of the History of the Rebellion*), the title page of which is dated
separately 1842.
Barker, p. 44, describes the single-volume 8° version
as "one of the most attractive of mid nineteenth-century
books printed at the Press; it remained in print until
the 1950's."

106W   1849   Oxford   7 vols.   8°

This is advertised as for the first time carefully
printed, etc. It contains the Irish material and the
Warburton notes. It is a slightly revised edition of
the 1826 version of Dr. Bandinel.

106X   1888   Oxford   6 vols.   8°

Edited by W. Dunn Macray, this is now the standard
edition, a painstaking re-collation of MSS with useful
notes, a fine index, and marginal dates, with other
apparatus which permits the reader to compare the accuracy of its readings with previous editions. Modern
spelling, alas. There are some few instances in which
Macray seems to misread the MSS, and a few questionable
matters of arrangement. It is a fine work of scholarship,
a labor of love and patience which could scarcely be
bettered (especially considering the present condition
of the MSS, especially Bodleian MS Clarendon 112) except
in respect of fuller notes and the correction of some

inaccurate dates. Some readers might wish for an
original-spelling edition.

THE LIFE ...

Of this work, there is no accurate edition; indeed, nothing
approaching a complete text. The autobiography which Clarendon began to compose shortly after his fall and flight, having
none of his papers with him, was meant as a record for his
children and posterity. It was therefore not written with
direct intention of printed publication, but rather for publication in the limited sense of availability to a select and
interested group. Its style, however, is formal, not unlike
that of the *History*, and no doubt Clarendon wrote, whatever
his professed intention, as if a larger audience were always
in mind. It rehearses much of the same matter as the *History*
of the Rebellion, although the focus here is much more upon
the activities of Mr. Hyde himself. It also gives us a
fascinating picture (which the *History* does not) of his education, upbringing, and early manhood in the company of, *inter*
alia, Ben Jonson, and the wits and poets. His story is continued to the Restoration. The MS account was cannibalized
by Clarendon to complete his *History* when other MSS of this
work finally arrived at his place of exile. For this reason,
the *Life* has always held second place to the *History* in
prestige.

The second part, which is essentially a vindication of
Clarendon's conduct as Chancellor between 1660 and 1667, is
commonly entitled the *Continuation of the Life*, as in the
first edition of 1759, but, confusingly, the same piece is
also sometimes entitled the *Continuation of the Grand Rebel-*
lion (also in the 1759 title). Put together, the parts comprise the autobiography of Clarendon, most simply referred to
as *The Life*. Parts of this work have appeared under the
titles *The Secret History of the Court and Reign of Charles*
the Second, The History of the Reign of Charles the Second
(Shebbeare's suppressed edition) and *Memoires*.

The circumstances in which the MSS of the *Life*, and a
very large collection of State and other papers, came to the
University Press and to the Bodleian Library are explained by
Dr. Bandinel in his Preface to his 1826 edition of the *History*
[106Q] and in W.D. Macray, *Annals of the Bodleian Library*
Oxford (Oxford: Clarendon Press, 1868), pp. 225-7; and in
F. Madan, *A Summary Catalogue of Western Manuscripts in the*
Bodleian Library at Oxford (Oxford: Clarendon Press, 1895),
vol. iii.

In contrast to the *History*, the *Life* sold very slowly.
710 copies of the 1759 folio edition of 2,000 still remained in 1814, and of these, 598 were sold as waste in
1818. A similar fate befell the octavo editions (Carter,
p. 363). Today, no edition of the *Life* is in print. A
new edition of *Selections from The History and the Life*
(Oxford, 1955), edited by G. Huehns, has recently
appeared.

150   THE LIFE OF EDWARD EARL OF CLARENDON, LORD HIGH CHANCELLOR
        of ENGLAND, AND CHANCELLOR of the UNIVERSITY of Oxford.
        CONTAINING, I. An Account of the CHANCELLOR'S LIFE from
        his BIRTH to the RESTORATION in 1660. II. A Continuation
        of the same, and of his HISTORY of the GRAND REBELLION,
        from the RESTORATION to his BANISHMENT in 1667. WRITTEN
        BY HIMSELF. Printed from his ORIGINAL MANUSCRIPTS,
        given to the UNIVERSITY of OXFORD, by the Heirs of the
        late EARL of CLARENDON.

        Oxford: Clarendon Printing-House, MDCCLIX

        This is the first folio edition of 2,000 copies, plus
        250 in large paper (Carter, p. 564).
        The frontispiece is an engraving of the portrait of
        Clarendon by Lely, matching those in the first folio of
        the *History*. There are also headpieces and tailpieces
        of a similar nature, and the engraved capitals designed
        by Aldrich are also used.
        The Preface explains how the papers came to Oxford.
        There is a succinct account of the relationship of the
        MSS *Life* to *History*. Directives for printing appear in
        full, no doubt to forestall any possible attempt at dis-
        crediting the text, as had happened in the case of the
        History.

150A   1759   Oxford   3 vols.   8°

        Printed in the same quantities as the folio edition.

150B   1760   Oxford   2 vols.   8°

150C   1760   Dublin   3 vols.   8°

150D   1760   Dublin   1 vol.   folio

150E   1761   Oxford   3 vols.   8°

        Described as the third edition, i.e., the third
        octavo Oxford edition.

150F   1798   Basil   5 vols. in 3   8°

    This continues from the 12 vols. in 6 editions of
the *History* [106M].

150G   1817   Oxford   2 vols.   4°

150H   1824   Paris, Rouen   4 vols.   8°

    A French translation (*Mémoires de Lord Clarendon*,
etc.). Reissued Paris, 1827, as part of a series of
English memoirs.

150I   1827   Oxford   3 vols.   8°

    Advertised as a new edition based on a fresh colla-
tion of the original MS.

150J   1843   Oxford   1 vol. and 2 vols.   8°

    The single-volume format is described by Barker,
p. 44, as "one of the most attractive of mid nineteenth-
century books printed at the Press; it remained in print
until the 1950's."

150K   1857   Oxford   2 vols.   8°

Section E

Oldmixon and the Genuineness of
The History of the Rebellion

Even in the first stages of composing *The History of the Rebellion* Clarendon, then Sir Edward Hyde, recognized its unsuitability for immediate publication because it would make mad work among friends and foes alike. First conceived in the spirit of factional polemic, it quickly took on the character of a philosophic treatise aiming at impartiality of judgment on all those who had fallen in either cause, and a preserving of their memories to posterity. Its publication was to be reserved for more propitious times, and, to give Clarendon his due, he remained undemanding of public notoriety. In his will he left the option of suppressing it, wholly or in part, to his sons and heirs. Political circumstance gave rise to its first appearance in print. Very soon after this event John Oldmixon, also according to the dictate of party politics, initiated what proved to be a bitter and protracted controversy concerning its authenticity.

This ripened into a classic Whig-Tory confrontation. Such was the prestige of Clarendon himself that the opening shots were fired exclusively at the editors of his work, the supposed managers of high-Tory politics. Gradually the range of the controversy broadened to include assaults on, and defenses of Clarendon's impartiality, which laid the foundations of seemingly unending party confrontation in the later eighteenth and in the nineteenth centuries.

Oldmixon himself, however, was on thin ice, and several well-meaning partisans were taken down with him. Working with what he was later forced into admitting as hearsay evidence, he began to cast doubt on the honesty of the Christ Church editors. He questioned whether the word "Rebellion" ever occurred in the original title, and then alleged tampering on a wider scale, eventually attacking the bias of the *History* and its style. Tory apologists rose to the battle, in which Oldmixon was indefatigable, until the grounds of his accusations completely disintegrated.

The text of the *History* was not, in fact, accurate, but not because of the reasons he had given. Johnson comments in summary style upon the outcome of the whole affair in *Idler* No. 65 (1759):

> Clarendon's history, tho' printed with the sanction
> of one of the first universities of the world, had
> not an unexpected manuscript been happily discovered,
> would, with the help of factious credulity, have been
> brought into question by the two lowest of all human
> beings, a scribbler for a party [Oldmixon] and a com-
> missioner of excise [Duckett].

Fortunately for Oldmixon, he did not live to endure this
verdict.

Henry Fielding, whose literary sensibilities had
been weaned on the products of this debate, reflects
more ironically on the wider prospect, in *Joseph Andrews*,
which began its public career in 1742:

> Notwithstanding the preference which may be vulgarly
> given to the authority of those romance-writers who
> entitle their books, "The History of England, the
> History of France, of Spain, etc." it is most cer-
> tain that truth is to be found only in the works of
> those who celebrate the lives of great men, and are
> commonly called biographers, as the others should
> indeed be termed topographers, or chorographers--
> words which might well mark the distinction between
> them; it being the business of the latter chiefly to
> describe countries and cities, which, with the
> assistance of maps, they do pretty justly, and may
> be depended upon; but as to the actions and characters
> of men their writings are not quite so authentic, of
> which there needs no other proof than those eternal
> contradictions occurring between two topographers
> who undertake the history of the same country, for
> instance my lord Clarendon and Mr. Whitlock, between
> Mr. Echard and Rapin, and many others, where, facts
> being set forth in a different light, every reader
> believes as he pleases, and, indeed, the more judi-
> cious and suspicious very justly esteem the whole as
> no other than a romance in which the writer hath
> indulged a happy and fertile invention.

There follows here a list of short titles displaying
the controversy in outline. The titles are then noticed
separately and discussed in items [111] to [142]. More
could be added if the purpose were an exhaustive account
of this controversy, but to do so would possibly distract
from the central focus of this bibliography.

1748   [TOWGOOD]   *An Essay towards attaining a true*   [142]
                        Idea of the Character and Reign
                        of K. Charles the first

111   [OLDMIXON, John]
       THE LIVES OF ALL THE LORDS Chancellors, LORDS Keepers,
       AND LORDS Commissioners, OF THE GREAT SEAL of ENGLAND;
       From WILLIAM the Conqueror, to the present TIME: But more
       at large of those Two Great Opposites, EDWARD Earl of
       Clarendon, AND BULSTRODE Lord Whitlock. With a PARALLEL
       of their ACTIONS. To which is added, An APPENDIX of
       many Rare and Valuable SPEECHES, LETTERS, &c. referring
       to the said LIVES. In Two Volumes. Necessary for the
       Readers of the Earl of Clarendon's and other Histories
       of those Times. By an Impartial hand.

       London: R. Burrough and J. Baker, 1708

           The original intention, we are told, was to compose
       lives of Clarendon and Whitelocke in parallel columns,
       which scheme was abandoned in favor of a Plutarchian
       method. Vol. i, therefore, is almost all given to a
       life of Clarendon, drawn from the materials of his auto-
       biography, but not arranged in his order. Vol. ii is a
       life of Whitelocke. Near the end of this volume is to
       be found an uninformative four-page parallel.
           In the life of Clarendon, Oldmixon remarks that
       Wood's *Athenae Oxonienses* was condemned to the flames
       by the Chancellor's Court at Oxford for libels against
       Clarendon, but that in practice merely a few sheets were
       destroyed. Warwick's character of Clarendon [105] is
       cited. There is a brief bibliography and a note that
       the MS History of Ireland was used without acknowledge-
       ment by Borlase.

114   [OLDMIXON, John]
       THE Secret History OF EUROPE SHEWING That the late
       Greatness of the French Power was never so much owing to
       the Number or Goodness of their Troops, and the Conduct
       of their Ministry at Home, as to the Treachery and Cor-
       ruption of the Ministers Abroad. [etc.]

       London: 1712

The administration of Clarendon (amongst others) is vigorously attacked. He argues that Clarendon hated the Dutch, but concealed his feelings. The most important of the nineteen charges against Clarendon in 1667, so Oldmixon thinks, was that of having betrayed his country to the enemy. He quotes part of Clarendon's reply (see *A Collection of Several Tracts* [129]) and leaves its credibility to be determined by the reader.

124 [OLDMIXON, John]
THE Critical History OF ENGLAND, Ecclesiastical and Civil: WHEREIN The Errors of the Monkish Writers, and others before the Reformation, are Expos'd and Corrected. As are also the DEFICIENCY and PARTIALITY OF Later HISTORIANS. And particular Notice is taken of

> The History of the 〕 〔 And Mr. Echard's
> Grand Rebellion. 〕 〔 History of England.

To which are added, REMARKS on some Objections made to Bishop Burnet's History of his Times.

London: J. Pemberton, MDCCXXIV

This sets out to show that the principles of the Revolution (1688) are true parts of the English constitution. Oldmixon doubts that Clarendon used the word "Rebellion" in the title of his *History*, and supposes that its published form is the work of the "Christ Church men." This history, along with Echard's, has done the greatest damage in modern times.

> The Beauty of Imagination and Colouring in the Earl of Clarendon's History charm'd them [common readers] so much, that they were not aware of the notorious Mixture of Falshood with Truth which runs through it.

He also observes that

> It has been said of the Earl of Clarendon, that his Lordship has remember'd more Minds than another Man could remember Faces; and it must be by a Miracle if the Likeness is always preserved.

Nevertheless, Oldmixon's criticism is generally cautious: when Clarendon's accuracy is called into account, it is balanced by generous appreciation of his artistry. His treatments of Echard and Burnet are not nearly as restrained.

125 GREY, Zachary
    A DEFENCE OF OUR ANTIENT and MODERN HISTORIANS, Against
    the Frivolous CAVILS Of a late PRETENDER to Critical
    HISTORY. IN WHICH The False Quotations and Unjust
    Inferences of the Anonymous Author are Confuted and
    Expos'd in the Manner they deserve. In Two PARTS. Knox
    begat Buchanan, Buchanan begat Milton, Milton begat
    Rushworth, Rushworth begat Ludlow, Ludlow begat S--dney,
    S--dney begat B--rnet, B--rnet begat B--nnet, B--nnet
    begat Old M--x--n, Old M--x--n, without Bastardy or
    Interruption, begat our Critical Historian. Page 56.

    London: Charles Rivington, MDCCXXV

        Part 2 is devoted to a defense of both Clarendon and
    Echard against Oldmixon. It is marked by a spirited
    controversialist style along party lines, complaining of
    the "too numerous succession of Antimonarchial or Repub-
    lican Historians."

126 [OLDMIXON, John]
    A REVIEW OF Dr. Zachary Grey's DEFENCE OF OUR ANCIENT
    and MODERN HISTORIANS. WHEREIN, Instead of dwelling
    upon his frivolous Cavils, false Quotations, unjust
    Inferences, &c. it is prov'd, (to his Glory be it spoken)
    That there is not a Book in the English Tongue which
    contains so many Falshoods in so many Pages. By the
    Author of the Critical History of England, Ecclesiastical
    and Civil, &c.

    London: J. Roberts, 1725

        This is a response of equal vigor, in full enjoyment
    of the controversy, despite a disavowal of any intention
    of starting or sustaining one. At this stage Oldmixon
    refrains from outright attacks on Clarendon's veracity.
    The one notable exception is that he doubts Clarendon's
    impartiality in his treatment of the murder of Ascham.

127 [OLDMIXON, John]
    CLARENDON and WHITLOCK COMPAR'D To which is occasionally
    added, A COMPARISON BETWEEN THE HISTORY of the REBELLION,
    AND OTHER Histories of the Civil War. Proving very
    plainly, That the EDITORS of the Lord CLARENDON'S History,
    have hardly left one Fact, or one Character on the Par-
    liament Side, fairly represented; That the Characters
    are all Satire, or Panegyrick, and the Facts adapted to

the one, or the other, as suited best with their Design.
By the AUTHOR of the CRITICAL HISTORY of ENGLAND, &c.

London: 1727

There was a second edition in 1737 in which the
author's identity was declared.

Here Oldmixon boldly proclaims his doubts about the
validity of the *History of the Rebellion*, which he first
hinted in his *Critical History* [124]. The accuracy of
the entire work is now impugned, and responsibility laid,
somewhat implausibly, even in the heat of partisan
politics, at the door of the editors. The amount of
actual evidence adduced for the charge of massive editorial interpolation and omission is slim in the extreme:
the presence of allegedly neologistic Gallicisms in the
text. Then, disarmingly, he asserts that whether or not
this might be true is a matter indifferent, since the
whole drift of Clarendon is to excuse the maladministra-
tion of Charles I.

He offers the following critique of Clarendon:

The stile of the History of the Rebellion is the
least historical of any that ever deserv'd the Name
of History. The periods are some Twenty, some
Thirty Lines in Length, so round, that we are lost
in the Circle, as much as in a Magician's; and
wherever we meet with such Declaiming in plain
Story, we may be sure that it is intended to amuse
us, as Legerdemains make Flourishes when they are
about to play Tricks.

130   [OLDMIXON, John]
THE HISTORY OF ENGLAND During the REIGNS of the Royal
House of STUART. WHEREIN The ERRORS of LATE HISTORIES
are Discover'd and Corrected; With PROPER REFLECTIONS,
And several ORIGINAL LETTERS from King CHARLES II.
King JAMES II. OLIVER CROMWELL, &c. As also the Lord
SAVILLE'S Famous Forg'd Letter of Invitation, which
brought the Scots into England in the Year 1640, And
gave Occasion to the Beginning of the CIVIL WARS. This
LETTER being never before publish'd, led the Earl of
CLARENDON, Bishop BURNET, Mr. ECHARD, Dr. WELWOOD, and
other Writers, into Egregious MISTAKES upon this Head.
To all which is Prefix'd, Some Account of the Liberties
taken with CLARENDON'S HISTORY before it came to the
Press, such Liberties as make it Doubtful, What Part of
it is CLARENDON'S, and what Not. The whole Collected

from the most AUTHENTICK MEMOIRS, Manuscript and Printed.
By the Author of the CRITICAL HISTORY of England.

London: John Pemberton, Richard Ford, Richard Hett,
John Gray and Thomas Cox, MDCCXXX

    Here in the preface is the substance of Oldmixon's
attack on Clarendon, which may be summarized as follows.
    Mr. Edmund Smith of Christ Church confessed on his
deathbed that he had altered the MSS of the *History of
the Rebellion*. There is an unsigned letter informing
Oldmixon that Smith died in the house of the letter
writer, having told him that the *History* was the work of
Aldrich, Smallridge and Atterbury. As an illustration
(the only one) of his charge, Smith pointed to the phrase
in Clarendon's character of Hampden: "He had a Head to
contrive, a Heart to conceive, and a Hand to execute any
villany."
    The *History of the Rebellion*, and the "preachments"
in it, ruined the country, and brought it to dishonor.
Oldmixon does not doubt that some of the *History* was
written by Clarendon, but claims others copied his style,
especially its redundancy of expression.
    Oldmixon needed to make way for his own history by
removing the rubbish of other historians (Clarendon and
Echard) which stood in his way.

131   CLARKE, John
    AN ESSAY UPON STUDY. Wherein Directions are given for
the Due Conduct thereof, and the Collection of a Library,
proper for the Purpose, consisting of the Choicest
Books, in all the several Parts of LEARNING.

London: Arthur Bettesworth, 1731

    Clarke, who was Master of the Grammar School, Hull,
under the influence of Oldmixon's findings, pronounces
on the validity of the *History of the Rebellion* ("corrupted up and down") and therefore omits it from his
recommended library. The evidence of corruption, he
says, is not contemptible.

132   ATTERBURY, Francis
    "I have lately seen an Extract of some Passages [....]"
7 pp.

Paris: MDCCXXXI

The date Oct. 26, 1731 is given at the beginning. There is no formal title, but the work was quickly known as Atterbury's *Vindication*. It was republished as such along with Clarendon's last will and testament in 1733 [137]. This first edition was evidently done in haste, for the printing is quite inaccurate.

133 OLDMIXON, John

Mr. OLDMIXON'S REPLY TO THE LATE Bishop ATTERBURY'S VINDICATION OF Bishop SMALLRIDGE, Dr. ALDRICH, and HIMSELF, FROM Some PASSAGES in the PREFACE to the HISTORY of the REIGNS of the STUARTS. RELATING TO Mr. EDMUND SMITH of Oxford's Discovery of INDIRECT PRACTICES in the publication of the HISTORY of the Grand Rebellion.

London: J. Pemberton, T. Cox, R. Ford, R. Hett, MDCCXXXII

Atterbury died in Paris, March 3, 1732, having been weak and ill for several years. The expectation of his death in that period was widespread; his infirmity was not concealed.

Oldmixon's reasons given here for delaying his reply are that despite Atterbury's remarks on his advanced age in his Vindication [132], he was in good health, and no one thought he would die. In *Vindication* Atterbury expressed the hope that although near death, he would outlive any acceptance of the allegations made against the *History of the Rebellion*. The allegations, retorts Oldmixon, can never be outlived. He adds, as if in further explanation of his delay, that he has suffered from gout and been living at a remove from London.

There follows a fresh set of allegations, e.g., that the words "scandalous reflection" in Atterbury's *Vindication* are surely not his words, but the interpolation of another. He confesses that Edmund Smith did not sufficiently distinguish the part played by Atterbury from those played by Aldrich and Smallridge in tampering with the *History*. "I do not pretend to be infallible in the Terms, my Information coming from Memory, almost thirty Years after the things were said and done." He has credible unnamed witnesses, but many are wary of coming forward. There is a further flurry of wild and unsupported allegations concerning people who saw the altered MS, all reliable witnesses. Nevertheless, Oldmixon has heard many which he rejected as "traditional, if not fabulous."

He cites insinuations made by him earlier in the
controversy, and wonders why they have not been answered
by the "Christ Church" men, and then recapitulates his
earlier materials at great length. Aspects of Atterbury's *Vindication* are contested, and there is an encomium of Smith and denigration of Atterbury. He concludes
with one new piece of information, on which he would say
more if he dare, and challenges the Christ Church editors
to produce the MS of the *History*.

134   [ANON.]
      Mr. OLDMIXON'S REPLY To the late Bishop of ROCHESTER'S
      VINDICATION OF Bishop SMALLRIDGE, Dr. ALDRICH, and Him-
      self, from the scandalous Reflections of the said
      OLDMIXON, Examin'd. Wherein is given An ACCOUNT of the
      numerous Alterations in Mr. DANIEL'S History, as 'tis
      printed in the Compleat History of England, of which
      Mr. Oldmixon has declared himself the SOLE EDITOR. To
      this is prefix'd A LETTER to the Reverend Subscribers to
      a late History, proving, that the Application of Cinna's
      Character to Mr. Hampden can be no Interpolation, being
      in an Original MS wrote by my Lord Clarendon himself.

      London: J. Wilford, 1732

      The author claims to have been shown the MS *Life* in
      Clarendon's hand in which Hampden is described as in
      History of the Rebellion ("He had a Head to contrive...."
      etc. See [130]). There was, he states, no interlineation
      in the MS. He was shown it by George Clark of the
      University.

135   [ANON.]
      THE CLARENDON-Family VINDICATED FROM THE Gross Falshoods
      and Misrepresentations OF JOHN OLDMIXON, Esq; Collector
      of the Customs for the Port of Bridgewater in Somerset-
      shire, Author of The HISTORY of the Stuarts, AND GEORGE
      DUCKETT, Esq; one of the Commissioners of his Majesty's
      Revenue of Excise. CONTAINING, I. Mr. DUCKETT'S Letter
      to Mr. OLDMIXON, concerning Mr. SMITH'S pretended Alter-
      ations to the Earl of CLARENDON'S History. II. The late
      Bishop of ROCHESTER'S (Dr. ATTERBURY'S) Defence of Him-
      self, Bp. SMALRIDGE, and Dr. ALDRICH, from the Aspersions
      laid to their Charge. III. The Attestations of Bp.
      TANNER, Mr. HEARNE, and a Gentleman of St. John's Col-
      lege in Oxford, relating to the Genuine Publication of

the Earl of Clarendon's History. IV. An Account of the
Assassination of the Earl of Clarendon when in his Exile.
In a Letter to Sir William Coventry, Secretary of State.
The Whole Address'd to George Duckett, Esq; defying him
to make good his Charge against the Noble Historian.

London: [E. Curll], MDCCXXXII

The vindicator charges that Duckett wrote the letter
telling of Smith's deathbed confession, and that everyone
knows Oldmixon to be the author of the *History of the
Stuarts* [i.e., 130]. Oldmixon's allegations are then
reproduced. A biography of Smith, which reveals that he
died in Duckett's house, is said to be by Jacobs (or
Jacob), and printed by Curll, or by Oldisworth. (However, the 1811 edition of Towgood [see 142] mentioned
that Johnson was responsible for the life of Smith, and
thus for revealing the truth of the controversy.)

Citing Rowe's preface to *The Tragedy of Lady Jane
Gray*, the author claims that Smith's papers were in
Duckett's hands. Reference is made to the question of
the character of Hampden, and most of Atterbury's *Vindication* is reprinted.

The testimony of Sir Clement Cotterel and of Mr. David
Jones is reported, with quotations from the latter, who,
in his turn, quotes Laurence Hyde's epistle in *History
of the Rebellion* to Queen Anne. Le Clerc's opinions on
Clarendon's characters are cited as a prelude to affirm-
ing that Clarendon did indeed apply Sallust's character
of Cinna to Hampden. The authority of T. Hearne, who
made an index to *History of the Rebellion*, is also
adduced.

The author knew of a learned bishop who had copies
of the original Clarendon characters, and would have
publicly appealed to him, but that his bookseller
"Mr. CURLL having formerly received a signal Favour from
his Lordship in the year 1712, (when he printed Sir
Thomas Browne's REPERTORIUM, relating to the Church of
Norwich)" wrote to him, and received a reply, which is
then quoted. This letter, from "Thom. Asaph Elect.,"
says that he never possessed any of the original characters. There is a letter from an unnamed Oxford man to
Le Clerc, and an excerpt from Le Clerc on Hampden.

Finally, there is Mr. Long's letter concerning the
attempt to assassinate Clarendon at Évreux, April, 1668.

The whole of this rather disorganized work may have
been compiled by Edmund Curll himself.

137   ATTERBURY, Francis
      Bishop ATTERBURY's VINDICATION OF Bp. SMALLRIDGE,
      Dr. ALDRICH, and HIMSELF, From the SCANDALOUS REFLEC-
      TIONS OF OLDMIXON, Relating to the PUBLICATION of Lord
      CLARENDON'S HISTORY. The SECOND EDITION. To which is
      added A TRUE COPY of the LAST WILL and TESTAMENT of
      Edward Earl of Clarendon.

      London: J. Wilford, 1733

          The first edition of this vindication is [132], and
      although this is called the second, the major portion of
      it appeared in the previous year (see [134], above). It
      is dated, as in the first edition, Paris, Oct. 26, 1731.
          Atterbury writes that he had recently seen Oldmixon's
      History, and cites the offending passages of the Preface.
      He points out that the quotation from the character of
      Hampden is itself misquoted. Oldmixon's allegations
      came to his attention when he was reading the 1730 edi-
      tion of *Bibliothèque Raisonée des Ouvrages des Savans
      de l'Europe*. From this he quotes the passage which
      claims that because he has been silent the allegation of
      forgery must be proven. Atterbury claims he had nothing
      to do with the preparation of *History of the Rebellion*
      for press, neither did Smallridge, nor did he know Smith.
      The task of textual revision was handed by Rochester to
      Sprat and Aldrich, and he attests to their probity. He
      also denies that anyone could fake or match the style of
      the "masterly hand." He explains that Smith bore a
      strong resentment against Aldrich, his governor at Christ
      Church, and that therefore it is most improbable that he
      could have had any share in the preparation of the
      History of the Rebellion.
          It is a finely written, dignified defense, which
      concludes by foretelling that Clarendon's *History* will
      continue to be read while Oldmixon's censure will be
      forgotten.
          Clarendon's will gives to his sons the right to dispose
      of his papers as they please, either by suppressing or
      publishing them.

138   [ANON.]
      THE LIVES OF THE English BISHOPS FROM THE Restauration
      to the Revolution.

      [London]: J. Roberts, 1733

The significant part is pp. 399-402, a section of
the conclusion, entitled "A CENSURE of Mr. Oldmixon's
Charge upon the Editors of the Earl of Clarendon's
History."

A copy in the Rylands Library carries the MS attribution of this piece to "Mr Williams."

139   [ANON. John Davys?]
CLARENDON AND WHITLOCK Farther compar'd. OR, A DISCOVERY
Of some gross MISTAKES Committed by Mr. OLDMIXON, In his
REMARKS on the HISTORY of the REBELLION.

London: J. Millan and Sk. Barett, MDCCXXXIX

In a judicious and carefully phrased preface, the
author admits to an admiration of Clarendon, but could
also criticize and find mistakes which Oldmixon has over-
looked. It is a scholarly work, proposing a real comparison of Clarendon and Oldmixon as a means of discovering the truth. He cites the offending passages in
Oldmixon, and demonstrates, *inter alia*, that Oldmixon
had not well read the *History of the Rebellion*.

140   BURTON, John
THE GENUINENESS OF Ld Clarendon's History OF THE REBELLION
PRINTED AT OXFORD VINDICATED. Mr. Oldmixon's Slander
Confuted. The True State of the Case REPRESENTED.

Oxford: 1744

Burton, a Fellow of Eton College, writes that his
vindication of Clarendon was drawn up twelve years earlier, and a portion thereof, just sufficient to refute
Oldmixon, printed in the *Weekly Miscellany*. Then he
awaited further controversy. This came, he remarks, in
a Reply to Bishop Atterbury, and a reply to the groundless reflections of Oxoniensis, but these were so weak
as to require no answer.

The point of this treatment at large is to inform
posterity of the controversy and thus do everything
needful to prevent any further attempts to raise groundless objections to the *History*. It is particularly
important to do so at this time, since most of those
concerned with the original MSS are now dead.

The central section is a leisurely and careful
examination of the charges involved and the principles
of the matter. In an appendix are Atterbury's

Vindication, Oldmixon's *Reply to Oxoniensis*, depositions
by several parties, Clarendon's Last Will and Testament,
and *Mr. Oldmixons Reply to the groundless and unjust
reflections upon him in three late Weekly Miscellanies.*
This is, therefore, a summary and conclusion of the controversy. There are also remarks on the genuineness of
Eikon basilike.

142   [TOWGOOD, Micaijah]
       AN ESSAY TOWARDS ATTAINING A TRUE IDEA OF THE CHARACTER
       and REIGN OF K. CHARLES the FIRST, And the CAUSES of the
       CIVIL WAR. Extracted from, and delivered in the very
       Words of some of the most authentic and celebrated
       HISTORIANS, viz. Clarendon, Whitelock, Burnet, Coke,
       Echard, Rapin, Tindal, Neale, &c.

       London: John Noon, MDCCXLVIII

           Towgood, a nonconformist controversialist of high
       repute in his day, sets out to demonstrate that no part
       of English history has been so misrepresented. He then
       repeats Oldmixon's charges in *The History of England*
       [130], adding that as the MS was never produced there
       can be little room to doubt. Clarendon's history, he
       says, is also in its nature very partisan.
           This work was reprinted in 1780 and again in 1811,
       when the Oldmixon passage was omitted.

Section F

Clarendon in Perspective, 1811 to the Present

By 1811 all Clarendon's major works had been published, if not
to complete satisfaction, at least sufficiently accurately to
allay the charges of suppression, dishonest editorial practice, and the like, which mark a great deal of the debate
about him in the eighteenth century. Much of the correspondence which had not been collected in *Clarendon State Papers*
remained either to be published, or to be noticed in the
century-long project, the *Calendar of Clarendon State Papers*
[193]. The correspondence with Sir Richard Browne is collected in an edition of Evelyn's *Memoirs* [214], and that of
John Mordaunt includes a number of letters from Hyde concerning clandestine negotiations immediately prior to the Restoration. Mr. Secretary Nicholas' correspondence is collected in
four volumes by the Camden Society [347], and is selectively
presented more recently by his descendant, Donald Nicholas,
along with a biography [287], while Lister's third volume
consists mainly of Clarendon letters from the Bodleian MSS
[263].

Although historians have always cherished state documents
and statesmen's correspondence, in the later nineteenth century renewed emphasis upon documentary sources in the search
for history *wie es eigentlich gewesen* caused private letters
on matters of state to achieve new prominence. In Clarendon
studies this is reflected in, for example, Gardiner's research
article [225]. Examination of other individual MS letters
and documents of Clarendon by Sir Keith Feiling [215 and 216]
inaugurates an attempt to illuminate some of the murky areas
of Restoration ecclesiastical politics. Exactly what Clarendon's aims were and where his sympathies lay in the Church
settlement is discussed by a number of scholars noticed in
the following section. As one of these, I.M. Green, represents the case, Clarendon seems to have been, like St. Paul,
"all things to all men." No one believes his account in *Life*
in all its particulars, yet the unearthed documents, which
might be presumed to lie behind the published facade and to
tell more truths, in this case do not settle the issue.
George R. Abernathy, Jr., degates it [163 and 164], with particular reference to Presbyterianism. Robert S. Bosher sees

Clarendon as a covert Laudian [185], John Miller, treating
the Catholics at the time of the settlement, also finds
Clarendon's mind difficult to read [281], and Anne Whiteman
thinks that finally his actions speak plainer than his equivo-
cal words [353]. Part of the problem lies in squaring a
statesman's theoretical utterances on toleration and comprehension with actions dictated by practical exigency and the
enforced compromises of politics. Another part of the problem,
as any student of the period will readily acknowledge, is
caused by the difficulties in terminology used to designate
minutely and uncertainly differentiated theological and ecclesiastical positions. Many works listed in the following
section discuss the meaning of these terms, and the nature of
liberal Anglicanism, which held as one of its tenets--probably
its major one--the abandonment in a spirit of Christian charity
of the bitter factionalisms denoted by this very terminology.
There is, of course, a great deal of special reference to
Great Tew, which must, as must its presiding genius, Lord
Falkland, be approached initially via Clarendon's memorable
evocation of its spirit in the *Life*. These passages are
quoted and discussed again and again, and the most frequently
quoted passage in all Clarendon is the great elegiac character
in the *History*.

To what extent is the liberal, tolerationist atmosphere
of Great Tew a determining factor in the philosophy and
statecraft of Clarendon is a question frequently posed. In
general, Great Tew emerges as a shining example of rational
enlightenment from an age of bitter atavistic squabbling.
(A tough-minded critique of this view is to be found in a work
difficult to come by, R.M. Krapp (alias Adams), *Liberal
Anglicanism: 1637-1647* (Ridgefield, Conn., 1944), not included
in this bibliography because of its very marginal bearing on
Clarendon himself.)

Clarendon's copious correspondence on state affairs has
become a source almost as important for historians of the
century as the *History* itself. During the period, however,
Clarendon's published works continued to appear in various
forms. Characters from the *History* and the *Life* appear in
anthologies with some frequency, as do other excerpts of his
writings. Seldom are they reproduced in original spelling as
in David Nichol Smith's excellent edition [313].

Of particular interest from the point of view of Clarendon's reputation are the reasons sometimes advanced for
these new editions. Thomas Arnold [171] writing in 1886 says
that Clarendon is too long for the modern reader. The Very
Reverend G.D. Boyle, writing in 1889 [187], recognizes in
Clarendon the phenomenon of a classic falling into neglect.
He attributes this to modern haste. In 1909, on the

tercentenary of Clarendon's birth, Sir Charles Firth observed
that Clarendon has had bad luck with his immortality. He is
said to be not well known even to Oxonians [219]. There are
signs, therefore, that toward the close of the nineteenth
century, and in the early years of the twentieth, Clarendon's
centrality in English history had begun to diminish. In 1912
Robert Jameson MacKenzie, who tells us candidly that he had
intended this publication to coincide with the tercentenary,
but could not make haste enough, remarks that Clarendon has
not maintained his place in the literature of the country,
and so with his edition [269] aims to alleviate the neglect.
He observes that the availability of Clarendon in popular
editions had dwindled--a complaint reiterated several times
subsequently, and made the subject of a debate in the letter-
columns of *TLS* by Professor H.R. Trevor-Roper [331]. In this
way he brings to public notice the very peculiar copyright of
the Clarendon Press in the works of Clarendon. Perpetual
copyright, designed to reap the profits of a work then seen
to be of surpassing importance, has resulted in its relative
obscurity. The *History of the Rebellion*, he tells us elsewhere [327], had been the best-seller of the eighteenth century. From its towering authority, it, and the reputation of
its author, slid into a remarkable eclipse. Trevor-Roper's
frequent and eloquent attention to Clarendon, not in the spirit
of reverence for a dead classic, but rather in appreciation
of his "modernity," has been largely instrumental in restoring
Clarendon to respectable academic attention. His assessment
has been confirmed by other eminent modern historians. This
partial restoration has gone hand in hand with some downgrad-
ing among modern historians of the emphasis on Puritanism as
the central dynamic of the English revolution. Alternative
hypotheses now abound, and basic questions have been asked
anew, to yield quite different answers, most notably in B.H.G.
Wormald's seminal revaluation [359].

     The twentieth-century academic research industry has
closely scrutinized every aspect of Clarendon's career,
writings, and statesmanship, including his influence on the
evolution of British governmental structures, as exemplified
in Turner's studies [339 and 340]. He remains, therefore, a
(qualified) authority on seventeenth-century affairs. For
some, notably Dame C.V. Wedgwood, he also remains the model
of good expository historical prose [350]. And there are
others who continue to admire his prose, especially as deployed
in his characters, if not his conclusions. But the tone of
modern scholarship is altered from that of the foregoing
century. Moral condemnation or praise are far less frequently
to be met with than in the nineteenth century, and attention
is often given to the usefulness, or correctness, of his

accounts, judged by the modern historian's criteria of accuracy. Thus, for example, Lawrence Stone's influential non-
treatment of Clarendon [316] is included here because it
epitomizes in the most firmly stated manner the differences
of assumption and methodology which mark off seventeenth-
century accounts from modern analytics.

   All of this change would have surprised nineteenth-century
commentators. To them Clarendon was controversial. Before
the groundswell of neo-Pyrrhonism washed over intellectual
history, it seemed possible, even desirable, to actually judge
as for good or ill the achievement of any public figure who
had indisputably changed the course of his country's history.
In the following section of this bibliography will be seen
instances too numerous to mention here of partisan treatments
of Clarendon, determined either to wipe away his authority,
or to enshrine it. On the one side Whig historians sought to
cast doubt, in some cases on Clarendon's moral probity, as
did George Agar Ellis [213], in others on his accuracy as an
historian, and often in the strongest terms they hailed his
demise. Peter Bayne, reviewing for *Contemporary Review* in
1876 [179 and 180], sees Clarendon's (then Hyde's) declarations
in the 1640's as stripped to the bare canvas, never to be
repainted. John Forster, the distinguished lawyer, thought
he had dealt a death-blow to Clarendon's authority [223], and
others frequently allude to his triumph. Yet none contest
that, in the words of an anonymous reviewer in 1852 [168],
there "is no name in English historical literature better
known or more frequently referred to."

   On the side opposed to Whig or "impartial" historians are
those who see Clarendon as remaining central. Perhaps von
Ranke's famous assessment made in 1875 [297] can best represent this view.

   The Whig versus Tory views of Clarendon are, therefore,
strongly expressed in that age of moral certainties. As Dame
C.V. Wedgwood observed, this was an epoch in which "moral
certainty was not only possible but natural" [226]. Those
who attacked, those who defended, and those who aspired to
impartiality could agree that their readers held their subject
in full view--he was big enough to assault, strategic enough
to defend, and too important to patronize. So Macaulay and
Carlyle, who rise vigorously to attack him, can allow him,
when vanquished, some qualities and dignity. The former can
write with great enthusiasm in his history of the seventeenth
century on why Clarendon as Chancellor was so detested, and
deservedly, but allows that his virtues as well as his vices
contributed to his ruin (a frequently imitated sentiment in
later writers). To Carlyle, equally at home with the grand
rhetorical denunciation, Clarendon was "a man of sufficient

unveracity of heart, to whom indeed whatsoever has veracity
of heart is more or less horrible," and yet despite his
"quilted dialect" Clarendon can speak some truth.[1] No more
than Macaulay does he feel the need to specify his evidence.
Neither need he introduce or explain Clarendon: what they have
to say is treated--by means of a rhetorical fiction--as if it
were what all men know to be true of him.

For another sort of reader unconcerned with party controversy or with the destiny of British institutions, Clarendon
is sometimes made the occasion of collections of illustrations,
engravings, and the like, with which to adorn their libraries.
Woodburn's Gallery [357] is one such, *A Catalogue of Portraits*
[167] another, and Mrs. Jameson's *Beauties of the Court of
King Charles* [249] a particularly charming third. Such treatments may be the forerunners of a brand of romantic and fanciful history which has enjoyed a considerable vogue in the
twentieth century. Amorous or secret histories of court
intrigue in the seventeenth century, often of French provenance, set a pattern for this diffuse genre. Clarendon, of
course, seldom stars in the romantic leads, which are reserved
for Charles II, the Earl of Bristol, and others of appealingly
cavalier proportions. However, in one product of the 1930's
he approximates to the role of a tragic victim [252].

The significance to a relatively homogeneous culture like
that of the British nineteenth century of Clarendon's constitutional, political, and literary dimensions was to be argued
or celebrated. It was sufficient to make some labor, as
others in the eighteenth century had done, to exumbrate their
family honor from the shadows of Clarendon's strictures on
their forebears. One of these is Ashburnham [172]. That
Clarendon would be almost eclipsed would have been to these
writers a most unlikely proposition. When his reputation was
at length revived, if that indeed is the case, it was on many
other grounds than those of party animosity or family honor.

Revaluation is a twentieth-century specialty. Hardening
distinctions between modes of knowledge (e.g., historical and
literary) and genres (e.g., character, memoir, essay, and the
multiple brands of historiography) which have been fostered,
perhaps, by academic territorialism, provide compartments in
which special criteria may be applied. They have the advantage of presenting more precise slices of Clarendon, minus
the moralizing. Controversy over details abounds, sometimes

---

1. *Oliver Cromwell's Letters and Speeches with Elucida-
tions* (London: Chapman and Hall, 1897), i, p. 81.

to the detriment of the longer and broader perspective. In
this connection Professor Veatch's treatment [345], idiosyn-
cratic as it is, is an enlivening view. Clarendon there
figures not as in a party debate, but in a new "battle of the
books": he is called in to help redress the balance of the
ancients against the moderns. But in much modern scholarship,
with its necessarily restricted and intense foci of interest,
it is seldom possible to see the man, his works, and his
actions as a whole without resorting to reiterations of the
grandly judgmental manner of the nineteenth century. Lister,
his best biographer [263], however, reminds us of what is
entailed in a judgment of his entire achievement:

> He might have been a more learned lawyer, a more able
> statesman, a more eloquent orator, a more accomplished
> writer, without being so remarkable a man. We must view
> combined in one individual the successful advocate, the
> prominent member of a legislative assembly, the learned
> judge, the sagacious minister, the great historian, the
> man so prompt and able in emergencies, as if the whirl-
> wind of political contention had been his proper element,
> --so calmly diligent in literary seclusion as if the
> studious cloister had been his fittest abode; we must
> view in all its fullness this marvellous combination: we
> must search through history, and see if it can furnish an
> analogous instance; and we shall then be better qualified
> to decide, how high the name of Clarendon should be
> placed, among those celebrated men of whom their country
> may be justly proud. [ii, p. 580]

METHOD: Entries are listed alphabetically by author or editor.
"--" in the item number column indicates a cross-reference.

162   Abbott, Wilbur C.   "The Long Parliament of Charles II."
      English Historical Review, 21 (April, 1906), 254-285.

      With the help of statistics showing the duration of
      sessions, number of divisions, and majorities achieved
      in them in the Commons during the cabal administration,
      Abbott is able to compare the Clarendonian and post-
      Clarendonian effectiveness of Parliament. In effect,
      Parliament grew less productive: sessions declined,
      divisions rose sharply, and majorities waned. It is
      paradoxical that as Parliament grew more independent, it
      also became more corrupt. Compared with the management
      of Parliament by Clarendon, in this later period, party
      lines gained in distinctness, the cabal was more dis-
      unified as an administration, and the Court influence
      declined. "The men who held power in the complex period

of the cabal have been bitterly attacked and but feebly defended. Yet it is to be remembered that they suffered, like the puritans, from the literary skill of Clarendon, in whose pages the evil they did lived after them."

In some respects (which Abbott goes on to describe), notably freedom of religion and the advancement of trade, this Parliament was an improvement over Clarendon's time. The main body of the essay is not concerned with Clarendon: comparisons with his administration and management set the scene for a detailed discussion of the Long Parliament of Charles II.

163 Abernathy, George R., Jr. "Clarendon and the Declaration of Indulgence." *Journal of Ecclesiastical History,* 11 (1960), 55-73.

Historians have relied on *Life* and Lister [263] in ascribing to Clarendon the role of opponent of the Declaration of Indulgence of 1662. A study of new material and a re-reading of *Life* show that he "consistently supported comprehension and toleration and that he was not responsible for the failure of the Declaration of Indulgence." Abernathy recognizes Clarendon as the author of the *Declaration concerning Ecclesiastical Affairs,* Oct. 25, 1660 [79], which declares his views on the matter. He details Clarendon's attempts to make good the promises of Breda despite the enthusiasm in the Commons for uniformity. Failing to make headway, Clarendon tried to persuade the King to use his prerogative powers, such as by suspending the Act of Uniformity for three months. Neither this device, nor attempts to introduce limited indulgence, progressed against the opposition of the Roman Catholics and the Bishops, both groups seeing Clarendon's aim as a concession to the Presbyterians.

Many writers have assumed that Clarendon's opposition to the Declaration of Indulgence in December, 1662, was an outcome of a struggle for power with Bennet. Abernathy denies that any such struggle took place. Clarendon, therefore, did not oppose the Declaration, but rather organized the King's retreat from it--a retreat caused by stiff Anglican and nonconformist opposition, especially in the Commons.

With reference to a document in Clarendon's hand (B.M. Sloane MSS 4107), closely resembling *Second Thoughts* [88], which he recognizes should be dated 1663, Abernathy convincingly argues that Clarendon's policy remained the same, that he attempted to bring it about, and that he did not repudiate it in 1662-63.

164 Abernathy, George R., Jr. *The English Presbyterians and
     the Stuart Restoration, 1648-1663. Transactions of
     the American Philosophical Society.* New Series,
     Vol. 55, part II (May, 1965), 101 pp.

This is a detailed narrative, supported by copious
documentary evidence, of the history of the Church
settlement up to the failure of the Declaration of
Indulgence. Clarendon is shown to have recognized as
early as 1649 that the Presbyterian interest was prepared to sacrifice strict Presbyterianism for the
monarchy. In steering the policies of the exiled Royalists he effectively committed Charles to a policy of
indulgence on the eve of the Restoration. Sections of
the Declaration of Breda for which he was directly responsible guaranteed ease of tender consciences and prepared
the way for attempted exercise of royal prerogative in
religious affairs. But the tide of Laudian Anglicanism
proved stronger than Presbyterianism, beset with disunity
and indecision, with the result that the comprehension
of nonconformists within the Church of England failed.
The Savoy Conference foundered in similar straits, so
that by March 1663, Clarendon and the King had come to
recognize the futility of their effort. "In the final
analysis, the Presbyterians lost at the Stuart Restoration through their disunity, their numerical weakness,
their indecision, their lack of a positive and consistent
policy, and their unwillingness to support Charles II
and Clarendon at the risk of gains for Catholics."
Part of this study was published in 1960 [163].

165 Airy, Osmund. *The English Restoration and Louis XIV.
     From the Peace of Westphalia to the Peace of Nimwegen.*
     London: Longmans, Green, 1888.

In his chapter "The Fall of Clarendon" Airy castigates
Charles' "base desertion" of Clarendon, and compares it
to the case of Strafford. The leading causes of his
demise are reviewed. He judges only one of the seven-
teen charges against Clarendon as plausible, and that is,
interestingly, that he attempted to promote a standing
army. There is a brief account of the circumstances
which gave rise to this allegation. That Clarendon's
virtues rather than weaknesses were a significant cause
of his fall is accepted, but Airy adds in conclusion
that the chief single cause was not personal at all.
It was his weak political theory. In effect he was not
a politician but a constitutional lawyer, who all his
life opposed encroachments on a system of law which was,

in his view, beyond argument or improvement. In the
changing patterns of Restoration politics his outlook
was essentially negative, and he could not adapt to the
need for populist strategies.

166   Allen, J.W. *English Political Thought 1603-1644.*
      N.p.: Archon Books, 1967. A reprint of the first
      edition, Methuen, 1938.

      The argument is that the Royalists were not defeated
in the long run because they succeeded in defining the
terms of the contest, and thus laid the foundation of a
possible later solution. Clarendon's *History* is cited
liberally, and a chapter entitled "The War of Manifestoes"
discusses the pamphlet war, but without treating Clarendon's role in detail. The *Answer to the Nineteen Propositions* [see 32A n.] is regarded as the major statement
of the Royalist interpretation of the constitution (a
view not shared by Clarendon). Allen concludes that
parliamentary arguments in this period were very feeble,
because in their attempts to base arguments on law they
masked essentially revolutionary concepts which in due
course led to the radical instability of English
government. On the manifestos Allen writes:

> It is not possible to say exactly how the long series
> of declarations issued in the King's name in 1642
> were actually drafted. Hyde, Falkland, and Culpepper
> must all, at least, have had a hand in them. But it
> may be said that they represented in the main the
> views of Edward Hyde. It may fairly be claimed for
> him that, of all the leaders on either side, it was
> he who best understood the situation.

He sees the resultant war as the outcome of a constitutional struggle in which neither side held moral
superiority.
      There is also an all too brief chapter on Great Tew
and its influence on ideas of religious toleration.

167   Anonymous. *A Catalogue of Portraits of Foreigners, who
      have Visited England, as Noticed by Lord Clarendon,
      Heath in his Civil Wars, Thurloe in his State Papers,
      &c. &c. &c.* London, [1814].

      A brief advertisement mentions the very inadequate
index to the *History of the Rebellion*, for which this
is a partial (and somewhat eccentric) corrective.

168 Anonymous. "Clarendon and his Contemporaries."
     Fraser's Magazine, 45 (1852), 341-352.

     A review of Lady Theresa Lewis' *Lives of the Friends
     and Contemporaries of Lord Clarendon* (1852) [262]. It
     rebuts her exoneration of Clarendon from the accusations
     of Whig historians, and specifically from those of
     Ellis [213]. Although his whole career is surveyed,
     attention is directed to the question of whether he,
     when Chancellor, was guilty of bribery and corruption.
     The question is of significance to the reviewer because
     there "is no name in English historical literature better
     known or more frequently referred to." Consequently the
     reviewer proposes calmly to assess the weight of evidence
     in what has become a heated controversy: "No man was
     ever more cordially disliked, or more industriously
     scandalized," and "No man's character has been more
     violently disputed."
     In the event the reviewer finds no adequate cause to
     dispel the fog of suspicion surrounding Clarendon's
     acquisition of his celebrated portrait gallery. Lady
     Lewis' industry, however, is graciously applauded.

169 Anonymous. "Clarendon's History of the Rebellion."
     Church Quarterly Review, 29 (1890), 30-49.

     This review of Macray's 1888 edition concerns itself
     with two main matters: a comparison of this with impor-
     tant earlier editions, and an appreciation of Clarendon's
     work. There is a great deal of description and discus-
     sion of the earliest editions, with speculation on the
     authorship of their preliminary matter. Macray's work
     is praised for its meticulous accuracy and for his tex-
     tual restitutions. One regret is that the want of a
     fully annotated *History* remains unsupplied. Clarendon's
     reputation has been subjected to waves of reaction, but
     now, the reviewer believes, after the post-1832 reaction
     has played itself out, it is possible to deal fairly
     again with this subject. Interestingly, the reason why
     this should be the case is said to be the fact of a
     contemporary revolt of the educated against the unedu-
     cated. Clarendon's cause in the 1640's, the reviewer
     claims, also represented "the revolt of the intellectual
     minority against the domination of a narrow unintellec-
     tual creed."
     Contemporary scholarship is taken into account with a
     caveat that it is "absurd to try Clarendon by the stan-
     dard of present historical criticism." Gardiner's
     judicious estimates are praised, but Forster is said to

have fashioned a "flail ... to thrash the life out of
Clarendon." Passages from the best known portraits of
the *History* are quoted, and some factual errors remarked.
An interesting observation draws attention to verbal
similarities between some sections of the *History* and
Machiavelli's *The Prince*.

170   Anonymous.   Review of Campbell, *Lives of the Lord Chan-
      cellors*.   *North American Review*, 65 (1847), 159-201.

This is little more than a synopsis of Campbell's
biography (pp. 186-92 are concerned with Clarendon) with
little critical estimation of it.   But it adds general
observations on the sentiments to which the reading of
this biography gives rise in the reviewer.   He remarks
on the amount of criticism and censure which Clarendon
has earned, but he, contrasted with the "heartless rowdy"
(Charles II), and the "base crew" of fellow statesmen, is
a monument of snowy purity to posterity.

171   Arnold, Thomas.   *Clarendon History of the Rebellion Book
      VI*.   Introduction by Thomas Arnold.   Oxford: Clarendon
      Press, 1886.

The reason for this edition is that the *History*,
although a classic, is too long and too costly for the
modern reader.   Sufficient information about the *History*
is given to make the excerpt intelligible.   There is a
brief biographical sketch of Clarendon, and full notes.

172   Ashburnham, George, 3rd Earl.   *A Narrative by John Ash-
      burnham of his Attendance on King Charles the First
      from Oxford to the Scotch Army, and from Hampton-Court
      to the Isle of Wight: never before Printed.   To which
      is Prefixed a Vindication of his Character and Conduct,
      from the Misrepresentations of Lord Clarendon, by his
      Lineal Descendant and Present Representative*.   2 vols.
      London: Payne and Foss, Baldwin and Cradock, 1830.

The almost interminable vindication (pp. 13-431 of
vol. I) takes pride in saying nothing against Clarendon
which cannot be found in the published works his own
friends have made available (i.e., *Clarendon State
Papers, Life*, and *History*).   One of the numerous appen-
dices in vol. II presents "The Memoirs of Sir John
Berkley [sic]," whose character is also severely treated
by Clarendon in the *History*.   Another appendix reprints
the characters from the *History* of Hertford, Southampton, Colepeper, Nicholas, and Sir Philip Warwick.   If

Clarendon were to be deprived of his characters, we
read, he would fall like quicksilver in a thermometer
from "summer heat" to "temperate." In another appendix
are letters from *Clarendon State Papers* in evidence to
support arguments made in the vindication. The point to
be made by this evidence is that Clarendon, then Hyde,
had himself deserted the King's service when he retired
to and remained in Jersey at the end of the Civil War,
rather than going to Paris where he might have offset
the force of the counsels of the Queen and Jermyn.
Clarendon is, therefore, to be seen as deficient in
loyalty compared with John Ashburnham who, whatever
blunders he may have made, stayed with the captive
monarch, and thus his right to criticize Ashburnham's
alleged duplicity is undermined.

173   Ashley, Maurice. *Charles II*. London: Weidenfeld and
      Nicolson, 1971.

      The chapter "Charles and Clarendon" is concerned with
      the period of Clarendon's ministry. Charles' public
      and private reasons for dissatisfaction with his Chan-
      cellor are discussed. The latter's incompetence in
      several vital public matters (especially naval affairs)
      is given some emphasis, and this appraisal helps Ashley
      toward his conclusion that Clarendon was not treated
      worse than, or as badly as, Strafford. (In this he
      takes issue with Airy [165]). Coolly judged in the
      light of politics there is no blame to be attached to
      Charles. "When things go wrong someone has to take the
      blame." Charles saved Clarendon's life by urging him
      to flee.

174   Ashley, Maurice. *England in the Seventeenth Century*.
      Harmondsworth, Middlesex: Penguin, 1970. First
      published in 1952; revised 1958, 1967.

      A general history of broad appeal, it does not focus
      on any single personality, and treats none in detail.
      Clarendon's unenviable notoriety gained through his con-
      nection with the Clarendon Code is discussed. He is
      said neither to have resisted it nor reduced its sever-
      ity, although he was an unenthusiastic supporter of it.
      Other reasons for his eventual downfall are listed.

175   Ashton, Robert. *The English Civil War: Conservatism and
      Revolution, 1603-1649*. London: Weidenfeld and
      Nicolson, 1978.

Although Clarendon's *History* is regarded as the best general account, to which only Gardiner's work can bear serious comparison (a remarkable reinstatement of Clarendon!), Ashton chooses to look farther back to discover "the entrance into these dark ways" than Clarendon himself recommends, into the decades prior to Charles' accession. One effect of this approach is that rather less attention than has been fashionable is paid to radical political movements, and more to the ways in which men of consequence, particularly Parliamentarians, came to view the relationships between Parliaments, Privy Councils, ministers, and Crown. An apparent benefit of the perspective thus created is a particularly lucid and persuasive account of the pamphlet war of the early 1640's. Hyde and Falkland, Pym, Hampden, et al. are shown in a subtle contest for frighteningly high stakes, contesting the political middle ground, projecting, distorting, or attacking a fragile structure of constitutional monarchy. Cavaliers "red in tooth and claw" provide a violent and unstable element in the political mix.

176 Aylmer, G.E. *The Struggle for the Constitution: 1603–1689*. London: Blandford Press, 1963.

This study is intended as an introduction to the period and is aimed at the senior school and, perhaps, college readership. Scholarly apparatus and documentation are, therefore, not on display. (This is in contrast with Professor Aylmer's immensely detailed administrative histories, *The King's Servants* (1961) and *The State's Servants* (1973), which contain some discussion of Clarendon, and citation of his works as source documents, often doubting their reliability.)

Simplifications are boldly made in an attempt to present an impartial view, and to instruct in historiographical methods and biases. Its conclusions are essentially those of Whig history. The role of Clarendon is firmly assessed: "the greatest contemporary historian ... was on the King's side in the Civil War, he was basically a Royalist. On the other hand he believed in constitutional, not absolute monarchy." The fullest treatment of him is in the context of his ministry. He is painted in the accepted manner as profoundly conservative, and in Parliament as assailed by Presbyterians and ex-Cromwellians on the one side, and on the other by eager "Young Cavaliers," which forced him into closer alliance with Anglican interests than he would have wished. In a

sense, the Clarendon Code is justly named. His probity
is defended in the light of the common practice of the
time, and his *History* is judged as amongst the greatest
in any age.

177 Baker, Herschel. *The Race of Time*. Toronto: University
     of Toronto Press, 1967.

The changing character of English historiography in
the period between Camden's *Britannia* (1586) and *The
History of the Rebellion* is the main area of inquiry.
A broadly ranging survey establishes a rich context for
the uses and forms of historical writing. "Mighty"
Clarendon is seen as a "modern" historian, and as such,
like Milton, contemptuous of predecessors, especially
those who, unlike himself, had no experience of practical
politics. An exposition of Clarendon's view on this
matter is found in *Essays Moral and Entertaining* [see
141].

178 Barbour, Violet. *Henry Bennet, Earl of Arlington:
     Secretary of State to Charles II*. Washington, D.C.:
     American Historical Association; London: Humphrey
     Milford, 1914.

Arlington was one of the three enemies of Chancellor
Clarendon to be held in most contempt by him. (Charles
Berkeley and William Coventry contended for fourth, if
Castlemaine be discounted.) He and Bristol and Buckingham (between whom no love was lost) were seen by Clarendon as the major political managers of his downfall.
Of these Arlington had received from Clarendon the
greatest degree of assistance during the Interregnum and
the later years of exile.
   In Barbour's painstaking and detailed biography one
can easily discern the course of their relationship and
the causes of enmity. In the chapter "The Fall of
Clarendon" the crisis of their political rivalry is
described. Barbour credits Arlington with originating
the advice to Clarendon to flee, rather than Charles.
At that time Commons and Lords were deadlocked, and this
advice may have been crucial.

179 Bayne, Peter. "Clarendon. Part I--Before his First
     Exile." *Contemporary Review*, 26 (1875-6), 912-937.

Apparently occasioned by the publication of the English
translation of von Ranke's *History of England* in 1875,
this is a lively critique of Hyde's politics in the

crucial early years of the Long Parliament. Bayne's perspective is colored by his regret over the disunion of
the Anglican Church in the 1870's, from which position
he considers what different choices Hyde could have made.
The most important of these is that Hyde might firmly
have laid hold upon the leadership of an opposition party
in the Commons at the time of the Remonstrance, and thus
been able to eschew the pernicious influence of the
Court party, especially that of Digby (later 2nd Earl of
Bristol) and the Queen. Bayne holds Great Tew's liberal-
ism in high regard and questions how Clarendon's idyllic
depiction of its spirit could co-exist with the tyrannical misery of England at that time. The interesting
answer is that speculative philosophy usually takes kindly
to despotism. This response is carefully placed here
(and in the second article [180]) to permit praise of
Clarendon's philosophic resilience along with a thorough
condemnation of his actions. "Hyde possessed literary
capacity to the measure of genius, but had no practical
talent." His literary efforts as royal penman in 1642-
43 were disastrous because with "lacquer" and "smooth-
ness of phrase" he disguised the fact that the monarchy
would make absolutely no concessions. Further, at
Uxbridge, Hyde had in his power the salvation of the
Church and King by means of accommodation to Alexander
Henderson's moderate Presbyterianism. Now, however,
"Churchmen of comprehensive and generous sympathies ...
may well regret the course adopted by Hyde in 1642."

180 Bayne, Peter. "Clarendon. Part II--After his First
     Exile." *Contemporary Review*, 28 (1876), 421-443.

The reviewer's political and religious sympathies are
much more strongly worded in this second article. He
seeks to demonstrate that the *History of the Rebellion*
is "comprehensively fallacious, incurably wrong," and
that the authority of that work is "totally worthless."
To argue his point Bayne takes a very interesting
position *contra* Ranke, namely that it is not in "point
of view" that Clarendon is accurate, and in "details"
wrong, but the reverse. Neither have the best authors
on the Puritan Revolution (in which tradition Bayne sees
himself) repeated Clarendon as Ranke asserts. Thus
emerges a picture of a Clarendon who in his *History* pro-
pounds a theory or delivers an opinion with placid
assurance that he is right, and then calmly jots down
facts demonstrating that he is wrong. The declarations
he penned are "plausible, well-worded documents" which

swayed simple-minded Cavaliers. They are now stripped
to the bare canvas: "No hand will ever lay that paint
again." In his enthusiastic pursuit of Clarendon he
follows him off the main track of English politics to
the well-known passage on the Spanish bullfight. Clarendon is rebuked for having nothing to say against the
inhumanity of bullfighting. On the other hand, the
"elaborate cowardice of modern Spain" which doesn't
dare to stage full-blooded bullfights is condemned.

How has Clarendon attained the wide currency and
authority to which Ranke attests? The answers are
three: his style (although this is often a liability);
his anecdotal skill; the interest of the established
clergy. The latter, as Bayne remarks, are condemned in
Clarendon's own words as men who "take the worst measure
of human affairs of all mankind that can write and
read." Hume is incidentally characterized as "a skill-
ful and unscrupulous literary artist" whose account of
the Puritan Revolution is simply Clarendon's.

After the "dark reserve of duplicity and falsehood"
in Clarendon's character is shown in its several manifestations, he turns to praise the steadfast philosophical cheerfulness of Clarendon in his last exile. In
historical hindsight we see a Clarendon who, because of
his partisan duplicity, falls short of being a "Shakespeare among historians," and who as statesman narrowly--
but fatally--failed to put England on a course which
would have wedded English law and liberty to ancient
monarchy, England to Scotland, and the Episcopal Church
to the leadership of Protestantism. (Seldom can a man
have failed by so little to do so much!)

181   Bennett, G.V. *White Kennett 1660-1728 Bishop of*
        Peterborough. London: S.P.C.K., 1957.

    Given the nature of his subject, Bennett is not con-
cerned extensively with Clarendon or his career, but
rather with the effect of the publication of the *History*
(1702-04) on party quarrels. Rochester, Kennett's major
political adversary, is said to have given "substance
and massive strength" to Tory orthodoxy by the publication of his father's work. Bishop Kennett, however,
who drew heavily on Clarendon, especially his characters,
thought the *History of the Rebellion* an excellent work
which by no means served one (the Tory) side only.

182   Beresford, John. *Gossip of the Seventeenth and Eigh-*
        teenth Centuries. London: Richard Cobden-Sanderson,
        1923.

Essays entitled "January 30, 1649," "Anne Hyde: Early Life and Marriage (1637-60)," and "Anne Hyde: Duchess of York (1660-71)" all draw on the authority of Clarendon, who is described as

> one of the greatest, if not the greatest statesman of the seventeenth century, and is still remembered by posterity as one of the greatest of English historians. But both as a statesman and as an historian his actions and his thoughts had their root in religious beliefs, and the Bible was to him, as it was to his arch-enemy, Oliver Cromwell, the foundation of secular life, and the source of all inspiration.

183   Bevan, Bryan. "The Downfall of Edward Hyde, Earl of Clarendon (1609-1674)." *Contemporary Review*, 211 (July, 1967), 208-211.

This is a review of the circumstances leading to Clarendon's fall, and an assessment of his career, both in broad, generalizing terms. It does not seem to add to the sum of Clarendon scholarship, being based largely on received opinion of a modestly sympathetic cast.

184   Bigham, Charles Clive, 2nd Viscount Mersey. *The Chief Ministers of England 920-1720*. New York: Books for Libraries Press, 1967. A reprint of the first edition, 1923.

Chapter XI presents brief lives of Clarendon and Danby in the Plutarchian manner. More emphasis is placed on the post-Restoration career of Clarendon, in keeping with the aim of the book as announced in the title. It is a compilation of standard sources, rather than a work of original scholarship. The conclusion stresses Clarendon's honesty in a corrupt age, comparing him to advantage with Danby: "The former looked backward and cherished his integrity; the latter looked forward and savoured bribery."

--   Bliss, W.H. *Calendar of the Clarendon State Papers*. See *Calendar of the Clarendon State Papers*, Vol. i [193].

185   Bosher, Robert S. *The Making of the Restoration Settlement*. London: Dacre Press, 1951.

This is an important and seminal study of a subject which has received renewed scholarly interest in recent times. Understanding of the process by which the Church

was re-established after 1660, and of the politico-
theology which guided it, depends to a considerable
degree upon interpretation of the role of Clarendon.
Bosher's detailed and documented treatment sees him as
the sustainer of the Laudian party in exile which managed
Anglican affairs because more moderate episcopalians
were unable to act in a concerted manner or exert their
influence. Bosher seems to argue that Clarendon mollified
Presbyterian sentiment with the ulterior motive of
softening resistance to the introduction of a Laudian
polity. Others have taken exception to this interpretation as a whole and in particulars. See also Abernathy
[164] and Green [229].

186 Bowle, John. *Hobbes and his Critics: A Study in Seven-
       teenth Century Constitutionalism.* London: Frank Cass
       and Company, 1969. A new edition with corrections,
       of the first edition, 1951.

Chapter VII is devoted to Clarendon's treatment of
Leviathan. It stresses the strong sense of practical
politics and statecraft in Clarendon's critique, and
links this to his upbringing and intellectual affilia-
tions. For this reason Clarendon's attack differs from
the many others which concentrate on either Hobbes'
religion or his geometry.

187 Boyle, G.D. *Characters and Episodes of the Great Rebel-
       lion Selected from the History and Autobiography of
       Edward Earl of Clarendon.* Oxford: Clarendon Press,
       1889.

Copious and well-chosen selections are ordered according to the sequence of books in the *History,* followed by
slighter excerpts from the *Life.* The discursive notes
are lively and full of interest, especially in their
treatment of the controversy over Clarendon's accuracy.
Boyle's succinct introduction centers on this theme,
preferring von Ranke's judgment [297] to the criticisms
of Forster [223]. Boyle remarks that Sir Walter Scott
had contemplated an annotated edition of the complete
writings of Clarendon, a project which has not yet been
undertaken. These selections, therefore, are an interim
measure, calling "attention to a great English classic,
who is perhaps too much neglected in days of haste and
occupation."

--   Bradford, Gamaliel. "A Great English Portrait-Painter."
       See Section F: Addendum [362].

188 Braudy, Leo. *Narrative Form in History and Fiction:*
      Hume Fielding & Gibbon. Princeton, N.J.: Princeton
      University Press, 1970.

      A chapter entitled "Clarendon & Bolingbroke" treats of
      Clarendon's complex sense of historical continuity, and
      of the tension in the *History* between the personal angle
      of vision and the broader perspective. "In some very
      basic way Clarendon does believe the true history of the
      civil wars to be a history of himself." Thucydides is
      seen as Clarendon's great exemplar. In an interesting
      approach to the *History* Braudy argues that it represents
      the elevation of personal perception to historical truth.
      Discussing the literary "character" Braudy claims that
      the examples of the genre in the *History* "set much of the
      tone for the eighteenth-century use of the 'character.'"
      Its enigmatic relationship to historical causality is
      also interestingly discussed.

189 Bridenbaugh, Carl. *Vexed and Troubled Englishmen 1590-*
      1642. Oxford: Clarendon Press, 1968.

      This is concerned mainly with the origins of the
      American people. In probing the reasons why Englishmen
      emigrated to America the author contests the account of
      Clarendon, which, he says, paints a picture of the
      felicity of England before the Civil War, alleging that
      this is a narrow view afforded members of a privileged
      class.

190 Brodie, George. *A History of the British Empire, from*
      the Accession of Charles I to the Restoration; with an
      Introduction, Tracing the Progress of Society, and of
      the Constitution, from the Feudal Times to the Opening
      of the History; and including a Particular Examination
      of Mr. Hume's Statements Relative to the Character of
      the English Government. 4 vols. Edinburgh: Bell &
      Bradfute, 1822.

      The Preface makes it quite clear that Brodie intends
      to dispute with Hume on all fronts. Hume's predisposi-
      tion was "unfavourable to a calm enquiry after truth"
      and impatient of the research necessary to an historian.
      Clarendon is employed extensively throughout as a source
      both of historical narrative and of character sketches.
      Brodie's own characters are assembled in the manner of a
      collage. The character of Falkland, for example, draws
      on Whitelocke and Carte, and paraphrases Clarendon
      throughout, but alters the weight of the final estimation.
      The method is curiously similar to that of Hume.

This is a decidedly Whig history, attacking Charles I
and his advisers, and doubting the veracity of Clarendon's
account.

--   Brown, K.C. *Hobbes Studies*. See Thomas, Keith. "The
      Social Origins of Hobbes' Political Thought" [321].

--   Browne, Sir Richard. *Correspondence*. See Evelyn, John.
      Memoirs [214].

191   Buff, Ad[olf]. *Die Politik Karls des Ersten in dem
      ersten Wochen nach seiner Flucht von London und Lord
      Clarendon's Darstellung dieser Zeit*. Giessen: [n.p.],
      1868. 45 pp.

This detailed analysis explores the possibility that
Charles I planned a *coup d'état* directly after his leaving
London. Activity in the Lords and Commons at the time is
compared with Clarendon's account.

192   Burke, Peter. *The Renaissance Sense of the Past*.
      London: Edward Arnold, 1969.

Hyde is described as the English Davila (historian of
the French civil wars), and his attempt to come to terms
with the meaning of the Civil War is briefly discussed
as an introduction to passages of quotation from the
History, illustrative of Clarendon's theory of history,
his class consciousness, and his use of prose characters.
The broader purpose of the book is to compare and contrast
the methods of major Renaissance historians.

--   Burton, Thomas. *Diary of Thomas Burton*. See Rutt,
      John Towill. *Diary of Thomas Burton* [309].

193   *Calendar of the Clarendon State Papers Preserved in the
      Bodleian Library*. 5 vols. Vol. I, to 1649, edited
      by O. Ogle and W.H. Bliss; Vols. II and III, 1649-1654
      and 1655-1657, edited by W. Dunn Macray; Vols. IV and
      V, 1657-1660 and 1660-1726, edited by F.J. Routledge.
      Oxford: Clarendon Press, 1869-1970.

The publication of this immense and necessary labor
was completed the year after the death of Routledge. It
is indispensable for Clarendon studies, and invaluable
to historians of the period covered. The final volume,
with an essay by its editor on the 1667 downfall of
Clarendon and an index to Vols. IV and V, also corrects
a number of errors of dating in *Clarendon State Papers*.

It is strange to read the reviewer for *The Athenaeum*, Oct. 5, 1872, complain "That the abstracts of these and other papers have not been given at greater length is unfortunate." It became necessary to reduce the length of abstracts even further in order to have any hope of completing the task. As it is, the modern reader will probably find the abstracts carefully made and sufficiently informative.

194   Campbell, Lord John. *The Lives of the Lord Chancellors and Keepers of the Great Seal of England from the Earliest Times till the Reign of King George IV.* 7 vols. London: John Murray, 1848. 3rd edition.

Volume III contains an epic life of Clarendon in ten chapters. This lavishness of treatment arises from the author's belief that Clarendon was central to the thirty most interesting years in English history, and his recognition that more praise and censure have been lavished on Clarendon than on any other public man in England. Almost all the available materials in print have been carefully combed to produce this detailed and remarkably accurate account. His judgment on Clarendon's early (pre-1650) career is highly favorable, but he has severe criticisms to voice on Clarendon's Chancellorship, especially his illiberality in matters of church discipline.

Lord Campbell was, of course, peculiarly well fitted to comment on the manner in which other supreme ministers of the crown exercised their power. He is also an astute critic of Clarendon's writing, praising the *History*, with all its faults in mind, as likely to be read when Hume is superseded, and remarking, interestingly, on the letters (in *Clarendon State Papers*) that they seem stiff and heavy, the more so when one considers that Clarendon was writing in the age of Dryden.

This is a fine biography, seldom consulted today.

195   Carlyle, E.I. "Clarendon and the Privy Council, 1660-1667." *English Historical Review*, 27 (April, 1912), 251-273.

This is a detailed account of how Clarendon organized the machinery of government according to his philosophy of constitutional royalism--a philosophy developed during the period of parliamentary opposition to the ministries of Buckingham and Strafford.

The first section of the article describes Clarendon's theory of administration, and pictures him as the

presiding genius behind the reconstitution of government.
He is shown to have consciously refused to play either
the role of favorite (like Buckingham) or that of adviser
to the monarch (like Richelieu and Mazarin). Under
Clarendon's guidance the Privy Council assumed a central
position.

The second section deals with organization of the Privy
Council, and describes its committee structures. In the
next section reasons for widespread (and ultimately
successful) opposition to Clarendon's system are explored.
The elaborate scheme was threatened and finally overthrown
by independent assaults of the Parliament and the King--
the two powers between which it was designed to mediate,
and to which it attempted to exercise varying degrees of
responsibility. The decline of Clarendon's own influence
was a consequence of the rise of a court party in Parliament (especially in the Commons), members of which were
inserted into Clarendon's committees against his advice
and contrary to his wishes.

The King is represented as disliking bureaucratic con-
trols, particularly over his financial supplies. Clarendon's recognition (documented from *Life*) that Charles
was attracted to French principles of government, which
appeared to leave the monarchy with greater autonomy, is
examined.

The fourth and final section, therefore, deploys the
foregoing evidence and analysis to account for Clarendon's
fall. Briefly, it was "due largely to the difference
between him and Charles with regard to principles of
administration." (This explanation--surely worthy of
more attention than it has received--differs from the
more commonly disseminated account, which attributes the
fall to Clarendon's irksome moralizing and denunciation
of Charles' personal life.) Clarendon ascribed his fall
to the ill will of Buckingham and Castlemaine (as in
Life), which was contributory, but not the main factor.
The disastrous outcome of the Dutch war also weakened
him, but was not the cause of his fall. Clarendon's own
misreading of the political situation, and his failure
to see his own blunders, are criticized.

196   Carter, Harry. *A History of the Oxford University Press*.
      Vol. I (to the year 1780). Oxford: Clarendon Press,
      1975.

      This is indispensable to an understanding of Oxford
      editions of Clarendon. The account of the Clarendon
      Trust which came to an end in 1868 when its funds were

used for the Clarendon Laboratory is also essential to
an understanding of the relationship of the Clarendon
MSS to the Press, and to the University.

-- *Catalogue of Portraits of Foreigners*. See Anonymous.
A Catalogue of Portraits of Foreigners [167].

-- Chadwick, Owen. *From Uniformity to Unity: 1662-1962*.
See Whiteman, Anne. "The Restoration of the Church of
England" [353].

197 Chapman, Hester W. *The Tragedy of Charles II in the
Years 1630-1660*. London: Jonathan Cape, 1964.

This is a colorful and rather sentimental contribution
to the history of the period, specifically that of exiled
Royalists during the Interregnum. Political realities
take second place to the development of a romantic portrait of Charles, which, although documented, is imaginatively unrestrained. The extensive treatment of
Clarendon may perhaps be characterized by the following
depiction of his influence:

> In fact Hyde's influence was more detrimental than
> that of Charles's most dissipated and irresponsible
> hangers-on. The Chancellor's sarcasms, his criti-
> cisms, his insistence that he himself was not, and
> never could be, in the wrong (why did others perse-
> cute and misunderstand him?), his determination to
> force the King into the mould of a high-minded, High
> Church, incorruptible ruler, drove Charles, who was
> really fond of him, into a series of petty evasions
> and broken promises.

The book is dedicated to Noël Coward.

198 Chassant, Alph. *Lord Clarendon*. Évreux: Charles
Hérissey, 1891. 44 pp.

This is an account of the attempted assassination of
Clarendon at Évreux in 1668. The author is amazed that
local historians of that town can write all kinds of
trivia, but omit mention of this important event. His
account is drawn from local archives.

199 Clarendon. *Essays Moral and Entertaining on the Various
Faculties and Passions of the Human Mind*. 2 vols.
London: reprinted for Longman, Hurst, Rees, Orme and
Brown, 1815.

This is a reprint of the usual essays, edited by James
Stanier Clarke, who dedicates it to Princess Elizabeth.
He sees them as a companion piece to Bacon's essays.

200   Clarendon. "The Life of the Earl of Clarendon," in
      Select Biography, Vol. VIII. London: Welton and Jarvis,
      1821.

      This volume is the last in a series, and is entitled
      "Philosophers," containing also a life of Bacon. The
      unnamed editor has neatly condensed the *Life*, retaining
      emphasis on the 1667 period.

201   Clarke, James Stanier. *Essays Moral and Entertaining.*
      See Clarendon. *Essays Moral and Entertaining* [199].

202   Coate, Mary. *Cornwall in the Great Civil War and
      Interregnum 1642-1660.* Truro: D. Bradford Barton,
      1963. First published Oxford University Press, 1933.

      Although a Wiltshire man, Hyde sat as M.P. for the
      Cornish borough of Saltash in the Long Parliament.
      Cornwall as a whole returned M.P.'s of a broad political
      spectrum. Hyde himself went up to take his seat animated
      with reformist zeal. Toward the end of the first Civil
      War he found himself again in Cornwall, now as a Privy
      Councillor and Chancellor of the Exchequer, with respon-
      sibility for the Prince of Wales. In effect he was the
      civilian director of Royalist policies in the West, find-
      ing himself repeatedly at odds with the military comman-
      ders, especially Grenville and Goring.
         Cornwall took more of his time and energy as a politi-
      cian than any other part of Britain, which is reflected
      in the detailed attention he pays to Western affairs in
      History of the Rebellion. He was particularly anxious
      for exact memorials of affairs there when composing the
      first half of *History* in the Channel Islands.
         Coate's treatment is also animated by a passionate
      attachment to the special qualities of this region, and
      a desire for accuracy and detailed documentation. The
      role of Clarendon as politician, and the authority of
      his works and correspondence, are cited with great
      frequency.

203   Coate, Mary. *The Letter-Book of John Viscount Mordaunt
      1658-1660.* Vol. 69 Camden Third Series. London:
      Royal Historical Society, 1945.

Mordaunt was one of the most active and important of
Hyde's correspondents during the Interregnum. He was
instrumental in building a Presbyterian-Royalist alliance, and preparing for military uprisings. His activities caused him to be brought to trial on a charge of
treason, and acquitted by the casting vote of the president of the court. From the multitude of incompetent or
untrustworthy Royalist agents conspiring the overthrow
of the republic, Mordaunt stands out for his valor and
determination, for which qualities Clarendon esteemed
him.

As the editor claims, these letters "fill in gaps in
the Clarendon, Nicholas and Ormonde correspondence."
Most of the letters concerning Clarendon are to be found
in *Clarendon State Papers* [155] or summarized in *Calendar
of Clarendon State Papers* [193].

204 Coltman, Irene. *Private Men and Public Causes*. London:
     Faber and Faber, 1962.

This is a seminal work on the morality of seventeenth-
century politics. It contains a finely perceptive
analysis of Clarendon's stand upon a matter of principle,
namely the death of Sidney Godolphin--a casualty of the
Civil War--contrasted with the attitude of Hobbes to this
event. (See also Clarendon's preface to *A Brief View and
Survey* [101].) It also treats the political views of the
Great Tew circle, especially those of Chillingworth,
Hales, Earle, and Falkland.

205 Craik, Henry. *English Prose*. 5 vols. London: Mac-
     millan, 1893-96.

Volume II, pp. 389-442, presents selections from the
History and the *Life*, with an introduction which stresses
Clarendon's skills as a character writer, and the influence of his irregular prose. Craik observes the habits
of oratory at work in shaping Clarendon's prose style,
which save it from pedantry, and make it "instinct with
the life and movement of human affairs."

206 Craik, Sir Henry. *The Life of Edward Earl of Clarendon
     Lord High Chancellor of England*. 2 vols. London:
     Smith, Elder, 1911.

This is, in effect, a Tory biography. It traces
Clarendon's history with detail, and tells the story
fluently, but without attempting to unearth new evidence
or to seek much further afield than the standard received

accounts of the time. Craik is highly inimical to
Lister's biography [263], said to be written in the
"true spirit of orthodox Whiggism." Lister himself is
"that most lukewarm of all biographers."

207   Cruttwell, Patrick. *The Shakespearean Moment.* London:
      Chatto and Windus, 1954.

      This is a widely ranging history of ideas which in-
      cludes a discussion of Clarendon's portrait of Falkland
      in the context of notions of character. Cruttwell
      praises its achievement of balance and impartiality, to
      which none of the poetry of the period managed to climb.
      He asks whether Clarendon's portrait of William Herbert,
      Earl of Pembroke (*Hist. Reb.*, i, 71-73), is a description
      of Shakespeare's patron.

208   Davies, G. "The Date of Clarendon's First Marriage."
      English Historical Review, 32 (July, 1917), 405-407.

      The date is usually and incorrectly given as 1629.
      In reality, as Davies shows, it should be the end of
      1631. He explains the probable cause of the initial
      error found in Lister's biography [263] and subsequently
      repeated. He remarks on Clarendon's early endurance of
      poverty, contrasting it with the love of ostentation
      which alienated many in 1667.

209   Davies, Godfrey. *The Early Stuarts: 1603-1660.* Oxford:
      Clarendon Press, 1959. First published 1937.

      Davies reviews, briefly, the process of composition of
      the *History* and *Life*, describing their salient character-
      istics. Clarendon's role in the events of the period is
      faithfully presented, particularly in 1641-43 when he was
      penman of Royalist declarations.

210   Davies, Godfrey. *The Restoration of Charles II: 1658-1660.*
      London: Oxford University Press, 1969. First published
      1955.

      Hyde's role in the achievement of the Restoration is
      traced, and his views as recorded in *History* are fre-
      quently cited. The Declaration of Breda is described
      as his "masterpiece," and the subtlety of its provisions
      is analyzed.

211   Davies, Godfrey. Review of: B.H.G. Wormald, *Clarendon:
      Politics, History & Religion, 1640-1660.* *English Histor-
      ical Review*, 67 (April, 1952), 271-275.

Davies represents as the central issues of Wormald's
study [359] the questions of whether Clarendon correctly
described his own attitude toward the Civil War, and of
whether Gardiner and Firth misrepresent Clarendon. He
is skeptical of the way in which Wormald reaches his
conclusions, and remarks that far from Gardiner's having
created a mythical Hyde (as Wormald asserts) the fact of
the matter is that Wormald is on his way to creating a
"mythical Gardiner." The distinctions Wormald draws
between phases of Hyde's activities and his attitudes
toward them are criticized as too subtle. In conclusion,
Wormald's book fails to demonstrate any need to rewrite
the history of the Puritan revolution.

--   Dover, George James Welbore Agar-Ellis, 1st Baron.
      Historical Inquiries. See Ellis, George Agar. *His-
      torical Inquiries* [213].

212   Ellesdon, William. "The Letter of William Ellesdon of
      Charmouth to the Earl of Clarendon concerning the
      adventures of Charles II in West Dorset on September 22,
      23 and 24, 1651," pp. 171-186. In Bradley, A.M.,
      *The Royal Miracle: A Collection of Rare Tracts, Broad-
      sides, Letters, Prints, & Ballads Concerning the
      Wanderings of Charles II. After the Battle of Worces-
      ter (September 3-October 15, 1651). With a Preface,
      Historical Introduction, Appendix, Bibliography, and
      Illustrations.* London: Stanley Paul, 1912.

Ellesdon puts Clarendon in mind of the services he
performed for Charles during the flight from Worcester.
His story is recounted in prolix detail.
      (In "A List of Pensions" printed in an appendix to
The Correspondence of Henry Hyde [248], it appears that
Ellesdon obtained a pension of £100 p.a.)

213   Ellis, George Agar. *Historical Inquiries Respecting
      the Character of Edward Hyde, Earl of Clarendon, Lord
      Chancellor of England.* London: John Murray, 1827.

This attack on Clarendon, largely animated by party
affiliation, starts from the assumption that "There is
no character to which history has been more indulgent."
The author testifies that "we have been all taught from
our childhood upwards to revere 'the Chancellor of human
nature' as one of the brightest ornaments that dignify
our annals." Ellis allows that he was better than those
cabal ministers "who succeeded in rendering the reign of
Charles II the most disgraceful period of English

history." He is not disposed to attack Clarendon's
achievements as an historian, but probes his supposed
personal integrity when Chancellor. How did Clarendon
acquire a spectacular gallery of portraits by Vandyke
and Janssen? He cites instances of Clarendon's rapacity
and corruption. The sale of Dunkirk is laid to his
account, as are numerous instances of alleged bribe-
taking. These are illustrated by quotations from contemporary sources. The Chancellor's apparent connivance
at plots to assassinate Cromwell, and his likening of
the death of Charles I to that of Christ, are indignantly
denounced.

214   Evelyn, John. *Memoirs Illustrative of the Life and*
        Writings of John Evelyn, Esq. F.R.S. Author of the
        "Sylva", &c. &c. Comprising his Diary, from the Year
        1641 to 1705-6, and a Selection of his Familiar
        Letters. To which is Subjoined, The Private Corres-
        pondence between King Charles I. and his Secretary of
        State, Sir Edward Nicholas, whilst his Majesty was in
        Scotland, 1641, and at other Times during the Civil
        War; Also between Sir Edward Hyde, Afterwards Earl of
        Clarendon, and Sir Richard Browne, Ambassador to the
        Court of France, in the Time of King Charles I. and
        the Usurpation. 2 vols. London: Henry Colburn, 1819.
        First published 1818.

The correspondence of Hyde and Browne is from 1646 to
1659. The letters, some of which appear in full in
Clarendon State Papers, are here given as a sequence,
copiously annotated.
    Evelyn's *Memoirs* contain many well-known references to
Clarendon, with whom Evelyn remained on very good terms,
no doubt because of their shared interests as scholars
and collectors. An entry for August 15, 1661, reads
"Came my Lord Chancellor (ye Earle of Clarendon) and his
lady, his purse and mace borne before him, to visit me.
They were likewise collation'd with us, and were very
merry. They had ben our old acquaintance in exile, and
indeed this greate person had ever ben my friend."
    There is a fine letter of Evelyn to Clarendon after
the Great Fire, dated November 27, 1666, which recommends
correct editions of the classics for use in grammar
schools, and leads to Evelyn suggesting his willingness
to plan a wholesale "Reformation of our English Presse."
    A letter to Pepys in 1689 recalls Clarendon's collection
of medals and the subjects of his famous portrait gallery,
named "promiscuously as they come into my memoirie."
This same letter has the following assessment.

He was a great Lover at least of Books, & furnish'd
a very ample Library, writ himselfe an elegant style,
fauour'd & promoted the design of the Royal Society;
and it was for this, and in particular for his being
very kind to me both abroad & at home, that I sent
Naudaeus to him in a dedicatory Addresse, of which I
am not so much asham'd as of the Translation.

Evelyn refers to the work of Gabriel Naudé under the
title *Gaspar Naudaeus, Instructions Concerning Libraries*
(1661).

--   Every, George. "Clarendon and the Popular Front." See
      Section F: Addendum [363].

215   Feiling, Keith. "Clarendon and the Act of Uniformity,
      1662-3." *English Historical Review*, 44 (April, 1929),
      289-291.

The two letters in question are from Sheldon to
Clarendon, August 30, 1662, and from Clarendon to
Ormonde, September 1, 1662. Both, drawn from Bodleian
MSS Clarendon, are brief. Feiling's purpose in bringing
them to notice is to authenticate his suspicion that
Clarendon's policy toward dissenters (both Puritan and
Catholic) was both less rigid, and less determinedly
Anglican, than Clarendon himself paints it in *Life*. The
crux of the matter, here in Feiling's article, and in
subsequent more exhaustive studies, is the recognition
that Clarendon's political actions in this difficult
period, in which many shades of religious opinion sought
freedom from potential restrictions, were motivated by
"political exigencies." This seems simple, but Clarendonian
and Tory representations of Clarendon's role had made him
appear as a politician who unbendingly exercised a single
principle. Feiling's brief notes inaugurate a fresh
inquiry into the ecclesiastical politics of these years.

216   Feiling, Sir Keith. *A History of the Tory Party: 1640-
      1714*. Oxford: Clarendon Press, 1950. Corrected from
      the first edition of 1924.

This is an important, seminal scholarly work. As it
concerns Clarendon it may be briefly summarized as an
account of his contribution to the formation of Tory doctrines, indeed of the Tory party. It is considered to
be a most important contribution. The efforts expended
by Clarendon to hold together the Royalist cause during
the Interregnum are treated in particular detail.

217 Feiling, K.G. "A Letter of Clarendon during the Elec-
        tions of 1661." *English Historical Review*, 42 (July,
        1927), 407-408.

     The letter is to Orrery, March 31, 1661, in the Bod-
     leian Clarendon MSS and is strongly anti-Presbyterian in
     sentiment. Feiling argues that it is evidence of Claren-
     don's inveterate dislike of Presbyterians, and thus
     helps to chart the "extraordinary vacillations" in his
     policy toward dissent during the crucial years of the
     Church's re-establishment.

218 Firth, C.H. "Clarendon's 'History of the Rebellion.'"
        English Historical Review, 19 (1904), 26-54, 246-262,
        464-483.

     The article is in three parts: Part I--"The Original
     History" (January, 1904), Part II--"The 'Life' of Himself"
     (April, 1904), and Part III--"Clarendon's 'History of
     the Rebellion.'" It is indispensable for an understanding
     of the composition of the *History of the Rebellion*,
     which involved a notoriously complex process of conflation
     of numerous MSS. Detailed scholarly investigation of
     Clarendon's sources, the working documents he requested
     and consulted at several stages of composition, coupled
     with references to his correspondence, both published in
     Clarendon State Papers and in the Clarendon MSS, provide
     a step-by-step account of the author at work. Evidence
     from contemporary commentators and modern historians
     supports judgments on the accuracy of the *History*, and
     other related matters.

     PART I: Firth is concerned to elicit Clarendon's evolving
     purpose in writing a work not originally intended as a
     great history. Early in the composition of "Original
     History" in the Scilly Isles, 1646, for example, Hyde
     saw his recording of errors and mistakes of the Royalist
     leaders as being "not so much for the information of
     future historians as for the practical guidance of those
     whose duty it might be to advise the King in the future."
     As each of Hyde's arguments and analyses is sifted,
     Firth tests its intention and validity, and finds himself
     in frequent disagreement, sometimes strongly expressed:
     "Hyde's account of the events of January and February
     1642 is a tissue of misrepresentations."
       There are also judgments on the success or otherwise
     of the architecture of the *History*. The inclusion of
     the many declarations in book IV, for example, is from
     an artistic point of view, "a great error. The progress

of the narrative is impeded and its coherence destroyed."
At other points the thinness of Hyde's qualifications is
remarked. Books VI and VII, describing the war, are
difficult because Hyde knew nothing about war, and had
very little first-hand experience. By 1648 events had
begun to catch up with the historian's narrative. Only
twenty lines of book VIII were written in spring, 1648,
and the rest of the *History*, therefore, belongs to a
later period of composition. Hyde became embroiled
again in practical politics, and was not to return to
his papers for twenty years.

PART II: This considers the *Life*, dated "23 July 1668"
at the start. Its narrative of events was carried to
the Restoration by 1 August 1670. The *Life* as published,
however, has half its interest removed because the best
parts were stitched into the *History*. When writing the
MS of *Life* Clarendon exercised greater freedom in censure of persons because the text was not now intended
for the King. It was, in effect, a "secret history" and
personal vindication. The portraits which result have
been greatly applauded (instances are cited), but in
truth they spring from his failure to understand the root
causes of the rebellion. "It is scarcely a paradox to
say that his vivid presentment of the actors sprang in
part from his imperfect comprehension of the drama itself." This insight is elaborated in some detail, and
the grand scale character of Falkland is examined.
   Firth leads us, therefore, to see that in the final
conflated *History* the politics are from the "Original
History," the portraits from *Life*. "He now inserted
characters not merely when the incidents of the narration
demanded but whenever he could find a pretext for indulging his predilection for that particular kind of composition."
   How trustworthy is the *Life* compared to the "Original
History"? Firth's answer is that because Clarendon lacked
materials, even the MSS of the *History*, it is much less
reliable. But he exonerates him from charges of dis-
honesty. The errors are "plainly due to a failing
memory, a memory that was confused, inexact, and
imaginative."

PART III: When in 1671 the English government relaxed
the severity of its laws concerning communication with
Clarendon, Laurence Hyde visited his father, and brought
some papers to him, including the "Original History."
As a result of this stimulus Clarendon completed the
History by June, 1672. Now one of his motives was desire

for fame as an historian, and another the hope that he
would be allowed to go home. This latter motive induced
him to suppress some of the more telling criticisms of
Charles I he had put in *Life*. Thus he completed the
work, which may be seen schematically as comprising
books I-VII, the "Original History" supplemented by passages from *Life*, 1668-1669, and books VIII-XVI,
supplemented by passages from the *History* written 1671-
1672, which also incorporates two major papers of 1646.
This scheme is then elaborated, and Firth concludes,
with instances, that the stitching process was not always
well done, giving rise to some contradictory accounts.
MS Clarendon 112 is examined in some detail to further
illuminate the composition process.

The matter of reliability in particular accounts and
portraits is treated at length. When it comes to the
Second Civil War, Clarendon's account "contains every
kind of error." The Protectorate is perfunctorily
treated. But the final book (XVI) is more interesting
and (surprisingly) Firth agrees, in the main, with
Clarendon's assessment of Monck. In conclusion he
observes that:

> In stating the causes of the Rebellion he had
> exaggerated the importance of personal influences,
> and attributed too much to the particular charac-
> teristics of individual men.... In recounting the
> Restoration his point of view had altered. It is
> now the current of human affairs which guides men's
> acts, whither they know not, whether they will or
> not. The individual actor, even when he seems to
> direct the course of events, is in reality their
> creature.

Although there is much with which to argue in Firth's
mainly negative judgment of Clarendon as an historian,
there is no more useful and exhaustive treatment of the
historian's sources than this. It will continue to be
essential.

219 Firth, C.H. *Edward Hyde Earl of Clarendon as Statesman,*
     Historian and Chancellor of the University. Oxford:
     Clarendon Press, 1909. 28 pp.

This pamphlet originated as a lecture delivered in
February, 1909, on the tercentenary of Clarendon's birth.
It was reprinted in:

219A Firth, C.H. *Essays Historical and Literary.* Oxford: ss,
     Clarendon Press, 1938.

This is a seminal document by one of the great modern pioneers of seventeenth-century historical scholarship. Firth reveres Clarendon's achievements as a statesman, appreciates his success as a pamphleteer, and criticizes the *History of the Rebellion* as the history of an essentially religious revolution which omits the religion. This criticism gained considerable currency by its frequent adoption and repetition, but may be treated with reservation. Firth also originates the interesting view that the *Life* is an essentially superior work to the *History*, and that this would be apparent were there a better edition available than the slipshod version of 1857 [150K]. He has comments to make on the reliability of the *History* and its sources, which are to be found more fully developed in his *E.H.R.* articles of 1904 [218]. Clarendon's prose style is thus summarized:

> It does not hurry his readers along with the rapid and irresistible rush of Macaulay's [History]. It has the ample, easy flow of a great river, that, as Tennyson says, 'moving seems asleep', but carries you to the end of the journey without haste and without noise.

When the lecture was first delivered Firth observed that Clarendon had become neglected: the *History* is on the shelves of every learned and cultivated man, but seldom read. "He has had bad luck with his immortality." By 1909 Clarendon had become a "vague and indistinct personality" even among cultivated Oxonians. The essay hopes to redress that balance by reminding readers of Clarendon's just place in history and literature.

220 Firth, Sir C.H. "The Royalists under the Protectorate."
     English Historical Review, 62 (October, 1937), 634-648.

This paper, originally an undelivered lecture, was prepared for publication by Godfrey Davies. It investigates the question of who was to have been comprehended, and how, in the Commonwealth political settlement. In this context Clarendon's attack on Hobbes [101] is cited, specifically his condemnation of the doctrine that the obligation of the subject to the sovereign lasts only so long as the latter may be able to protect him. In the event, argues Firth, the government did nothing to encourage Royalist cooperation, and the Royalists, even if passive, were unseduced. There are comments in passing on the nature of published Royalist sentiments.

221 Forrest, James R. "Clarendon on the Stage." *Modern
     Language Review*, 69 (April, 1974), 250-253.

     The article is concerned primarily with a discussion
of the propriety of the stage and its likely effect on
youth, with which question Clarendon's *A Dialogue Concerning Education* concludes. Forrest recognizes that
this dialogue follows by advancement of theme *A Dialogue
on the Want of Respect due to Age*, both of which appeared
in the 1727 *A Collection of Several Tracts* [129, 129A]. He
seems to be unaware of the fact that they were printed
separately [152, 154]. *The Dialogue Concerning Education*
is described as "a humane document of uncommon social
significance that incidentally exhibits Clarendon's not
inconsiderable dramatic gifts."
     That Clarendon himself might have been well disposed
to the theater is surmised from his involvement in the
1634 Inns of Court production of Shirley's *The Triumph
of Peace*. That he might have disliked Restoration
theater is suggested by his having been "plainly perso-
nated" in *The Country Gentleman,* supposedly by the 2nd
Duke of Buckingham (his hated adversary). What Forrest
wishes to demonstrate, however, is that, given the evidence of the dialogue, Clarendon was especially disturbed
by the impersonation of males by females and *vice versa*;
as he writes, the "promiscuous acting the Parts of Men
and Women."

222 Forster, John. *Arrest of the Five Members by Charles the
     First, A Chapter of English History Rewritten*. London:
     John Murray, 1860.

     Forster's exposés of Clarendon's biases and inaccura-
cies were greeted in Whig circles as decisive in dis-
mantling his authority. They are in large part based
upon the then unpublished parliamentary diary of Sir
Simonds D'Ewes, and strike at Hyde's politics in the
Long Parliament--a phase of his career which he represents in *Life* and *History* dressed in re-ordering hindsight.
     Throughout this work there is point-by-point refuta-
tion of Clarendon's "studied misrepresentation" of the
affair. D'Ewes stands for the prosecution. This is
not, however, the primary work in Forster's attack, and
he refers the reader to the earlier Remonstrance study
wherein is conclusive proof of the faithlessness and un-
trustworthiness of Clarendon.

223 Forster, John. *The Debates on the Grand Remonstrance,*
     November and December, 1641. With an Introductory
     Essay on English Freedom under Plantagenet & Tudor
     Sovereigns. London: John Murray, 1860.

Forster probes Hyde's conduct at the time of the Bill
of Attainder of Strafford. The division of votes on
that matter is commonly, he writes, viewed as a test of
parliamentary opinion at that time. Hyde did not vote
against it, and may have voted for it, because it is
certain he did vote for the bill to perpetuate Parliament
to which royal assent was given the same day. He implies
that Clarendon was behind the erasure from the journals
of both Houses of his vote for the Attainder. However,
the MS journal of Sir Simonds D'Ewes tells the story.
The early actions of Hyde and the later recollections of
Clarendon are, therefore, contradictory.

> Much of the confusion is undoubtedly due to Claren-
> don, the assiduous efforts of whose later life to
> blacken the characters of the leading men of the
> parliament, are read with implicit belief by so many
> to whom it never occurs to remember that at the out-
> set of his life Mr. Hyde had acted cordially with
> those men.

There are also aspersions cast on the first editors of
the *History* who had not the "filial courage" to print
some of the admissions Clarendon makes about his two-faced
conduct at this time. Now in the new edition it stands
as a shameless avowal. Thus Clarendon's account is quite
unreliable, and others, such as that of Sir Ralph Verney,
are to be preferred.
     Every detail of Clarendon's treatment of the Remon-
strance period is challenged by Forster. There are
lengthy footnote quotations which praise his "exquisite
art" in order to point the factual unreliability more
strongly. His judgment on Clarendon is perhaps represented best in this excerpt:

> Clarendon's *History of the Rebellion* should be de-
> posed from the place it holds in our literature.
> Its rare beauties of thought and charm of style, the
> profound views of character and life which it clothes
> in language of unsurpassed variety and richness, its
> long line of noble and deathless portraits through
> which its readers move as through a gallery of full-
> lengths by Vandyke and Velasquez, have given and
> will assure to it its place as long as literature re-
> mains. But, for the purpose to which it has mainly

been applied by many past writers since Clarendon's
death, as well as by writers not prejudiced or partial it should never have been used. The authority
of its writer is at no time more worthless, as when
taken upon matters in which he played himself the
most prominent part; and his imputations against the
men with whom he was once leagued as closely as he
was afterwards bitterly opposed to them, are never
to be safely relied upon.

Forster has now brought him to face the charges of the
men he has traduced, and the testimony of D'Ewes: "The
result is decisive against Clarendon. It is not merely
that he turned King's evidence against his old associates, but that his evidence is completely disproved."
This work was first published in vol. I of *Historical
and Biographical Essays*. 2 vols. London: John Murray,
1858.

224 Foxcroft, H.C. *The Life and Letters of Sir George
     Savile, Bart. First Marquis of Halifax*. 2 vols.
     London: Longmans, Green, 1898.

There is a chapter entitled "Introduction to Political
Life--Relations with Lord Chancellor Clarendon." It is
as much concerned with the enmity between Clarendon and
William Coventry, as with Halifax. Much use is made of
Life, especially of passages in which Clarendon characterizes Coventry with a passion little short of hatred.
Although she judges Coventry a very sane man, Foxcroft
finds Clarendon's conduct excusable because opposition
to him was so frequently identified with unscrupulous
intrigue. His dislike of Coventry was extended to
Savile, on the grounds of his reputed atheism and
loose conduct.

225 Gardiner, Samuel R. "Draft by Sir Edward Hyde of a
     Declaration to be Issued by Charles II in 1649."
     English Historical Review, 8 (1893), 300-307.

As he recounts in the *History*, Clarendon drew up a
document at The Hague in the first months of 1649 aimed
at recovering the throne for Charles II, but the members of the council, all but a few, and each for
different reasons, took exception to it. It is, nevertheless, the germ of the Declaration of Breda. The
draft is in the Bodleian Clarendon MSS.
Following a solemn denunciation of the proceedings
leading up to Charles I's death, the document proposes

remedies, including a national synod with foreign
divines represented to settle disputes in religion. It
offers an act of indemnity excluding only those who consented to the death of the King. It calls upon other
princes to recognize the threat to themselves inherent
in the theories and claims of the English regicides and
thus to make available material assistance to enable
Charles II to regain his rights.

Gardiner reports an endorsement on the document which
claims that parts of this paper were incorporated in a
manifesto drafted after the battle of Worcester.

226 Gardiner, S.R. *History of the Great Civil War 1642-1649*.
     4 vols. London: Longmans, Green, 1893. First published
     in 3 vols., 1886-91.

Gardiner's work on the seventeenth century commands
enormous respect among historians. It is now a fashion
to modify and soften his judgments, for they too held
great sway. His criticisms of Clarendon have been very
frequently repeated, and, as is often the case with
highly authoritative opinions, simplified for the sake
of convenience. Given his standpoint, Clarendon must be
seen as deficient in his treatment of the religious issues
of the English revolution. Briefly stated, Clarendon did
not give due weight to religious sentiment as a primary
motivating force in men's actions. Yet in practice,
Gardiner is not as censorious as is sometimes imagined.

In Vol. III of this work is a passage which, perhaps
as well as any other in his scholarly writings, conveys
his views. "It was not Puritanism, but the very opposite of Puritanism--the expansion of the reasoning
intelligence--which held the main current of thought in
the seventeenth century." Cromwell labored to dam it,
but in vain, for Hyde would ultimately "step into his
place."

His account of the *History* stresses the inaccuracies,
but is magnanimous in exonerating Hyde from any willful
departure from the truth. Nor does he regard the
History as a party pamphlet--it rises much above that
level of partisanship. "He could not descry the larger
issues to which the work of his generation was tending,
and was bereft of the imaginative power which sometimes
enables statesmen to perceive what will be the working
of forces not yet called into existence.... His History
is chiefly important as a revelation of himself and of
the beliefs which outlasted the victory of 'Puritanism.'"

C.V. Wedgwood, more sympathetic to Clarendon, sees that
"any writer dealing with the first half of the seventeenth
century must take up a position in relation to the late
Samuel Rawson Gardiner. Gardiner wrote in an epoch when
moral certainty was not only possible but natural" (*The
King's Peace 1637-1641*. London: Collins, 1955). Wormald
sees his reassessment of Clarendon [359] as "inevitably
a critical commentary upon the work of S.R. Gardiner."

227 Gibson, Robin. *Catalogue of Portraits in the Collection
     of the Earl of Clarendon*. Published privately by the
     Paul Mellon Centre for Studies in British Art, 1977.

This timely and welcome work continues the inquiry
begun by Lady Theresa Lewis [262], and satisfactorily
answers the allegations made by Ellis [213] that Clarendon
plundered Royalists for goods, pictures, and money. In
particular, he is said to have extorted paintings for
his burgeoning gallery in exchange for giving ear to the
complaints of impoverished Royalists. Gibson establishes
that most of the pre-Civil Wars paintings in the collection are copies of originals still, for the most part,
in the family collections for which they were painted.

This is the best and most fully documented history to
date of the formation and subsequent fortunes (and misfortunes: fire, debt, etc.) of this gallery--the most
famous of its time. "Despite its uncertain history ...
the Clarendon collection survives today as a remarkable
evidence of the vision of Edward Hyde, the 1st Earl."

The paintings, handsomely reproduced in black and white
photography, are described in detail.

228 Grant, A.J. *English Historians*. London: Blackie, 1906.

In the introduction Grant discusses Clarendon's *History*, comparing it to Thucydides' on the ground of their
use of character sketches. The similar fate of both
men, banished from their countries, is remarked, but the
inner spirit of the *History* is quite different.

He concludes, "For a century and a half it fixed the
ideas of English men with regard to the prominent actors
in the great Puritan revolution. Its prestige was
destroyed, as by a sledge-hammer by the publication of
Carlyle's *Cromwell*; but the book remains one of the
foremost of English historical classics."

In the second part is a selection of passages (the
character of Cromwell; Charles II's escape from Worcester)
intended to contribute to understanding of the methods
and styles adopted by historians of different periods.

This is prefixed by a note on Clarendon's probable falsi-
fying of sources, coupled with praise for the style, and
especially for the character sketches.

229   Green, I.M. *The Re-establishment of the Church of
      England, 1660-1663.* Oxford: Oxford University Press,
      1978.

Strangely, Baxter and Clarendon give similar accounts
of the settlement--that despite early concessions to
Puritans, Charles II and his ministers aimed at a strict
episcopalian settlement. Why do these natural enemies
describe thus the ecclesiastical politics of the years
1660-1663?

In Green's intricately devised narrative Clarendon's
role is prominent throughout. His conclusions are em-
bodied in a final chapter on "Clarendon and the Clarendon
Code" which is summarized and, of necessity simplified,
as follows. Green's argument is audacious, and at
variance with those of Bosher [185] and Abernathy [164],
and also, as it sometimes must be, with Clarendon's.
Green admits, or rather recognizes, that it is very difficult to read Clarendon's mind. His writing (correspondence, declarations, etc.) displays a "striving after
effect" which now acts as a screen to "conceal his more
intimate thoughts." Essentially, despite cautions about
Clarendon's autobiographical perspectives, Green sees
him as a high church Anglican on whom the need to pro-
pound and execute Charles' tolerationist aims sat un-
easily. Clarendon found it difficult to run with the
royal hare and hunt with the Cavalier hounds. Actually
he deplored royal policy, and was distressed by the degree
of accommodation of nonconformists which he was obliged
to defend.

The strain was too much. Not only for Clarendon, but
also for the King who, in 1667, supported "attacks on
Clarendon with a vigour which was not only unusual for
one of his languid disposition, but also did him little
credit." Subsequent to the Chancellor's fall, as many as
eighteen of the twenty-two bishops present at one sitting
defended Clarendon, and in 1668 emerged a group of die-
hard Anglicans known as Clarendonians.

In these vicissitudes before his second exile Clarendon
grimly hung on to office "perhaps from a sense of innate
superiority to Charles II's other ministers." He remained his own man, it seems, but was destroyed as a
consequence.

230   Green, John Richard. *History of the English People.*
      4 vols. New York: Harper, [1878-80]; London: Mac-
      millan, 1877-80.

      Green holds the *History* in low esteem except as a
      "literary" document marked by "nobleness of style and
      the grand series of character-portraits which it embod-
      ies." As an historical source it is marred by the
      "deliberate and malignant falsehood with which he has
      perverted the whole action of his parliamentary oppon-
      ents." When the *History* ceases to deal with the first
      Civil War it becomes "tedious and unimportant." As a
      statesman Clarendon was correct to see that three great
      institutions--prerogative of the Crown, authority of the
      Church, and the free will of Parliament--were to be pre-
      served in balance, which was the point at which the Long
      Parliament reforms had aimed when he deserted it. In
      1660 expectation of uniformity in the Church was a
      fiction.

231   Greenslade, B.D. "Clarendon and Hobbes' *Elements of Law.*"
      Notes & Queries, 202 (1957), 150.

      This clarifies a point in *Brief View and Survey* [101]
      where Clarendon recalls having written for Hobbes'
      De Cive, translated into English. Greenslade thinks
      Clarendon's memory to be at fault here, and that the
      book which he meant was *Elements of Law.* The argument
      is developed with considerations of dating.

232   Hale, J.R. *The Evolution of British Historiography from
      Bacon to Namier.* Cleveland and New York: Meridian
      Books, 1964.

      This is, in effect, a greatly expanded version of
      Grant's *English Historians* [228], with a full introduc-
      tory essay. In the section on Clarendon are general
      remarks concerning the conflation of the *History* and its
      contemporaneous character, along with a brief treatment
      of Clarendon's shift from moderate and critical Royalism
      to his becoming spokesman for the crown. Clarendon's
      deficient understanding of Puritanism is balanced by his
      grasp of detail, in which respect he is "wiser than
      Raleigh and subtler than Bacon." The portraits espec-
      ially deserve praise, and their possible origin in
      Elizabethan notions of humours is suggested. The *History*
      is the "supreme example of how far a historian can be
      saved from bias and externality by an understanding of
      human nature." There are also selections from Clarendon.

233   Hales, John. *Tract Concerning Schism and Schismatics,*
      Wherein is Briefly Discovered the Original Causes of
      all Schism; by the Ever Memorable Mr. John Hales, of
      Eton College; to which is Prefixed a Character of the
      Author, by Edward Earl of Clarendon, Lord High Chancel-
      lor of England, and Chancellor of the University of
      Oxford. A Tract for the Times. London: Hamilton
      Adams, [1883?].

      The character of Hales is from the *Life.*

--   Hardacre, P.J. "Clarendon and the University of Oxford."
      See Section F: Addendum [364].

234   Hardacre, P.H. "Portrait of a Bibliophile I: Edward Hyde,
      Earl of Clarendon, 1609-1674." *Book Collector,* 7
      (1958), 361-368.

      By means of a diligent search of *Clarendon State*
      Papers [155] Hardacre traces the acquisitions of Claren-
      don after 1643, when his personal library in Middle
      Temple was taken by authority of a Parliamentary Ordi-
      nance, and sold to Robert Reynolds. A picture of Claren-
      don as indefatigable book collector (and reader!) is
      vividly drawn. Hardacre also looks at the bindings of
      Clarendon's library post-1660.
      Before the dispersal of the library it numbered some
      6,350 volumes. "The absence of reference to belles-
      lettres in Clarendon's correspondence is striking, es-
      pecially in view of his remarks, in his autobiography,
      about his youthful association with playwrights and
      poets. Closest to his heart were the 16th and 17th
      century historians and religio-political controversial-
      ists." He read what other erudite men did not care for.

235   Hardacre, Paul H. *The Royalists during the Puritan*
      Revolution. The Hague: Martinus Nijhoff, 1956.

      The narrative of the growth and sustenance of the
      Royalist party and of those who controlled its fortunes
      in the Interregnum makes frequent mention of Clarendon's
      role, with reference to his accounts. His influence on
      policies towards the Catholics and other religious minor-
      ities at the Restoration is also discussed in detail.

236   Hartmann, Cyril Hughes. *The King's Friend: A Life of*
      Charles Berkeley, Viscount Fitzhardinge Earl of Fal-
      mouth (1630-1665). London: William Heinemann, 1951.

Berkeley's fortunes as a young Royalist in exile were
intimately bound up with Clarendon. Indeed, Clarendon
had succeeded in blocking the proposed marriage of
Berkeley to Lady Morton (with whom Clarendon seems, on
the evidence of his letters, to have been very affectionate). Later Berkeley revenged the injury by traduc-
ing the reputation of Hyde's daughter at the time of her
marriage with James, Duke of York. In *Continuation of
the Life* Clarendon gives an indignant account of his
scandalous behavior.

In this biography, therefore, Clarendon figures prominently, and the rancorous relations between the young
courtier and the Chancellor are examined in some detail.
The depth of Clarendon's animosity toward a man whose
person he despised, and whose political behavior (an
ally of the Bennet [Arlington]-Coventry faction) he
resented, can be gauged by his remarkable obituary of
Berkeley, slain in the battle of Lowestoft against the
Dutch, 1665. In this section of the *Life* Clarendon
records the King's inordinate "passion for the loss of
this young favourite, in whom few other men had ever
observed any virtue or quality which they did not wish
their best friends without; and very many did believe
that his death was a great ingredient and considerable
part of the victory."

237 Hayward, John. Letter to *Times Literary Supplement*,
        February 24, 1950.

This follows H.R. Trevor-Roper's letter of February 17,
1950 [331], "The Copyright in Clarendon's Works." It
agrees with his views and adds that Clarendon's *Life*
deserves to be known. Two requests for permission to
reprint excerpts from Clarendon have been refused by the
delegates of the Press.

238 Hayward, John. Letter to *Times Literary Supplement*, March 10,
        1950.

Like Trevor-Roper, March 10, 1950 [332], Hayward
ridicules the notion that the existence of a few copies
of a poor edition of the *Life* constitutes "availability"
of Clarendon's works.

239 Heatley, D.P. *Studies in British History and Politics.*
        London: Smith, Elder, 1913.

An essay entitled "Bacon, Milton, Laud: Three Points
of View" presents the three basic positions to be

discussed by excerpts of *A Ful and Plaine Declaration
of Ecclesiastical Discipline* (1558), Hooker's *Ecclesiastical Polity*, and Clarendon's *Religion and Policy* [161].
There is also a note on Clarendon's criticism of Hobbes.

240 Hexter, J.H. *The Reign of King Pym*. Cambridge: Harvard
     University Press, 1941.

Insofar as Hexter considers Clarendon's role, it is to
the reliability of the *History of the Rebellion* that he
turns his attention. Here, he argues, is the source of
the myth of Pym as leader of a war party. From the
middle of 1642 Hyde's information on London matters must
have been sketchy or based on rumor, yet there are moments
when the "circumstantial character of Hyde's tales must
give us pause." This phenomenon is explained in such a
manner as to lead to the conclusion that although Clarendon must be used with great caution, there is often a
kernel of substantial truth, thanks to his special
sources.

241 Hill, Christopher. "Clarendon and the Civil War."
     History Today, 3 (October, 1953), 695-703.

This is a provocative and valuable article which draws
attention to Clarendon's attitude towards class divisions.
It argues that the concept of the Civil War as a class
struggle was not foreign to seventeenth-century and
later commentators, but that it ceased to be acceptable
to the English middle classes after the events of 1848.
Then the picture of the 1640's as a Puritan revolution
gained currency and is especially ably argued by Gardiner
[226]. After Gardiner, the most telling criticism of
Clarendon is that he wrote the history of a religious
conflict, but omitted the religion. Hill argues, therefore, with copious citation of instances, that the
History of the Rebellion is not about a Puritan revolution, but about a class struggle. "Clarendon makes no
bones about describing the line up of the civil war as a
class division." He himself, as a moderate reformer at
the outset of the Long Parliament, who thought he could
make omelettes without breaking eggs, was acceptable as
a leader in 1660, although, in fact, he was already too
old-fashioned. Charles II at his Restoration was much
better equipped to deal with the new bourgeois world
than was his Chancellor. Indeed, by Clarendon's own
account, at the heart of Charles' adaptability was his
contempt for antiquity. Clarendon, on the other hand,
although a Baconian in many things, held to an idealized

hierarchical society which he thought he had experienced
in the 1630's. A real transfer of power had taken
place, so that Clarendon's victory in 1660 was more
apparent than real. As a historian, his social analysis
is acute, but he "underestimated the passion for justice
and equality which might animate the ordinary man."
Even Clarendon's style is old-fashioned (and here Hill
seems to overstate his case), reflecting the "idealized
feudal society of his youth," and lacking the urgency of
Parliamentary pamphlets, especially of the Levellers and
Diggers. He concludes that "the future, in prose as in
politics, lay with the ex-parliamentarian Pepys and the
ex-Cromwellian soldier John Bunyan."

The essay, here illustrated with engravings from the
1702-04 edition of the *History* and a portrait of Anne
Hyde, was reprinted as "Lord Clarendon and the Puritan
Revolution," in *Puritanism and Revolution.* London:
Secker and Warburg, 1958, pp. 199-214.

242 Hill, Christopher. *Intellectual Origins of the English
     Revolution.* Oxford: Clarendon Press, 1965.

     His chapter "Ralegh--Science, History, and Politics"
refers to Clarendon throughout. The book is an interesting and fully documented history of ideas, which develops
a context in which Clarendon, *inter alia*, may be more
fully understood than hitherto.

243 Howard, Alfred. *The Beauties of Clarendon, Consisting
     of Selections from his Historical and Moral Works.*
     London, Glasgow, Dublin, 1833.

     This is Vol. XIII in the series *The Beauties of
Literature,* 15 vols.
     The Clarendon section is bound with *The Beauties of
Hume.* It consists chiefly of characters, prefaced with
a warning against Clarendon's prejudices when drawing
portraits of enemies. A final section, "Moral Extracts"
is drawn not from *History,* nor from *Life,* but *Essays.*

244 Howat, G.M.D. *Stuart and Cromwellian Foreign Policy.*
     New York: St. Martin's Press, 1974.

     It is generally agreed that Clarendon was little
interested in foreign policy. Howat's study seems to
confirm this assessment, characterizing Clarendon as
standing for "strong executive government, exclusive
Anglicanism and a pacific foreign policy." His fall
is briefly described. As an "avuncular figure" and a

"moralist" he was irksome, and dispensable. But his departure did nothing to ease Charles II's relations with
the Commons.

245 Huehns, G. *Clarendon: Selections from The History of
     the Rebellion and The Life by Himself.* Oxford: Oxford
     University Press, 1978. First published 1955.

For this new edition there is a new introduction by
H. Trevor-Roper [330] replacing an earlier one by the
editor which, after a brief biography, discussed his
work with reference to comments by Lister, Firth, Pepys,
Warwick, Saintsbury, Abbott, Stauffer, Burnet, et al.
This is no doubt the most accessible and compendious version of Clarendon in print. There are helpful historical
commentaries before most sections.

246 Hughes, J. *The Boscobel Tracts, Relating to the Escape
     of Charles the Second After the Battle of Worcester,
     And his Subsequent Adventures, &c. &c. &c.* London:
     T. Cadell; Edinburgh: William Blackwood, 1830.

This originated in what was felt to be a need to im-
prove Clarendon's account, which is a "tissue of blunders
and inaccuracies." Several accounts are collected.
Clarendon's is judged to have no bad moral effect, and
is well told, but there is a need to correct small
matters in point of accuracy. A recent account by Sir
Walter Scott in a letter to the editor brought the need
for this project to his attention.
   See also Matthews' *Charles II's Escape from Worcester*
[276].

247 Hutton, William Holden. *The English Church from the
     Accession of Charles I to the Death of Anne (1625-
     1714).* New York: AMS Press, [n.d.]. First published
     by Macmillan, 1903.

This is Vol. VI of *A History of the English Church.*
8 vols. Edited by W.R.W. Stephens and William Hunt.
   The recent spate of scholarly contributions to the
history of the Restoration Church settlement has scarcely
noticed this work. It deserves some attention.
   Clarendon is represented as being alarmed by the force
of revived Laudianism, and thus as a moderate. Mention
is made *passim* of his influence on ecclesiastical affairs.
In discussing *A Brief View and Survey* [101] Hutton con-
centrates on what Clarendon condemns in Hobbes' views
concerning the power of the monarch in matters of belief.

"It was in short the essential immorality of Hobbes'
doctrine that most conspicuously affected Clarendon: but
there was a special animosity in his mind because it
seemed to him that Hobbism approximated very closely to
the casuistry of Rome."

Hutton discusses Clarendon's *Religion and Policy* [161],
especially the recommendation that English Catholics
should simply abjure the claimed political power of the
Papacy, after which Papists' religious beliefs, in themselves, would not be injurious. Although Clarendon
defends the Church against foreign aggression, he would
deny the Erastian position of complete Church dependence
on the state.

On the historical influence of the *History* he observes
that in the high Toryism of Anne's reign it was read
with avidity as a defense of "Church and King"--which is
something of a distortion.

248 Hyde, Laurence. Meditations on the Anniversary Day of
     Lord Chancellor Clarendon's Death; Containing Obser-
     vations on his Life and Character; and Reflections on
     the Conduct of his Enemies, Friends, and Relations,
     about the Time of his Banishment. Written by his Son
     Laurence Hyde, and Left Unfinished.

     This is vol. I, pp. 645-650, of *The Correspondence
     of Henry Hyde, Earl of Clarendon and of his Brother
     Laurence Hyde, Earl of Rochester; with the Diary of
     Lord Clarendon from 1687 to 1690, Containing Minute
     Particulars of the Events Attending the Revolution:
     and the Diary of Lord Rochester during his Embassy to
     Poland in 1676.* 2 vols. London: Henry Colburn, 1828.
     Laurence Hyde had been permitted twice to visit his
     exiled father, and it is Clarendon's discourse with
     him "more like a friend, and upon more equal terms,
     than like a father" on these occasions which are the
     initial subject of this meditation. His filial indig-
     nation against his father's enemies is, of course,
     strongly attested, but so too is his disgust with those
     of Clarendon's supposed friends (their identities are
     unspecified) who, "weary of supporting wronged inno-
     cency," spoke more bitterly against him when he fled
     than those who first prosecuted his destruction had
     done.
     Laurence Hyde also criticizes his own part which
     amounted to advising his father to withdraw himself
     from England rather than confronting his accusers in
     Parliament, and for consenting to the act of banishment.

With a further self-accusation about to be made, the
document breaks off.

Another cause of disquiet which looms large is the
apostasy of his sister, the Duchess of York. The English
Church is castigated for having taken so little care to
strengthen her against Romish blandishments (see also
[103]). He is grateful for her death because it prevented
her probable open confession of Catholicism.

Contrasting with the family anguish in this examination
is the picture he draws of his father's serenity of mind
in exile. His time was "wholly taken up in writing or
reading some good work, (for which that age that shall
have the happiness to have them revealed to them, will
certainly esteem him.)"

249   Jameson, Mrs. *The Beauties of the Court of King Charles
       the Second; A Series of Portraits, Illustrating the
       Diaries of Pepys, Evelyn, Clarendon, and Other Con-
       temporary Writers. With Memoirs Biographical and
       Critical.* London: Henry Colburn, 1833.

In pen portraits of the court beauties the testimony
of *Life* is frequently employed, and delicately elaborated.
In the matter of the King's demand that Castlemaine be
admitted to the Queen's bedchamber, Clarendon is pictured
as proceeding with "true diplomatic art" in a mission
deeply distasteful to him (compare Trowbridge [337]).
Not that this availed him--he withdrew from a contest in
which he "had cut such a sorry figure."

250   Jamison, Ted R., Jr. *George Monck and the Restoration:
       Victor without Bloodshed.* Fort Worth, Tex.: Texas
       Christian University Press, 1975.

This is a reconsideration of Monck's role in effecting
the Restoration, against the opinions of Clarendon who
minimized his importance, choosing to regard him as an
unwitting tool of providential design. Jamison is
probably correct in arguing that Clarendon (for a variety
of reasons) underestimated Monck's abilities, as well as
misconstruing his intentions. Most important among the
latter was the assumption that Monck himself would aim
for the throne.

251   Jessup, Frank W. *Background to the English Civil War.*
       Oxford: Pergamon Press, 1966.

This is a composition of excerpts from relevant primary
documents intended as a supplement to a British television

series. *The History of the Rebellion* is frequently
quoted.

252 Jones, Maurice Bethell. *Restoration Carnival: Catherine
     of Braganza at the Court of Charles II.* New York:
     Julian Messner, 1937.

> Exasperated, Charles summoned Clarendon. If he had
> poisoned Catherine's mind, he obviously could do the
> most to make her reasonable. "The Queen seems to
> trust you, Edward," he said.
>
> Clarendon's pale watery eyes regarded him paternally.
> He was distressed by Charles's ways....

Which reduces him in due course to impotent observer of
the great house he will never see completed:

> The Chancellor, a wreck beaten by tumbling waves,
> went in his wheel-chair, clinging to false hope, to
> watch the masons labouring. At last he heard that
> parliament talked of sending him to the Tower....
> For a long time he sat watching them in the pale
> November light, and after they had finished and gone
> home he stayed to gaze over the countryside towards
> the Hampstead hills, till they were lost in blackness.

A most fluid and unusual treatment of Clarendon, vastly
entertaining.

253 Judson, Margaret Atwood. *The Crisis of the Constitution:
     An Essay in Constitutional and Political Thought in
     England 1603-1645.* New Brunswick, N.J.: Rutgers
     University Press, 1949.

The central matter is an account of the struggle in
the Long Parliament and growth of respect for the law.
There is a good deal of emphasis on Clarendon's view of
the balance necessary in the constitution between King
and subject. In pursuing this line the author sees
herself as disagreeing with Wormald [359] who holds that
the theory of a balanced constitution did not then pre-
vail, and that Hyde did not, therefore, believe it.

254 Kaye, Percy Lewis. *English Colonial Administration under
     Lord Clarendon 1660-1667.* Baltimore: Johns Hopkins
     Press, 1905.

It is frequently alleged that Clarendon had no great
interest in colonial affairs, the forward policy of
Cromwell stagnating during his Chancellorship. Nor did

he have much interest in foreign affairs in general.
Indeed, his deficiencies in this regard are often seen
as major causes of his downfall, especially his failure
to deal with the Dutch maritime threat to English com-
mercial interest. Kaye, however, recognizes that,
although Clarendon was not necessarily its originator, a
consistent colonial policy came into being under his
administration. The policy was simple: that the colonies
(i.e., North America) should contribute solely to the
wealth of the mother country. Clarendon organized sub-
committees of the Privy Council to activate and oversee
this policy. After his fall the management of colonies
weakened and fell into disorder.

The detailed ramifications of colonial policy are the
main subject of this study. In general, his attempts
to strengthen the operation of royal prerogative in
colonial matters ran into stern local oppositions. After
him his successors had neither the energy nor confidence
to enforce his notions.

255   Kenyon, J.P. *The Stuarts*. Fontana/Collins, 1970. First
      published London: Batsford, 1958.

This is a general and popular history of a broad
period, which necessarily relies on generalizations.
Views of Clarendon are generally unsympathetic, and inadequate when Kenyon treats Charles I's reign. Others
are difficult to justify if Clarendon's state papers
for the Interregnum are examined. One such view refers
to the 1660's when

> his political development intermitted by war and
> exile, Clarendon had remained frozen in the attitude
> of 1641, when he was a "Country" back-bencher. He
> was thus the only "gentry" chief minister of the
> century, and his pathetic attempt to focus the day-
> to-day administration of a semi-modern state on a
> moribund Privy Council, and his refusal to form a
> permanent "Court interest" in the Commons on the
> grounds that this would be contrary to "the consti-
> tution", reflect the views of the "Country" opposi-
> tion in 1679 and again in 1701 and 1710. He
> deliberately reduced Charles II to the same position
> *vis-a-vis* parliament as his father in the twenties.

256   Keynes, Geoffrey. "A Footnote to Donne." *The Book
      Collector*, 22 (Spring, 1973), 165-168.

A fascinating exercise in detection proves (beyond reasonable doubt) that Clarendon was the author (signing himself "Edw. Hyde") of the twenty-line poem "On the Death of Dr. Donne." Appearing under this title at the end of the posthumous collection of Donne's *Poems* (1633), and earlier, at the end of *Deaths Duell* (1632), as "An Epitaph on Dr. Donne," the poem has been attributed to Edward Hyde (or Hide), the future Chancellor's cousin, a well-known divine, which attribution Keynes himself accepted until he came to prepare the fourth edition of his *Bibliography of Donne*. A manuscript volume of Donne's poems (the one known as "EH") in Keynes' possession contains on fly-leaves at each end four specimen signatures of Hyde's name. Comparing them with other authenticated specimens of Hyde's signature at several times (including that found in the Matriculation Subscription Book of Oxford University, 31 January 1622), Keynes concludes that Hyde owned this MS copy of Donne's poems, and that on the fly-leaves he tried out some of the figures of speech which occur in the poem. It is, he remarks, the product of a "clever and 'ratiocinating' mind." The elegy is then produced as printed in 1633.

257 Knights, L.C. *Further Explorations.* London: Chatto & Windus, 1965.

This collection of essays--originally delivered as lectures--contains the influential "Reflections on Clarendon's *History of the Rebellion*." Although it acknowledges the thinness of its historical scholarship, the essay is a valuable and sensitive treatment of Clarendon's broad outlook, and of his literary method. The *History*, which is compared extensively with Trotsky's *History of the Russian Revolution*, is seen as something more than a partisan apology. It represents a long tradition of cultivated and cultured manners, animated with a fundamental respect for persons and moderation. Several characters are brought to the fore as a means of examining Clarendon's method. This is described as working from "within," from a balanced knowledge of the whole man. Defects in the characters he describes are moral. Knights observes that Clarendon's style is much more fluid in the characters than in the linking narrative. By way of a further critique of Trotsky, he concludes that Clarendon's way of writing about politics and history keeps alive cultural values which are, in the final analysis, more important than political programs.

The essay first appeared in *Scrutiny*, 15 (Spring, 1948).

258 Knights, L.C. *Public Voices: Literature and Politics with Special Reference to the Seventeenth Century*. London: Chatto & Windus, 1971.

The substance of five Clarck Lectures delivered at Cambridge, 1970-71, is here presented in essay form. The fourth is relevant in this context: "Tension and Commitment: The Falkland Circle, Clarendon and Marvell." It expands upon, and adds fresh estimates of Clarendon to those found in the earlier essay reprinted in *Further Explorations* [257]. The *History* is seen as a monument to the qualities of the Great Tew circle.

259 Lacey, Douglas R. *Dissent and Parliamentary Politics in England, 1661-1689*. New Brunswick, N.J.: Rutgers University Press, 1969.

Although the career of Clarendon is not an issue central to this study, it is included here because of a succinct discussion of his impeachment, which argues that Presbyterian support for the Chancellor emanated from his earlier tolerationist attempts to safeguard their interests, and from their dislike of the managers of his downfall, especially of Buckingham. There is also a review in discursive footnotes of scholarship on the question of Clarendon's role in the Church settlement. Feiling, Abernathy, Bosher, and Witcombe are discussed.

260 Lamont, William, and Sybil Oldfield. *Politics, Religion and Literature in the Seventeenth Century*. London: Dent; Totowa, N.J.: Rowman and Littlefield, 1975.

The complex thematic organization of this book (which lacks an index) makes it difficult to use except as a course textbook. It attempts to bring together "historical" and "literary" perspectives in works of seventeenth-century writers. Selections from Clarendon are presented, notably his character of Cromwell.

261 Leatham, James. *Two Royalists: Spalding and Clarendon. A Comparison and a Contrast*. Cottingham: Cottingham Press, [1910?], 8 pp.

Leatham, a little-noticed, but prolific writer on Scotch literary and socialist topics, produces here a Plutarchian character study of men very unlike in their

social origins: "One became a great name in the republic
of English literature (although he hated republics), ...
the other was a local annalist, a parochial gossip."
They were similar insofar as they were amateurs of the
pen in days when writing was uncongenial; both were
"law-'n'-order" advocates and, above all, both excelled
in literary portraiture. Fine use is made, by way of
illustration, of Spalding's spirited, naive, rugged
prose, and its human insights.

Clarendon's portrait of Falkland, praised for its
loving loquacity and verbal intensity, is of a national
antitype to the Scotch writer. He argues staunchly
against the modern vogue for lazy fiction. Why has no
publisher the wish to publish popular versions of the
works of these men?

John Spalding was clerk to the consistorial court of
the diocese of Aberdeen, and was author of an unfinished
account of the troubles in Scotland, 1642-45.

262 Lewis, Lady Theresa. *Lives of the Friends and Contempo-*
     raries of Lord Chancellor Clarendon: Illustrative of
     Portraits in his Gallery. 3 vols. London: John
     Murray, 1852.

The lives Lady Lewis chooses to write are of Falkland,
Capel, and the Marquis of Hertford. In each instance a
good deal of her information is drawn from Clarendon's
accounts. There is also an interesting inquiry into the
contents of the portrait gallery acquired by Clarendon,
which is based on contemporary evidence. This is
mustered with a view to dispelling the doubts cast by
Ellis [213] and others on the way in which Clarendon came
by the portraits. (See also Gibson [227].) There is
valuable evidence concerning the dispersal of the
gallery, which was closely related to the fortunes of
Clarendon's successors. Similarly, the second part of
the introduction treats the Clarendon MSS.

263 Lister, T.H. *Life and Administration of Edward, First*
     Earl of Clarendon; with Original Correspondence and
     Authentic Papers Never Before Published. 3 vols.
     London: Longman, Orme, Brown, Green, and Longmans,
     1838.

Lister aims at an "impartial" and documented study of
Clarendon as a public man, one on whom "more praise and
censure have been lavished, than, perhaps, on any other
character in the whole circle of English history." While
there is perhaps some truth in the censure of Craik

[206], Lister's handling of the sources available to him is masterly, and, as the title announces, he presents a number of interesting documents as well as a short anno- tated bibliography of Clarendon's work. In short, it remains a most useful study, and Lister's "coolness," if it is such, toward the politics of his subject is not obtrusive.

The third volume, a collection of letters and papers from original sources, was published in 1837.

264 Lockyer, Roger. *The History of the Great Rebellion*. London: Oxford University Press, for the Folio Society, 1967.

An unscholarly compilation intended, perhaps, for collectors of fine modern bindings.

--   M., E. "Lord Clarendon--A Striking Figure in the Legal History of England." See Section F: Addendum [365].

265 MacDiarmid, John. *Lives of British Statesmen*. London: L.A. Lewis, 1838. First published 1807.

Biographies of four statesmen, More, Burleigh, Straf- ford, and Clarendon are presented. That of Clarendon is compiled mainly from *Life* (1759), with some use of *History* and other standard contemporary sources (White- locke, Rushworth, etc.) with occasional reference to letters from *Clarendon State Papers* [155]. It is a sym- pathetic account, largely uncritical of Clarendon's veracity, and taking him at his own word. Nor are Clarendon's critics and enemies assailed in partisan spirit. It is essentially a tale of "undeviating virtue" intended to arouse compassion, not envy, in the reader. He does, however, observe that Clarendon's religion was clouded with prejudices, and then promptly excuses it as a weakness inseparable from humanity.

266 MacDonald, Hugh. *Portraits in Prose*. London: Routledge & Sons, 1947. First published 1946.

Works of the twelfth to the earlier twentieth century are represented. The texts of characters by Clarendon (seven in all) are taken from Nichol Smith's *Characters of the Seventeenth Century* [313]. Of Clarendon's the Introduction remarks simply that they are "quite indivi- dualised" and that Clarendon was impartial only "within certain limits." What these might be is undisclosed.

267 MacGillivray, Royce. "Clarendon among the Pre-Claren-
       donians." *Humanities Association Bulletin*, 20 (Fall,
       1969), 9-19.

The coinage "Pre-Clarendonian" designates historians
who wrote of the Civil War prior to the 1702-04 publication of the *History*. It is used to set the stage for a
subtle and penetrating inquiry into certain disputed
characteristics of Clarendon's historiography. The *History* is perhaps the most persuasive of all accounts of
the Civil War, and is accessible to twentieth-century
interests, if for no other reason, as a "study in the
pathology of rebellion." As a history of a Puritan revolution it has, of course, been criticized notably by
Firth and Gardiner. MacGillivray takes this criticism
first, reviewing some of Clarendon's own remarks on
religion and concluding he gives the bare "minimum of
description warranted by the mere existence of the
phenomena." In fact there is a wide diversity of opinion
among the pre-Clarendonians on this issue, which does
not reflect republican versus Royalist party lines.
Even when they do see religion as important, they do not
agree as to what religion or in what way. More important
to contemporaries was the question of whether the rebellion was plotted in advance.

Clarendon rejects the deep conspiracy theory somewhat
falteringly. But is there a discrepancy between his
account of the causality of the rebellion and the causality of the Restoration? MacGillivray pushes on from
Wormald's [359] rejection of Firth [218] when he answers
the question in the affirmative. The key to understanding Clarendon's coherence of analysis is the seventeenth-
century theory of first and second causes which explains
a supposed variety of ways in which God intervenes in
human affairs. It is tempting to explain away Clarendon's
view of the Restoration "miracle" as a foible or as
the consequence of his want of detailed information. In
fact, the miraculous account is deeply ingrained in other
seventeenth-century historians.

Very few of Clarendon's interpretations can be called
original. They are all paralleled in other writers.
His achievement is "a masterly synthesis in admirable
prose."

The essay concludes with an examination of Clarendon's
treatments of Cromwell and Charles I. Sir Philip Warwick's account is compared, and, in the case of Cromwell,
found to be very similar. On Charles I it is Clarendon
who is conventional; Warwick stands apart. Clarendon's

figure of Charles is dim and enigmatic. For some reason, perhaps "inward disquiet," he does not paint a living picture of the King.

268 MacGillivray, Royce. *Restoration Historians and the English Civil War*. The Hague: Martinus Nijhoff, 1974.

Chapter VII of this study constitutes the most interesting re-evaluation of Clarendon in recent years. The whole study, as defined in the title, is dominated by the recognition that "Clarendon's *History* is so formidable an achievement that all historians writing about the war before its publication have an air of prematureness." The subject matter of the chapter specifically devoted to Clarendon cannot be compassed on the same scale as that afforded the other historians (principally Heylyn, Fuller, Hobbes, Hacket, Rushworth, Nalson, Whitelocke, Baxter, Ludlow, Mrs. Hutchinson, and Burnet). Consequently MacGillivray has made judicious use of other scholarly accounts in order to abbreviate his own narrative. Foremost of these are Lister, Firth, Bosher, Hill, Trevor-Roper, and Wormald. With the view of the latter that Hyde in the early 1640's was a "Parliamentarian" not a "Royalist" he takes exception. The author's understanding of Clarendon places heavy emphasis upon his sense of the importance of friendship and practical experience (for both of which there is ample evidence), upon the theoretical consistency of the beginning and end of the *History* (*contra* Firth), and upon Clarendon's differentiated loyalty (in descending order of importance) to monarchy, the King (Charles I), and the Royalists. Finally he grapples interestingly with the notions that Clarendon was "a conventional and even platitudinous thinker" who writes with "formidable power," and that he was a narrowly Anglo-centric historian (in *History of the Rebellion*). That he is by no means narrow and insular is witnessed by *Religion and Policy* [161]: "a good corrective to any temptation to think of Clarendon as a narrow man."

269 MacKenzie, Robert Jameson. *War-Pictures from Clarendon Being Selections from the History of the Great Rebellion and Civil Wars in England by Edward, Earl of Clarendon*. Oxford: Clarendon Press, 1912.

The introduction says that this work sprung from an attempt to commemorate the tercentenary of Clarendon's birth in 1909, but was delayed. Clarendon, great writer though he is, has not maintained his place in the current

literature of his country. There is need of a volume
to mediate between Clarendon and the public, for only
Boyle's 1889 anthology [187] is now available.

The text is taken from Macray's 1888 edition. There
are illustrative portraits and cursory notes.

270   Macleane, Rev. Douglas. "Clarendon the Historian." In
       Alice Dryden, ed., *Memorials of Old Wiltshire*. London:
       Bemrose & Sons, 1906.

As the collection title suggests, this is concerned
with the association of the Hyde family with Wiltshire.
There follows an assembly of miscellaneous facts concerning, and comments on, Clarendon, including Aubrey's
treatment of Clarendon's death. The facts that the
Clarendon Press building was erected in 1713 out of the
profits of the *History of the Rebellion*, and that the
Clarendon Laboratory was erected in 1753, are recorded.

Macray, W. Dunn. *Calendar of the Clarendon State Papers.*
See *Calendar of the Clarendon State Papers*. Vols. II
& III [193].

271   Macray, W.D. *Notes which Passed at Meetings of the
       Privy Council Between Charles II and the Earl of
       Clarendon, 1660-1667, Together with a Few Letters,
       Reproduced in Fac-simile from the Originals in the
       Bodleian Library*. London: Nichols & Sons for the
       Roxburghe Club, 1896.

This is a lavishly produced volume, prepared by the
editor of the 1888 edition of *History*. He observes that
these are probably the sole papers of this character to
be preserved, private oral communication being then, as
now, forbidden. Typically, Clarendon preserved such
scraps of information.

Part of this appears in *Clarendon State Papers*, Vol.
III, part in Lister's biography [263], but in each case
with little attempt at order or annotation.

272   Madan, Francis F. *A New Bibliography of the Eikon
       Basilike of King Charles the First With a Note on the
       Authorship*. Oxford: Oxford University Press, for
       Oxford Bibliographical Society Publications, N.S. 3
       (1949), 1950.

In deciding in favor of Bishop Gauden's authorship,
Madan cites Clarendon's letter to Gauden, which urges
him to maintain his silence, and seems to recognize his

claim, as irrefutable proof. Gauden was, however, working from Charles' own state documents, and the extent to which they were fashioned by Clarendon is probably very considerable. (See also H.R. Trevor-Roper, "'Eikon Basilike': The Problem of the King's Book" [334].)

273 Manning, Brian. "The Aristocracy and the Downfall of Charles I." In Brian Manning, ed., *Politics, Religion and the English Civil War*. London: Edward Arnold, 1973.

Arguing that Charles I's style of government provoked grievances among the aristocracy, and that only civil war was able to make some rediscover the identity of their interests with those of the Crown, Manning uses *History*, *Life*, and *State Papers* of Clarendon as his principal sources. He discusses Hyde's role in the development of a king's party in the Commons up to the attempted coup of the Five Members affair. He believes that one reason why young men like Digby, Falkland, Hyde, and Bridgeman appeared as the King's supporters in the House is that the opposition was dominated by old, powerful aristocrats--an oligarchy, in the ranks of which young men could not easily rise.

274 Marriott, J.A.R. *The Life and Times of Lucius Cary Viscount Falkland*. London: Methuen, 1907.

Falkland's memory was immortalized in one of the best-loved passages in Clarendon. This biography relies, inevitably, very heavily on Clarendon's accounts. As the author remarks in Bibliographical Note, "Clarendon, Clarendon, toujours Clarendon." Of the *History of the Rebellion* Marriott offers the following curious judgment:

> The *History* has two grave shortcomings: It fails altogether to gauge the strength of the forces which were at work to produce the great upheaval of 1640; and it attributes too much importance to the play of personal idiosyncracies. But its merits and defects alike contribute to its perennial fascination. As an analysis of the causes of the Rebellion it is wholly inadequate; as a gallery of contemporary portraits it is interesting and valuable beyond all verbal computation.

This seems to be an emphatic version of the received opinion of S.R. Gardiner [226] commonly held at the turn of the century, and revised by subsequent scholarship.

275   Mason, John E. *Gentlefolk in the Making: Studies in the*
      History of English Courtesy Literature and Related
      Topics, 1531-1774. Philadelphia: University of
      Pennsylvania Press, 1935.

      Although Mason's treatment of Clarendon is not exten-
      sive, it is included here because he deals with an almost
      entirely neglected aspect of Clarendon's work, namely
      the philosophical essay. He points out that "A Dialogue
      ... Concerning Education" [152] follows Plutarch "On the
      Training of Children." Another essay "On Youth and Age"
      condemns the French influence on post-1660 English
      youth.

276   Matthews, William. *Charles II's Escape from Worcester:*
      A Collection of Narratives Assembled by Samuel Pepys.
      Berkeley and Los Angeles: University of California
      Press, 1966.

      Charles delighted himself, and bored his auditors, by
      compulsively recounting his "miraculous" escape.
      Clarendon's account in the *History* can be corrected by
      comparing it with the other versions. This also mentions
      the account in *Clarendon State Papers* [155].

277   McAdoo, H.R. *The Spirit of Anglicanism: A Survey of*
      Anglican Theological Method in the Seventeenth Century.
      London: Adam & Charles Black, 1965.

      Where McAdoo is concerned with Clarendon it is largely
      in the context of the development of Great Tew theology.
      His late works, "Of the reverence due to Antiquity"
      (*Tracts*, etc.) and *Animadversions* [97], are several
      times cited and discussed. Chillingworth's influence on
      him is also mentioned. Clarendon believed that antiquity
      should be looked at critically, and, on the whole, has a
      higher regard for modern theological learning than for
      that of the Church fathers. This is because of Great
      Tew's latitudinarian emphasis on those traditions which
      are universal rather than in contention.

278   McGee, J. Sears. *The Godly Man in Stuart England:*
      Anglicans, Puritans, and the Two Tables, 1620-1670.
      New Haven and London: Yale University Press, 1976.

      The author anticipates that Clarendon will be the most
      familiar of the Anglican voices to be heard in this
      treatment of two broadly distinguished traditions of
      piety--the others would be more obscure. In what speci-
      fic sense Clarendon was "Anglican" is not debated. His

Contemplations [129] are said to "reflect throughout his
confidence that his religion had given him a coherent,
connected version of the truth, a conception of an ideal
standard of behavior against which he could measure his
own actions and everyone else's." The *Contemplations*
are almost always neglected. Here they are given thorough exercise, although little is said of their relationship to Clarendon's political thought.

279 McLachlan, H. John. *Socinianism in Seventeenth-Century
     England*. London: Oxford University Press, 1951.

This study follows Tulloch [338], who is frequently
acknowledged, in discussing the rational theology of
Falkland and the Great Tew circle, and, inevitably, in
using Clarendon's account. This, however, he supplements
with remarks by Thomas Barlow (Bodley's Librarian, 1642-
1660) on Falkland's library. Clarendon's account of
Hales is also used. There is also a reference to the
preface to the Lushington sermons [113].

--   Mersey, Second Viscount. *The Chief Ministers of England
     920-1720*. See Bigham, Charles Clive. *The Chief
     Ministers of England 920-1720* [184].

280 Miller, Amos C. "Joseph Jane's Account of Cornwall
     during the Civil War." *English Historical Review,*
     90 (1975), 94-102.

Jane, who wrote a rebuttal of Milton's *Eikonoklastes,*
had been a Member in the Long Parliament for Liskeard,
while Hyde sat for the neighboring Cornish town of
Saltash. Like Hyde, and other Royalists, he fled to
the Netherlands after the final defeat of the Royalist
forces in the West, and there he died in 1658. It was to
him that Hyde appealed, when composing the *History*, for
a relation of events in the West, and particularly for
an explanation of why that area, once so devoted to the
royal cause, changed its allegiance. Although, as Miller
points out, Hyde did not use directly much of Jane's
account when composing that manuscript "concerning the
western business" (commonly referred to as MS Western
affairs), what he read there confirmed his opinions of
the misgovernance of Sir Richard Grenville, whom he so
roundly condemns in the *History* (see also Granville
[136]). Grenville claimed that the civilian Royalist
Council, dominated by Hyde, by its interference caused
the Royalist defeat.
The latter part of the article reprints Jane's account.

281 Miller, John. *Popery and Politics in England: 1660-*
     1688. Cambridge: Cambridge University Press, 1973.

     The succinct account of Clarendon's treatment of
     Catholic interests at the Church settlement complements
     the several recent scholarly examinations of his atti-
     tudes toward Protestant dissenters in the same period.
     Miller accepts Bosher's view [185] that Clarendon wished
     for full episcopacy, but was not himself dogmatic in
     matters of liturgical practice. His attitude toward
     dissenters is, however, difficult to discern, and this
     is equally true of his attitude to Catholics. He was
     unaffected by the anti-Catholic furore of 1641, and on
     several occasions after the Restoration can be shown to
     have acted in the Catholic interest. Some contemporaries
     thought that he tried to split Catholic opinion, and
     expel the Jesuits. The failure of Catholics to achieve
     toleration is also attributable to a feud between Bristol
     and Clarendon, which led, in 1663, to Bristol's ill-
     fated attempt to impeach the Chancellor.

282 Millward, J.S. *Seventeenth Century.* London: Hutchinson
     Educational, 1961.

     This is essentially a schools text, part of the "Por-
     traits and Documents" series. It is a useful and well-
     chosen compilation of contemporary source materials
     including six portraits by Clarendon, several other
     excerpts from the *History* and Clarendon MSS, and the
     portrait of Clarendon by Burnet [123].

283 Mintz, Samuel I. *The Hunting of Leviathan: Seventeenth*
     Century Reactions to the Materialism and Moral
     Philosophy of Thomas Hobbes. Cambridge: University
     Press, 1969.

     Hobbes is reputed to have boasted that Clarendon could
     make no hook strong enough to fasten *Leviathan.* In his
     attempt to pull out Leviathan with an hook, Clarendon
     chose to cast in matters of religion, according to
     Mintz. In this opinion he is at odds with Bowle [186],
     who thought Clarendon's attack to be aimed at considera-
     tions of statecraft. Mintz's canvas is wider than
     Bowle's, and the *Brief View and Survey* [101] is not
     treated on its own account or systematically. He empha-
     sizes Clarendon's appreciation of the power of Hobbes'
     ironical and witty style to mask the most odious
     opinions.

284 Mo[od]y, [Christopher Lake]. A Review of *Religion and Policy*. *Monthly Review*, 74 (1814), 51-60.

The reviewer, in sympathy with Clarendon's views, reiterates the salient features of the argument of *Religion and Policy*, with copious quotation. The argument is very pertinent to current disputes, he claims, and he urges Catholics to "rest assured of the good intentions" of Clarendon, which were designed to bring about a Catholic-Protestant rapprochement. They should not regard the book as inspired by party animus.

Identification of the reviewer, who was a clergyman in Turnham Green, is made by B.C. Nagle, *Index to Monthly Review 2nd Series*. Oxford: Clarendon Press, 1955.

-- Mordaunt, John. *The Letter-Book of John Viscount Mordaunt*. See Coate, Mary. *The Letter-Book of John Viscount Mordaunt* [203].

285 Murdock, Kenneth B. *The Sun at Noon: Three Biographical Sketches*. New York: Macmillan, 1939.

Murdock has carefully chosen the term "biographical sketch": he does not wish to imply exhaustive research or predominantly scholarly perspectives. The three sketches are of Elizabeth Cary, Lucius Cary, and John Wilmot, Earl of Rochester. That of Lucius Cary, Second Viscount Falkland, is much the longest. It draws very heavily on Clarendon who "eulogized him with a dignity and beauty never since equalled, and told the story of his time with shrewdness of observation and splendor of phrase."

286 Nenner, Howard. *By Colour of Law: Legal Culture and Constitutional Politics in England, 1660-1689*. Chicago and London: University of Chicago Press, 1977.

A valuable investigation of the relationship of a common-law culture and politics in the period--a topic frequently misrepresented. Often the constitutional battle has been represented as law (Parliament) versus prerogative (Crown), which is a premise of Whig history.

The impeachment of Clarendon is treated in some detail, which gains a great deal in lucidity from Nenner's careful exposition of the principles involved. The event was an important test of Parliament's claim to uphold the law. This was a fragile claim in view of recent history, and put under further strain by uncomfortable comparisons of Clarendon's case with Strafford's. The significance

of precedence in this instance is illuminatingly discussed. Parliament retained its image, but only (Nenner's
analysis seems to suggest) because Commons and Lords were
locked in stalemate--"the Lords refused to sacrifice the
earl on the altar of common fame for an end that the
Commons considered politically desirable." Clarendon's
departure provided the resolution.

287   Nicholas, Donald. *Mr. Secretary Nicholas (1593-1669).*
      His Life and Letters. London: Bodley Head, 1955.

Hyde and Nicholas shared the hardships of the Royalist
exile. Their friendship was lifelong, and Nicholas also
gave steadfast and devoted service to the Stuarts. He
emerges from these pages as a kind of lesser Clarendon.
He had also planned to write a history of the Civil Wars;
had a gallery of portraits including those of Charles I,
Clarendon, Ormonde, Laud, Charles II, and James, Duke
of York; received a visit from the indefatigable Evelyn.
He also suffered from gout. A great deal of Clarendon's
correspondence with Nicholas is here presented.

--   Nicholas, Edward. *The Nicholas Papers.* See Warner,
      George F. *The Nicholas Papers* [347].

288   Nicolson, Harold. *The Development of English Biography.*
      London: Hogarth Press, 1933.

Nicolson writes of seventeenth-century biography with
an air of peevishness. He believes that biography should
be the product of psychological realism and therefore
laments the supposed influences of Plutarch and Theophrastus. Without apparent evidence, he thinks that the
influence of French romance portraits (such as those of
Madame de Scudéry) "is very important in the work of
Clarendon." In similar vein he observes that "Clarendon
had learnt much from the classics and even more from his
long residence in France." He avers that Clarendon was
the first great English historian, and the first to lay
down that problems in history are concerned primarily
with human personality--"his own history, therefore, is
in fact a gallery of portraits." They should have been
better done, but the *History* is the fusion of two books,
and Clarendon was steeped in the French manner. "His
characters are admirably composed, but they lack distinc-
tive relief; his dramatic sense is stronger than the
pictorial; he is synthetic rather than analytical; he has
little concern with personal idiosyncracies. Clarendon's
method is thus to personify qualities."

He ends on the rather menacing note that "We shall have franker and fuller autobiographies than we have yet been accorded."

289   Norrington, A.L.P.   Letter to *Times Literary Supplement*, March 3, 1950.

He points out that H.R. Trevor-Roper's claim that the delegates' of the Press reasons for exercising their perpetual copyright of Clarendon must be either silly or deep, should be modified in view of the fact that the *History* and the *Life* are still in print: "seldom have so many words been made available to so few readers for so long at so low a price."

290   Norrington, A.L.P.   "The Copywright in Clarendon." *Times Literary Supplement*, July 7, 1950.

He explains the intention of the 1773 Act (Trevor-Roper, Feb. 17, 1950 [331] gives 1774) allowing perpetual copyright to Oxford University Press.   To date the delegates have refrained from giving permission for the printing of extracts, but have not proceeded against those who did so without authorization.   (Trevor-Roper, March 10, 1950 [332], cites MacDonald's *Portraits in Prose* (1946 edition) [266] as a work which does not acknowledge permission.)   However, the delegates now propose to give permission for extracts from Clarendon to be quoted in books printed by other presses, provided that permission is sought in the usual way.   He adds that it is proposed to bring out an edition of Clarendon's *Life*, the latest of which has now gone out of print.   (Up to 1980 no such edition has appeared.)

--   Nuttall, Geoffrey F.   *From Uniformity to Unity: 1662-1962*. See Whiteman, Anne.   "The Restoration of the Church of England" [353].

291   Ogg, David.   *England in the Reign of Charles II*.   2 vols. Oxford: Clarendon Press, 1934.

Clarendon's role is, of necessity, frequently mentioned.   His post-Restoration politics are treated in some detail, but his attitudes and actions pre-1660 are only passingly alluded to.   "His real character can be as little determined from his own eulogy as from the diatribes of his opponents."   Firth [218] is his guide to the real character, and Ellis [213] to the opponents' views.   The picture of Clarendon thus drawn, and subsequently invoked is somewhat sentimental: it accepts the

often repeated view that Clarendon was suited by nature
to a static world; that in 1660 he led the chosen people
out of the wilderness, and would have been better advised (from, presumably, the viewpoints of posterity and
dramatic neatness) to have stopped there.

-- Ogle, O. *Calendar of the Clarendon State Papers*. See
   Calendar of the Clarendon State Papers. Vol. I [193].

-- Oldfield, Sybil. *Politics, Religion and Literature in
   the Seventeenth Century*. See Lamont, William.
   *Politics, Religion and Literature in the Seventeenth
   Century* [260].

292 Ollard, Richard. *The Image of the King*. London: Hodder
    and Stoughton, 1979.

The characters and actions of Charles I and II (more
emphasis on the latter) are described in a manner "dis-
engaged from the difficulties of historical detail."
There is no attempt made to break new ground; the work
is rather a lucid narrative from an intimate biographical
perspective. Clarendon figures centrally both as a major
source of information and character analysis, and as a
participant. He is described as "the best servant of
the Stuarts," and his judgments on the characters of the
two monarchs (*inter alia*) have a "rare value." Correspondence drawn from *Clarendon State Papers* [155] is used
to elaborate the characters of *History* and *Life*, or to
supply their deficiencies.

293 Pearl, Valerie. *London and the Outbreak of the Puritan
    Revolution: City Government and National Politics,
    1625-43*. Oxford: Oxford University Press, 1964.
    First published 1961.

Clarendon is cited frequently as a close and penetra-
tingly critical observer of London politics in the crucial early years of the Civil War. Indeed, Pearl thinks
more highly of Clarendon's accuracy of analysis (though
not of dates) than she does of Firth in his three *EHR*
articles [218]. It now seems clear that Clarendon was,
for a period of time, well-informed about London activities, and not simply a purveyor of Oxford gossip.

294 Plummer, Rev. Alfred. *English Church History from the
    Death of Charles I to the Death of William III*.
    Edinburgh: T. & T. Clark, 1907.

The second of four lectures which comprise this book, entitled "Restoration and Retaliation," deals with the years 1660-1678, and in so doing makes a number of references to the part played by Clarendon in the Church settlement. Plummer's account is neither novel nor searching for its time. He presents a summary of Clarendon's attitudes. Although a firm friend of the Constitution and of the Church, Clarendon failed, apparently because he was rather out of touch with the realities of English political life. He was "really a stranger" to England, and it is therefore "wonderful that he did not make even more mistakes than can be attributed to him." One of the causes of his destruction was the religious intolerance of nonconformity; another was the base ingratitude of Charles.

295 Prall, Stuart E. *The Puritan Revolution: A Documentary History*. London: Routledge & Kegan Paul, 1968.

The bias of this collection is indicated sufficiently by the title, and the method of selecting excerpts is evidently a consequence of Prall's assent to the classic formulation in Crane Brinton, *The Anatomy of Revolution*. The single substantial excerpt from the *History of the Rebellion* deals with the manner in which the rival Civil War armies were raised. In his Introduction Prall remarks that Hyde and about forty percent of the Commons, with the majority of peers, joined the emerging Royalist cause: "The truly interesting question, in fact, is not what were the causes of opposition to the king, but rather, what caused the emergence of the king's party during the first two years of the Long Parliament?" Strangely, the answer to this question remains unsought by Prall.

296 Raab, Felix. *The English Face of Machiavelli: A Changing Interpretation 1500-1700*. London: Routledge and Kegan Paul; Toronto: University of Toronto Press, 1964.

This seminal work contains an interesting account of Clarendon's understanding of Machiavelli, and more particularly, his treatment of Cromwell (in *History*) as the Machiavellian ruler of *virtu*. He uses Clarendon's commonplace books for 1646-47 (MSS Clarendon 126, 127) as evidence of his close reading and appreciation, noting that Clarendon must have been using Dacres' translation of *Discourses*. Unlike most of his contemporaries, Clarendon understood Machiavelli in the round, although he failed to grasp the depth of his republican sympathies. Al-

though the *History of the Rebellion* declares itself,
in an early passage, as a kind of providential history,
in reality its close attention to causality marks it as
a Machiavellian work. Clarendon's Machiavelli is
"politic" Machiavel, and nowhere does Clarendon feel the
need to apologize for his "wickedness" or atheism.
Clarendon, in short, was one of a very few in his time
and place who really grasped the significance of Machiavelli, and pushed aside the theatrical image of him as a
villain.

297 Ranke, Leopold von. *A History of England Principally in
      the Seventeenth Century.* 6 vols. New York: AMS Press,
      1966. First published Oxford: Clarendon Press, 1875.

Volume VI contains criticisms of the major sources
von Ranke has employed. The first of these is Clarendon.
One of the valuable services he renders is an estimation
of Clarendon's significance in a European context--a
context all too infrequently invoked. The seventeenth
century he sees as a period especially remarkable for
the number of leading statesmen who gave accounts of
their own times in either histories or memoirs.   In
France there were Sully, Richelieu, and De Retz, in Italy
Davila, Sarpi, and Pallavicini, in Germany Khevenhiller
and Chemnitz, not to list others of lighter vein or those
who remain unpublished. "Among these famous contemporaries Lord Clarendon with his History of the Rebellion
takes a front place."
There is a detailed description of the Bodleian MSS
of *History*, and an account of its composition. This is
surely the foundation of Firth's treatment in 1904 [218].
Ranke's is more clear-cut than Firth's, less troubled by
questions of motive. For example, Ranke sees but two intentions, the first to write a history and the second to
write a biography. Incompatibilities arising from this
condition do not disturb him.
His detailed discussion of the *History* is in two
parts, books I-VIII and the later books. (This is
slightly misleading for the modern reader, for Ranke
includes *Continuation of the History* as part of the
History, whereas it is much more commonly seen now as
part of *Life*.) This discussion also serves as a biography of the author. He is, however, alert to incon-
sistencies in Clarendon's narrative, to factual errors
and to instances in which Clarendon's judgments suffered
when he was insufficiently informed of events. He is
also interested in the sources Clarendon tapped for

accounts of the Civil War. The conclusion is that he
probably does not owe much to the communications of anyone other than Walker. Ranke argues that, in a sense,
Walker's account is the King's who revised and corrected
the manuscript. "Hence when Clarendon follows Walker it
is a work of the King's that he is adopting."

In the latter books of *History* Ranke notices that
Clarendon is much more in the foreground of events and
attributes this to the biographical intention. He also
tests the trustworthiness of Clarendon's account of
various key personalities such as Cromwell and Monck.

In the final consideration of what he calls the three
great parts of Clarendon's work, Ranke regards them, although differing from each other in viewpoint, as "held
together by the author's unity of view." What makes
this underlying unity is described:

> It is perfectly true, as has been said, that it is
> difficult to tear oneself away from the book, when
> once one is deep in it, especially the earlier sec-
> tions; one converses with a living, intelligent,
> and powerful spirit. His sketches of character are
> unequalled in the English language.

The educated world's view of the English seventeenth
century is determined by Clarendon.

> The best authors have repeated it; and even those
> who combat it do not get beyond the point of view
> given by him; they refute him in details, but leave
> his view in the main unshaken. Clarendon belongs to
> those who have essentially fixed the circle of ideas
> of the English nation.

298 Richardson, Alan. *History Sacred and Profane*. London:
     S.C.M. Press, 1964.

Clarendon and Burnet are seen as not strictly historians, because they do not recreate an age that is
dead and gone, but rather make their own age live for us.
That is why Clarendon and Burnet may be read for enjoy-
ment and profit by other than historians.

The book examines a very useful historiographical
spectrum in which the works of Clarendon may be understood.

299 Richardson, R.C. *The Debate on the English Revolution*.
     London: Methuen, 1977.

This is not an addition to the history of the period,
but a view of the many controversial interpretations of
it, and an attempt to understand the reasons why the period continues to provoke fresh controversy. The impact
of Clarendon's *History* is regarded as fundamental.
Richardson's treatment of this theme is an expansion of
his thesis expressed in "The English Revolution and the
Historians" [300], with more generous quotation and analysis. Particularly interesting is the treatment of the
role played by Clarendon's son in the transmission of the
History: "More of a Tory than his father, Rochester
helped to ensure that Clarendon's more subtle masterpiece
would be denounced by Whigs as partisan, Tory history."
    This is a very useful addition to our understanding of
(among other matters) the central influence of Clarendon
on the English historical tradition.

300 Richardson, R.C. "The English Revolution and the Historians."
        Literature and History, 1 (March, 1975), 28-48.

    This is a comprehensive and lucid treatment of the
historiography of the 1640-1660 period. Clarendon's
work is seen as a central foundation of Tory history,
and the variety of reactions to it (Whig and "impartial")
is chronologically traced. Richardson subscribes to the
view that "Clarendon in fact ranks much more highly as a
historian than as a politician." His major work is
regarded as "a historical classic." His account of the
history of the period, despite its quality of magisterial
balance and impartiality, provokes the storm of criticism
and counter-interpretation which shows how controversial
a subject the Revolution remains.
    The article is expanded and elaborated in *The Debate
on the English Revolution* [299].

301 Roberts, Clayton. *The Growth of Responsible Government
        in Stuart England*. Cambridge: University Press, 1966.

    Clarendon's political theories and practice figure
prominently in the first half of this study which traces,
in effect, the evolution of the exercise of power under
Stuart monarchs from favorites via Privy Council to prime
ministers. Clarendon (as Hyde) developed and advocated
a form of responsible government by means of a body of
men of independence, reputation, means, ability, and
integrity: the germ of a strong Privy Council. Charles I's
predilection for private advices, despite lip service to
Hyde's views (on which he based much of his thinking in
the pamphlets of the 1640's), rendered the system futile.

It was under Charles II that Clarendon rejected for
himself the title of prime minister (as being too newly
translated from the French) and strove instead to introduce a governmental system in which a small Privy Council
played the key role. However, Clarendon's concept of
this as the old established English method (and here
Roberts endorses Carlyle [195]) was ideal, not historical.
Clarendon obstinately refused to recognize that Charles
paid merely token respect to his ideal until retrospec-
tively, in *Life*, he admitted as much.

The "balance of government" had broken down by 1667.
Its architect (Clarendon) lacked the will or power to
preserve it; Charles II and Parliament grew weary of it.

Chapter 5 (partly based on "The Impeachment of the Earl
of Clarendon" [302]) examines the years 1660-1667.

> Few Lord Chancellors have defended the laws of
> England with greater steadfastness than the Earl of
> Clarendon. Yet the House of Commons impeached him
> in 1667 for attempting to subvert those laws.
> Standing guard over the English constitution, he
> was accused of plotting its ruin. Less guilty than
> Bacon, he suffered a harsher fate. More innocent
> than Lord Keeper Finch, he endured the same painful
> banishment from the England he loved.

302 Roberts, Clayton. "The Impeachment of the Earl of Clarendon."
     Cambridge Historical Journal, 13 (1957), 1-18.

Roberts assesses the merits of several accounts of
Clarendon's impeachment and determines that there were
two general causes of the event: the personal animosity
of Charles II, and the aspirations of rising politicians.
He is careful to distinguish the dismissal from the impeachment, and shows that not all the main political
figures favored both. He also argues that Clarendon
himself confused the main motives and the strength of
his antagonists. George Villiers, 2nd Duke of Buckingham,
appears as the mastermind of the anti-Clarendon cabal
(surely also Clarendon's view), which was composed of
many disparate groups and interests welded together for
the occasion by hatred of the Chancellor. Roberts does
not, however, give due weight to the reasons for long-
standing mutual animosity between Buckingham and
Clarendon.

The detailed examination of circumstances reveals just
what a "close run thing" the dismissal of Clarendon really
was. Finally, Roberts shrewdly demonstrates that impeachment was more significant than dismissal, for the latter

would have implied acceptance of a degree of monarchial
independence which Parliament was unwilling to concede.
    Parts of this essay are reprinted in *The Growth of
Responsible Government* [301].

303   Robinson, Thomas H.   "Lord Clarendon's Moral Thought."
      Huntington Library Quarterly, 42 (Winter, 1979), 37-59.

    Although neither systematically developed nor very
original, Clarendon's moral thought deserves to be
examined as a contribution to Arminian humanism. This,
as derived from Great Tew, consists largely in following
the consequences of a belief in the sovereignty of reason, and in the supremacy of "works" over "faith."
Robinson naturally directs his attention to the broad
stream of ethical humanism which flows through the essays
(*Tracts*, etc.) and the *Contemplations.*
    The Church of England was the ground in which Clarendon
thought that humanism had most firmly rooted. He was
neither "Anglo Catholic," nor Laudian fanatic, nor authori-
tarian Tory. To more narrowly define his position,
Robinson examines some of the misconceptions concerning
Arminianism. For Clarendon and the Great Tew circle
the legacy they held from Erasmus meant a latitudinarian-
ism on a European, not just English, scale, and it sought
to emphasize those matters on which Christians stood
united, and it downplays dogmatic scripturalism.
    To the formation of Clarendon's mature moral thought
went much more of Aristotle than of Plato (in contrast
to those other latitudinarians, the Cambridge Platonists).
But if Clarendon is Aristotelian, it is an attitude probably derived as much from Cicero and the Scholastic
philosophers as from Aristotle himself. This influence
might be summarized in the axiom that the pursuit of
happiness is also the pursuit of virtue--despite the
Fall, man is inclined to choose to do good. "It is not
from Original Sin, or the corrupt Nature of Mankind,"
Clarendon wrote in one of the essays, "but from the
Corruption of their Manners, that Men are more afraid
of any temporal Disgrace, any present Disadvantage than
of eternal Punishment."
    The article concludes with considerations of Clarendon's
attitudes toward the possibility (and, as he saw it, the
fact) of human progress. This Baconian posture Robinson
sees as a consistent development of his ethic, not an
intrusion upon it.

304 Roebuck, W.G. "Charles II: the Missing Portrait."
     Huntington Library Quarterly, 38 (May, 1975), 215-224.

   This attempts to answer the question why there is no
full portrait and scarcely any characterization of
Charles II in the *History of the Rebellion*. It examines
briefly the composition of the work to discover the
operative principles in Clarendon's selection of details
concerning Charles. It examines letters written to the
King and others at the time of the *History*'s completion
and after, to show Clarendon's hopes that this work would
secure his recall from exile. The significance of this
motive to the *History* is considered. Clarendon's understanding of Charles II's character is contrasted with
that of Halifax.

305 Roebuck, Graham. "A 'New' Portrait by Clarendon."
     Notes and Queries, 20 (May, 1973), 168-170.

   Re-examination of Bodleian MS Clarendon 122 reveals
that instead of containing three characters or portraits
(as printed in *Clarendon State Papers*) it has a hitherto
unnoticed fourth. The three recognized and named by
Clarendon's eighteenth-century editors, for Clarendon
left them without titles, are of Digby, Berkeley, and
Bennet. The fourth, which has been printed as if it
were part of that of Sir Henry Bennet, may be of George
Villiers, second Duke of Buckingham. The probable purpose of this group of portraits and the literary quality
of the "new" one is considered. The latter is then presented as it appears in MS.

306 Røstvig, Maren-Sofie. *The Happy Man: Studies in the
     Metamorphoses of a Classical Ideal*. 2 vols; Vol. 1,
     1600-1700, Vol. 2, 1700-1760. Oslo: University Press;
     Oxford: Basil Blackwell, 1958. First published in one
     vol., Oslo: Akedemisk Verlag; Oxford: Basil Blackwell,
     1954.

   Vol. 1 is concerned with Anglican ideals of retreat
and retirement, and their classical sources. In passing
Røstvig notes that Falkland's attempt, but ultimate
failure, to live the life of retired moderation was a
consequence of the pressure of the time, and she cites
as evidence passages from Clarendon.

--   Routledge, F.J. *Calendar of the Clarendon State Papers*.
     See *Calendar of the Clarendon State Papers*. Vols. IV
     & V [193].

307   Rowse, A.L.   "Books in General." *New Statesman and*
         Nation, 27 (February 12, 1944), 111. Reprinted in his
         English Spirit (1944).

      This section of the weekend review is given over to a
      reappraisal of Clarendon, one of the classics of our
      literature "which few enough have heard of, let alone
      read." Rowse chooses to praise the qualities of the
      Life, although bearing in mind its incompleteness after
      it was dismembered to make the final *History.* Clearly
      Rowse has Firth's analysis [218] in mind, tacitly dis-
      senting from his evaluation of the characters in *Life,*
      and openly differing with him over Firth's claim that
      Clarendon was one of the few men in English history who
      rose from low social estate to high political office.
      His condition was not obscure, but well connected. He
      seems tacitly to agree with Firth, however, in the view
      that Clarendon had no notion of the social forces which
      underlay the Civil War--he was "an actor in these events."
      Then he illuminates the country gentleman qualities in
      Clarendon's personality and prejudices. There is also
      praise for the subtlety of Clarendon's prose style, well
      fitted as it was to explore the psychology of the age.
      Finally, it is to the Great Tew influence that Rowse
      looks to explain the sustaining power in the work of
      Clarendon's final exile--and this is lyrically expressed.

308   Russell, Conrad.   "Introduction." In Conrad Russell, ed.,
         The Origins of the English Civil War. New York:
         Barnes & Noble, 1973.

      Part of the rationale governing this collection of
      recent essays runs thus:

         The English Civil War is perhaps the outstanding
         example of the need of each generation to re-write
         its own history, and it is impossible to survey its
         origins without surveying also the origins of the
         discussion of its origins. Any such discussion must
         begin with Edward Hyde, Earl of Clarendon, whose
         History of the Great Rebellion, written shortly after
         the event, could draw on knowledge we may now never
         possess. For Clarendon the moralistic overtones of
         the story involved a collapse in respect for estab-
         lished institutions: the abandonment of the text,
         "fear God: honour the King." For him this contempt
         for established authority appeared to be implicit in
         Puritanism, and therefore he thought the seeds of
         the second revolution were necessarily contained in

the first. However, underneath his moralistic message Clarendon is telling a rather different story.
This is an essentially *political* story, a story of
mistaken decisions and missed opportunities. He
thought it would have been possible for the King to
reach a settlement with the leaders of the Long
Parliament and was constantly prepared to make statements to the effect that the war would not have
happened if one or another thing had happened differently. It is precisely these statements which
must be denied by all the various schools that hold
an English Revolution was inevitable.

Despite this challenge, none of the essays seems to
attempt such a revaluation.

309 Rutt, John Towill. *Diary of Thomas Burton, Esq. Member
     in the Parliaments of Oliver and Richard Cromwell,
     from 1656 to 1659: Now First Published from the Origi-
     nal Autograph Manuscript. With an Introduction,
     Containing an Account of the Parliament of 1654; From
     the Journal of Guibon Goddard, Esq. M.P. Also Now
     First Printed*. 4 vols. London: Henry Colburn, 1828.

This is a Whig history of the querulous sort. It complains of long scholarly neglect of the Interregnum out
of deference to restored royalty. There are a number of
references to Clarendon, each tending to cast doubt on
Clarendon's accuracy, honesty, and historical value.
One of the more unusual complaints is against the practice of prefixing biblical mottoes to each book of the
History--a practice "now justly exploded."

310 Saintsbury, George. *Dryden*. London: Macmillan and Co.,
     1881.

The author's assessment of Clarendon's style is presented in a survey of the individualism of seventeenth-
century prose which, he claims, required reformation in
order to become suitable to everyday use. Part of this
deserves to be quoted:

     Clarendon has shown how genius can make the best
     of the worst style, which from any general point of
     view his must probably be pronounced to be. In his
     hands it is alternately delightful or tolerable: in
     the hands of anybody else it would be simply fright-
     ful. His parentheses, his asides, his endless invo-
     lutions of phrase and thought save themselves as if
     by miracle, and certainly could not be trusted to
     save themselves in any less favoured hands.

311   Saintsbury, George. *A History of English Prose Rhythm.*
      London: Macmillan, 1922. First published 1912.

      This now quite neglected work surveys an enormous
      historical range from Greek and Latin prose rhythms to
      "George Meredith: his Meredithesity." It is bemusing to
      the modern reader for whom the purpose of such a study
      remains unevident. Its ornate, byzantine structure of
      chapters, interchapters, and appendices covers hundreds
      of pages with elaborate and frequently bizarre prose.
      The faults of Clarendon's style--examined in a chapter
      entitled "The Concurrence of the Plain"--"are almost
      universally known even to the casual student of the
      subject." These faults seem to lurk in his lengthy
      periods which might, or, on the other hand, might not
      be remedied with punctuation:

          The slightest alteration usually, not seldom
          none at all, save a simple reform of the punctuation,
          would meet the case. But often also it would not;
          and Clarendon has allowed himself to be drawn into
          complicated, and certainly not admirable, *anacolutha*
          of construction.

      A consequence, it seems, is that "you must not demand
      from Clarendon *ce qu'il n'a pas* but only *ce qu'il a.*"
      And,

          Balance and antithesis positively assist compre-
          hension (though with the danger, which we shall see
          fully illustrated below, of sometimes giving to non-
          sense an air of comprehensibility), so balance and
          antithesis are admitted. But we discern few other
          devices of art.

      Where Clarendon may be supposed to have attempted a
      higher strain of harmony "with burst of trumpet or dying
      fall of lyre" we sometimes get "wretched things, blunted
      gossip-phrase, without selection, appropriateness or
      cadence of any sort." With this Saintsbury promptly
      shifts his attentions. Recent Clarendon studies have
      not resumed them.

312   Schwoerer, Lois G. *No Standing Armies: The Antiarmy
      Ideology in Seventeenth-Century England.* Baltimore
      and London: Johns Hopkins University Press, 1974.

      Clarendon's part in the long controversy here described
      and analyzed is not great, but anti-militarist sentiment
      played an important part in Clarendon's fall from power.
      In the charges against him in 1667, that he favored a

standing army was placed first, thus arguing the per-
ceived impact on Parliamentary opinion of the anti-
militarist phobia. There seems to be some basis in fact
for this suspicion, inasmuch as Clarendon defended the
establishment of the Guards in 1661 against the strong
objections of Southampton. But that he favored military
rule is a quite different matter. Parliament rejected
the charge by a vote of 172 to 103, and thus "law muted
hysteria."

In treating the 1642 period Schwoerer remarks that
Charles I's barrage of declarations and responses (many
concerning the militia) was written mainly by Hyde, and
had the effect of winning adherents to the cause. She
then looks at the battle of pamphlets and observes that,
"Curiously enough, there is no evidence that Edward Hyde
contributed to the exchange of pamphlets."

-- Singer, Samuel Weller. *The Correspondence of Henry Hyde.*
See Hyde, Laurence. *Meditations on the Anniversary
Day of Lord Chancellor Clarendon's Death* [248].

313 Smith, David Nichol. *Characters from the Histories &
Memoirs of the Seventeenth Century, with an Essay on
the Character and Historical Notes.* Oxford: Clarendon
Press, 1918.

One of the four parts of the introductory essay is
devoted to Clarendon. It is a fine, lucid account of
the composition of the *History* and of Clarendon's intentions. The indebtedness to Firth [218] is acknowledged,
but in scope it goes beyond the limits Firth set for his
discussion. The *Life* is examined and appraised as a discrete work--"by far the most elaborate autobiography
that had yet been attempted in English." A second topic
is Clarendon's art of character writing. To look at its
beginnings Smith chooses *The Difference and Disparity*
[73] in the belief that it is "a somewhat laboured composition ... a young man's careful essay." His later
characters owe so much, as Smith argues, to the habits
of friendship and conversation which the younger Hyde
cultivated, the blessings of which never failed him.
The manner of his treating character subjects is percep-
tively described: "He starts from the centre and works
outwards. This is the reason of the convincingness of
his characters, their dramatic truth."

Thirty-seven of the characters are chosen for inclusion, twenty-seven of these from "Manuscript Life."
They are presented in their original spelling--the only

considerable and accessible selection of Clarendon's to
provide this luxury. The notes deserve praise for their
detail and excellence of judgment.

314   Stephen, Sir James Fitzjames. "Clarendon's 'History of
      the Rebellion.'" *Horae Sabbaticae*, 1st ser. London:
      Macmillan, 1892.

      The viewpoint of this article (first printed in *The
      Saturday Review*) is a surprising and tonic mélange of
      contempt for Clarendon's (alleged) interpretation of
      history, and sensitive appreciation of his literary
      skills. Neither side of the balance, however, is unequi-
      vocal. Treating Clarendon's explanations of the cause
      of the Civil War in brief summary, Stephen concludes
      that it is "a simply childish notion." He eventually
      softens this view by observing that "science was not then
      invented." Similarly, while some characters and scenes
      from the *History* (excerpts seldom quoted by other com-
      mentators) are warmly admired, and compared to their
      advantage with the products of other literary genres,
      Stephen zealously repunctuates and edits other passages
      to "show that Clarendon might, with hardly an effort,
      have made his book as brilliant as it is impressive."
      Perhaps the intention of these manoeuvres is to revive
      interest in "a well-established classic" which has suf-
      fered the common fate of being widely known, and seldom
      read.

315   Stephen, Sir James Fitzjames. "Lord Clarendon's 'Life.'"
      Horae Sabbaticae, 1st ser. London: Macmillan, 1892, pp.
      329-347.

      "Few men have sung their own praises with such calm
      assurance" claims Stephen, with appropriate illustration.
      The stately gravity with which this central purpose of
      the *Life* is accomplished goes hand in hand with a per-
      sistent deceitfulness. As in his essay on the *History
      of the Rebellion* [314] the author is highly critical of
      Clarendon's blinkered perception of political realities.
      This criticism is, however, difficult to reconcile with
      the statement that he "was one of the very few who clearly
      understood the nature of the struggle between the King
      and the Parliament, and took part emphatically and pas-
      sionately for the King; and this although in the earlier
      part of his career, he was as well aware as any one of
      the existence of great abuses which required a remedy."
      The essay ends on a demonstration of the "wonderful
      clumsiness" of Clarendon's prose.
         It first appeared in *The Saturday Review*.

316 Stone, Lawrence. *The Causes of the English Revolution 1529-1642*. London: Routledge & Kegan Paul, 1972.

Stone believes the revolution of 1642 is the first great revolution of world history. If that is the case, and if its roots are as deep as his dates imply, then narrative accounts, especially those of a "rebellion," will not suffice to provide an understanding of it. He, therefore, chooses a rigorously analytical method, rather than a narrative. Seeing the revolution in this perspective, and being, in his own description, an "agnostic liberal," he places little credence in either Clarendon's method or in what he has to say. For example, Royalists' "propaganda, repeated subsequently by Clarendon was concerned to cast doubts on both the purity of motives and the social standing of their opponents." To concentrate, as C.V. Wedgwood and others do, upon Clarendon's Great Rebellion is to miss the essential problem. The war itself is easy to explain, but the more important question is why most of the established institutions of the State and Church collapsed two years before the war. "There is reason to think that those who had opposed the Crown on purely constitutional and political grounds in the 1620's and 1630's tended to swing back to the King with Sir Edward Hyde in 1642."

317 Stoye, J.W. *English Travellers Abroad 1604-1667. Their Influence in English Society and Politics*. London: Jonathan Cape, 1952.

This study of a fascinating topic has some peripheral interest for Clarendon studies because it deals with the career of William Aylesbury, Clarendon's brother-in-law, who acted as agent for George Villiers, Second Duke of Buckingham, on the Continent, and also translated Davila's *Civil Wars*--which may well have influenced Clarendon in his writing of the *History*.

318 Styles, Philip. "Politics and Research in the Early Seventeenth Century." In Levi Fox, ed., *English Historical Scholarship in the Sixteenth and Seventeenth Centuries*. London and New York: Oxford University Press, for the Dugdale Society, 1956.

This is a fine, detailed discussion of interest in historical research in the period with a view to answering the question whether its influence would determine the sides taken in the Civil War. Who would foresee that

Falkland and Hyde, Pym, and Hampden, all interested in
historical research, would end on opposing sides?

319 Sutherland, James. *English Literature of the Late
     Seventeenth Century.* Oxford: Clarendon Press, 1969.

The main entry on Clarendon, summarizing his achievements, compares him with his adversary, Milton. It is
to the *History*, adjudged to lie somewhere between formal
history and memoir, that he looks: "The final impression
made by Clarendon is of the quite exceptional wisdom of
the man."

320 Tanner, J.R. *English Constitutional Conflicts of the
     Seventeenth Century 1603-1689.* Cambridge: Cambridge
     University Press, 1928.

There have been many reprints of this frequently cited
study, which deals with, *inter alia*, the development of
oppositions in the Long Parliament, and therefore with
Hyde's and Falkland's emergent leadership of a moderate
group. The *History* is frequently quoted in illustration
of views of the time.

Clarendon's policy of comprehension in the Restoration
settlement is discussed. Tanner claims that in October,
1660, Clarendon drafted the Declaration on Ecclesiastical
Affairs, offering to accept a revision of the Prayer Book
and an establishment of limited episcopacy. But this
initiative was rapidly superseded by the zeal of the
Pension Parliament for the inaptly named Clarendon Code.

When Clarendon was impeached, the situation was not
unlike that when the 1st Duke of Buckingham was attacked,
but Charles was not prepared to dissolve Parliament.
This marks an important stage in the growth of the power
of Parliaments. Clarendon's fall was an emancipation for
Charles, who tended toward tolerationist, but not compre-
hensivist policies.

Compared with Shaftesbury, "Clarendon stands for
steadiness, stability, the restoration of the old order,
hostility to new ideas--but Clarendon was old enough to
be no longer impressionable when the Civil War broke out.
Shaftesbury, on the other hand, had been educated in a
period which had seen the collapse of all fixed principles
and traditional ways of thinking."

--   Taylor, Dick, Jr. "Clarendon and Ben Jonson as Witnesses
     for the Earl of Pembroke's Character." See Section F:
     Addendum [366].

Theobald, J. Anwyl. "Clarendon and Machiavelli." See
Section F: Addendum [367].

321 Thomas, Keith. "The Social Origins of Hobbes' Political
     Thought." In K.C. Brown, ed., *Hobbes Studies*. Oxford:
     Blackwell, 1965.

     Here is an interesting and detailed discussion of
     Hobbes' attitudes toward the aristocracy, and his views
     of the aristocratic ideal, in which Clarendon's charac-
     ter of Falkland figures largely. Light is shed on the
     relationship of both Hobbes and Clarendon to Sidney
     Godolphin (see also the introduction to *A Brief View and
     Survey* [101]). Hobbes' objections to the aristocracy
     are shown in relation to those of the Great Tew circle.

322 Thompson, James Westfall. *A History of Historical
     Writing*. Vol. 1. Gloucester, Mass.: Peter Smith,
     1967. First published by Macmillan, 1942.

     In this vast survey Clarendon is given his due place
     as the "greatest historical writer of this [17th] century
     of stirring issues and great men in English history."
     It is largely a digest of Clarendon's career, but also
     briefly charts the controversy over the accuracy of his
     details and the interpretation of events in *History*.
     The question of his prose style is discussed in similar
     manner, with quotations from critics of varying views.

323 Tillyard, E.M.W. *The English Epic and its Background*.
     London: Chatto and Windus, 1954.

     In the chapter on Clarendon Tillyard compares him to
     the great epic historians of antiquity in an elaborate
     context developed by his survey of the epic form from
     earliest examples. For his view of the structure of the
     History--which bears on the question of whether it has
     epic form--he relies on Firth [218]. Clarendon ulti-
     mately thought of himself as the English Thucydides, but
     there is also a consciousness of the achievement of
     Tacitus. "That Clarendon in building up this book meant
     to compete with the great historians of antiquity cannot
     be doubted." Interestingly, Tillyard discerns Homeric
     qualities in the opening structure of the *History*. As
     in the *Iliad* Homer begins with the quarrel of Agamemnon
     and Achilles, so Clarendon deals with the fatal influence
     of Buckingham in getting Parliament dissolved and alien-
     ating men's affections from the King.

In the final analysis, Clarendon cannot compare with
the great epics--his work lacks the requisite shape,
distorted as it is by a mass of detail and digression.
His partisanship in the struggle he describes is also a
hindrance which one does not encounter in the great epics.
"He possesses no clear conception of the way history
evolves.... And this lack is fatal to the general epic
effect."

324 Townshend, Dorothea. *George Digby Second Earl of Bristol*.
     London: T. Fisher Unwin, 1924.

At frequent intervals Clarendon found himself in con-
tact and conflict with the subject of this lively biography. The *History* reports his extraordinary behavior--
disastrous to the Royalist cause--in the Civil War.
Clarendon State Papers contain a good deal of the considerable correspondence pertaining to their relationship, and the *Life* (i.e., the *Continuation*) describes
Bristol's ludicrous impeachment of Clarendon in 1663,
and after his period of disgrace, his public reappearance
in 1667 on cue for the Chancellor's downfall. These and
other necessary sources (e.g., Carte MSS) are well sewn
into Townshend's vigorous narrative.
     She is particularly effective in dealing with the im-
peachment, which Clarendon appears to have greeted with
contempt. Writing to Ormonde in July, 1663, he speaks
of the "excellent charges the good Lord Bristol" was
bringing against him. Nevertheless, in the basic design
they foreshadow the successful ones four years later.
When Clarendon went into exile he composed (MS Clarendon
122) four portraits of his chief enemies, Bennet,
Berkeley, Buckingham, and Bristol (see Roebuck [305]).
That of Bristol is the longest he ever composed. It
pictures a highly talented, ludicrous, self-contradictory
figure, but even then with some residual affection, for
they had once been close, and the more staid Clarendon
admired his panache.

325 Trevelyan, George Macauley. *England under the Stuarts*.
     London: Methuen, 1930. First published 1904.

This edition is the fifteenth--some indication of the
immense popularity and respect this study has enjoyed.
Trevelyan's outlook is essentially developed from Whig
history, and characterized by a strong sympathy for the
values of English nonconformity. Its qualities are well
known and loved: thoughtful, judicious, sonorous prose
and an application to detail. The treatment of

Clarendon is sparse--much slighter, in point of space
alotted, than one would expect. Hyde's role in the Long
Parliament, for example, is hardly touched. Why this
should be so emerges from a consideration of the kinds
of remark passed, which add up to a quite unflattering
picture. He is called slightingly "law-ridden Hyde"
and "constitutional Hyde" who was "employed to indite
manifestoes, in which the King appeared as the guardian
and his enemies as the destroyers of law." His consti-
tutionalism in the Civil War steadily loses ground to
the violent Cavaliers, and his attempt to make the
Cavalier Parliament work at Oxford is doomed: "no Parliament could flourish in that uncongenial soil." In 1660
(no mention of his activity during the Interregnum)
Clarendon returns with his "bitter Anglicanism," and
gives his name to the Code which "broke for ever the pre-
tension of Puritanism to political supremacy." Although
Trevelyan avoids directly claiming Clarendon's authorship of the Code, he tacitly assumes it. "The present
under Clarendon was worse than the past under Laud."
When it comes to his 1667 fall, Trevelyan presents an
elegantly penned analysis of Clarendon's political iso-
lation, and concludes that "he was too ready to sacrifice
his dignity as a man in order to retain his office as
Chancellor" and that he "recalls the sordid side of Coke
or Bacon." "Clarendon had lost the nobility of Hyde."
In this observation we catch a hint of Trevelyan's
reasons for so disliking Clarendon. Earlier he writes
that in the *History* Clarendon has raised a lasting monument of English prose to Falkland (whose death is seen
as frankly suicidal). Only in his second exile did
Clarendon (in Trevelyan's eyes) redeem himself, entering
"the pure presence of the friend who had deserted him on
the field of Newbury, of whose love he had once been
worthy and was again worthy at the end."

326 Trevor-Roper, H.R. "The Anti-Hobbists." In his *His-
     torical Essays*. London: Macmillan, 1957; New York:
     Harper & Brothers, 1958.

     Clarendon and Bramhall are selected as the serious con-
     tenders for catching *Leviathan*, because they attacked
     the heart of his philosophy. Trevor-Roper believes that
     the two elderly statesmen did land *Leviathan*, and with
     remarkable ease, for when the carcase had decomposed it
     left behind merely "a few disconnected stage properties."

327   Trevor-Roper, H.R. "Books in General." *New Statesman
      and Nation*, 42 (July 28, 1951), 101-102.

      The occasion of this section of the Week-end Review,
      but not its topic, is the publication of Wormald's
      Clarendon [359]. There is only one reference to Wormald--
      to his laborious argument. Trevor-Roper's real concern
      is to interest the general reader in Clarendon's achieve-
      ments. These include the *History*, "one of the serenest,
      most majestic narratives that any man has ever written
      of events which have engulfed him," and the Restoration,
      his greatest work in politics, which was characteristic-
      ally a work of conciliation.
      The process of composition of the *History* is related,
      and its quality of modernity praised. When other
      accounts have grown dated, Clarendon's stands in
      "undiminished stature." He did not share the "greater
      illusions" of modern social historians, and to his keen
      economic sense which Marxist historians find in the work
      he adds an "endless tapestry of wonderful portraits."

328   Trevor-Roper, H.R. "Clarendon and the Great Rebellion."
      In his *Historical Essays*. London: Macmillan, 1957; New
      York: Harper & Brothers, 1958.

      The failure of Clarendon as a statesman is contrasted
      with his success as a historian. There is particular
      attention to the composition of the *History*, and he is
      represented as the English Thucydides. When, after many
      reassessments, one now reads it, one is surprised to
      find how "modern" Clarendon is. His incomparable por-
      traits are given glowing tribute.

329   Trevor-Roper, H.R. "Clarendon and the Practice of History."
      In *Milton and Clarendon*. Los Angeles: William Andrews
      Clark Memorial Library, U.C.L.A., 1965.

      This is an important account of Clarendon's political
      and literary careers which presents a number of reassess-
      ments of prevailing opinion, tending toward the vindica-
      tion of Clarendon's accuracy in interpreting events
      leading to the first Civil War. The "toryness" of the
      History and its reception is also discussed, and the
      formulation of Clarendon's religious and political ideas
      is traced back to Great Tew. He is placed finally in
      the mainstream of European philosophical historiography.

330   Trevor-Roper, Hugh R. "Clarendon's 'History of the Rebel-
      lion.'" *History Today*, 29 (February, 1979), 73-79.

This article appears later as the Introduction to
G. Huehns (ed.), *Clarendon, Selections from the History
of the Rebellion and the Life by Himself* [245]. Here it
is handsomely illustrated with portraits of Clarendon,
Henrietta Maria, and Anne Hyde, and with several contemporary prints and engravings. It does not appear to
embody fresh research, nor lead to novel conclusions,
but rather presents a balanced and lucid synopsis of
Professor Trevor-Roper's views developed in more detail
elsewhere. It is, in effect, a narrative of Clarendon's
career, which concludes by judging the *History* as the
"greatest contemporary history of the Seventeenth-century
Revolution in England," which, although contrary in many
points to Whig interpretation, has continued to find
able defenders.

331 Trevor-Roper, H.R. "The Copyright in Clarendon's Works."
     Times Literary Supplement, February 17, 1950.

This is a letter which investigates the circumstance
leading to the vesting of perpetual copyright in Clarendon's works in the O.U.P. It weighs the performance of
the Press against its obligations. In 1888 the Press
published Macray's edition of *The History of the Rebellion* "which now rests, with dull finality, like a monumental tombstone on the grave of its benefactor." The
highly profitable early editions of *History* and *Life*
have led to the building of the "new" printing house (the
Clarendon building) which now houses parts of the University administration, and, in 1868, to the building of
the Clarendon laboratories.
The sequence of correspondence ensuing from this letter
is Hayward [237], Norrington [289], Trevor-Roper [332],
Hayward [238], and Norrington [290].

332 Trevor-Roper, H.R. "The Copyright in Clarendon's Works."
     Times Literary Supplement, March 10, 1950.

Replies to Norrington's letter of March 3 [289], and
challenges the official assertion that Clarendon's works
are "available" by pointing out how incomplete all editions of the *Life* are. A projected edition of Clarendon
for World Classics in 1946 (Trevor-Roper suggested it
should be of the *Life*) was rejected. The 1946 edition
of *Portraits in Prose* by MacDonald [266] contains only
seven Clarendon characters for a total of 7,500 words.

333 Trevor-Roper, Hugh. *Edward Hyde, Earl of Clarendon.*
     Oxford: Clarendon Press, 1975. 29 pp.

This is a printed version of a lecture "Delivered
before the University of Oxford on 2 December 1974 to
mark the tercentenary of Clarendon's death." Hyde's
connections with Oxford (he was until his banishment the
University's Chancellor) and his special affection for
it is eulogized at the outset. But then it argues that,
paradoxically, Clarendon's real affection for Oxford
started at Great Tew. What then was the influence of
Great Tew on his subsequent career? Much has been
written about that *convivium philosophicum* to various
conclusions, but the essence of its ideas is clear: the
Great Tew circle followed Erasmus and Hooker and was
guided in the early seventeenth century by Hugo Grotius.

Clarendon's progress after that splendid epoch of the
1630's is narrated with affectionate attention to his
own writings, including the familiar letters and the
essays. There is also some exploration of another
theme to which Trevor-Roper has devoted some of his
expertise, namely the cultural continuity of rational
religious ideas and scepticism, especially during the
Interregnum. After 1660, for reasons sensitively
examined, Clarendon lost some of the flexibility and
openness of his Great Tew ideals. His later years are
presented here as almost heroic in their indefatigable
industry and stoic cheerfulness. In time he was vindicated, in a sense, by the party politics of the eighteenth
century. But this is not the best perspective from which
to judge him, anymore than one would judge Milton by the
later Whigs and Nonconformists. His greatness ultimately
lies in the *History*, and in the courage which turned
the course of history.

This work was reprinted as "Clarendon," *Times Literary
Supplement*, January 10, 1975.

334 Trevor-Roper, H.R. "'Eikon Basiliké': the Problem of the
     King's Book." In his *Historical Essays*. London:
     Macmillan, 1957; New York: Harper & Brothers, 1958.

This is a review of F.F. Madan's *A New Bibliography
of the Eikon Basilike* [272]. Bishop Gauden's "blackmail"
of Clarendon is described and (with Madan) Trevor-Roper
concludes: "It is an extraordinary fact that his great
History of the Rebellion, which he left in manuscript,
contains absolutely no reference to the famous work
which had been so effective in those years as the gospel
of his party. There seems only one reasonable interpretation of that silence: that Clarendon disbelieved in
the royal authorship but was unwilling, even in a book

written for posterity, to divulge the secret which would
have pleased no one except the shade of Mr. Milton."
The subsequent history of the authorship controversy is
succinctly recounted.

335 Trevor-Roper, H.R. "The Fast Sermons of the Long Parlia-
     ment." In his edition, *Essays in British History Pre-
     sented to Sir Keith Feiling*. London: Macmillan, 1964.

Although Clarendon is not the focus of this masterly
account of the role and influence of the pulpit, his
observation that "the first publishing of extraordinary
news was from the pulpit; and by the preacher's text,
and his manner of discourse upon it, the auditors might
judge, and commonly foresaw, what was like to be next
done in the Parliament or Council of State" is the
starting point of the discussion, in which Clarendon's
general interpretation is strongly vindicated.

336 Trevor-Roper, H.R. "The Good and Great Works of Richard
     Hooker." *New York Review of Books*, 24 (November 24, 1977).

This is a review of W. Speed Hill's edition of the
Preface and Books I-V of *Of the Laws of Ecclesiastical
Polity*. Hooker's reception, and the subsequent history
of his work, are shown to be closely allied to the industry
of the Great Tew circle, especially Sheldon, Morley,
Hammond, Earle, and "the political leader of them all,
Edward Hyde." Reasons for the close verbal resemblance
of the opening of Clarendon's *History* to that of *Eccle-
siastical Polity*, which has been remarked by Gardiner
and others, are here expanded. Hyde realized that
Hooker's foreboding in the 1580's of evil times for the
Church had finally in the 1640's become the reality.
Further,

> Even in his English style, even in his personal
> tricks of style, Hyde shows the ever-present influence
> of Hooker: those long, serpentine sentences majestic-
> ally uncoiling, clause after clause, now smooth and
> sinuous, now coruscating with a sudden, sharp
> malicious flicker--how can we avoid comparing it
> with Hooker's similarly articulated style.

He also compares the fate of Hooker's work with that of
Clarendon--to appear fifty years after its author's
death.

337 Trowbridge, W.R.H. *Court Beauties of Old Whitehall:*
     Historiettes of the Restoration. New York: Charles
     Scribner's Sons; London: T. Fisher Unwin, 1906.

     The manner of Clarendon's opposition to Castlemaine is
     characterized as tactless. He sided with the Queen who
     wished to reject Lady Castlemaine as lady of the bed-
     chamber, "with his customary tactlessness," and thus
     incurred her undying enmity. This is illustrated by a
     particularly vehement missive from Charles to the Chan-
     cellor warning of the consequences of meddling in the
     Countess' affairs. Trowbridge supposes that Castlemaine
     herself dictated the letter. Although the title of the
     book suggests that reasons of amorous intrigue will take
     priority in accounting for state affairs over other,
     more orthodox, perspectives, Trowbridge is skeptical of
     the alleged influence of Castlemaine on Clarendon's fall.
     He was rather the victim of "unforseen [political] com-
     plications," and his "want of tact." "In the place of
     one Minister who made a single mistake--the Dutch War--
     public opinion got the Cabal."

338 Tulloch, John. *Rational Theology and Christian Philosophy*
     in England in the Seventeenth Century. 2 vols.
     Edinburgh & London: William Blackwood and Sons, 1872.

     In a lengthy chapter on Falkland's moderate churchman-
     ship, the authority of Clarendon's accounts in *Life* and
     History is frequently invoked. Tulloch discusses Claren-
     don's portraits of Falkland, praising the "magic of his
     art," the "ideal enthusiasm," and the warm coloring.
     The effect has made it difficult to perceive Falkland's
     achievement in full daylight. Walpole's criticism (in
     Royal and Noble Authors [148]) that Clarendon has caused
     Falkland to be greatly overestimated is discussed.
     Tulloch allows some truth in this, but proposes to view
     Falkland as a rational and moderate thinker, in which
     role he may be properly observed. The ensuing account
     deals with the Great Tew group (drawing on *Life*) and with
     Falkland's part in the root and branch debates (drawing
     on *History*). Clarendon is also frequently cited in a
     chapter on John Hales.

339 Turner, Edward Raymond. *The Cabinet Council of England*
     in the Seventeenth and Eighteenth Centuries 1622-1784.
     2 vols. Vol. II edited by Gaudance Megaro; introduc-
     tion by E.R. Adair. New York: Russell & Russell, 1970.
     First published in 1930.

This examines the development of government by committees and particularly the evolution of cabinet
government. Clarendon is important to the study as a
rich source of information on the working of committees
(along with the notes of Secretary Nicholas) and as
being instrumental in promoting the system. In his
Chancellorship the committee for foreign affairs began
to take a major part, having become a place for the discussion of the most secret affairs. The reasons behind
the sale of Dunkirk (fatal to Clarendon's popular reputation) are discussed in an examination of one of the
matters which typically occupied this committee.

How confidential were these secret councils? Strafford
was brought to the block for words alleged to have been
spoken in a secret council. Clarendon's account of this
is examined. His later views on the value of secret
committees were not shared by Charles II. He makes use
of the notes privately passed between King and Chancellor
at this time. See Macray, W.D. [271].

Turner also shows how, during the first half of the
period he surveys, the terms "junto," "cabal," and
"cabinet" were frequently regarded as synonymous.

340   Turner, Edward Raymond. *The Privy Council of England in
       the Seventeenth and Eighteenth Centuries 1603-1784.* 2
       vols. Baltimore: Johns Hopkins Press, 1927-28.

This study of the Privy Council complements Turner's
work on the development of the Cabinet [339]. Clarendon
is an important source of information, especially for
the period of his Chancellorship. These two studies
necessarily overlap at a number of points.

341   Underdown, David. *Royalist Conspiracy in England 1649-
       1660.* New Haven: Yale University Press, 1960.

The role of Clarendon is inevitably ubiquitous in
this painstaking, meticulous account. As the author
remarks, "Hyde, who exercised general supervision after
1652, has left every historian in his debt for his
careful stewardship of his papers as well as for his
later writings." The Bodleian MSS Clarendon, *Clarendon
State Papers* [155], and *Calendar of Clarendon State
Papers* (vols. I-IV) [193] are the major sources of information on the web of abortive Royalist plotting. It is
a daunting subject not only because of the sheer bulk of
evidence, but also because much of it is in cypher.
Underdown has contributed a useful appendix on this
subject.

342 Ure, Peter. *Seventeenth-Century Prose, 1620-1700.*
     Harmondsworth, Middlesex: Penguin, 1956.

The cross section of brief excerpts, not chosen with a
view to presenting only "purple passages," contains part
of the character of Cromwell, a passage from *Life* concerning Sir Edmund Varney, seldom anthologized, and philosophical reflection on the past and his youthful credu-
lity from *Continuation of the Life.* In the Introduction
Ure observes that, like Milton, Clarendon was little
influenced by Senecan style, especially when he composed
his characters.

343 Vale, V. "Clarendon, Coventry, and the Sale of Naval
     Offices, 1660-8." *Cambridge Historical Journal,* 12
     (1956), 107-125.

Among historians there has been a strange lack of
interest in Sir William Coventry. His abilities and
industry earned praise from his contemporaries, with
the notable exception of Clarendon. Coventry had
organized a rival Court party in Parliament to oppose
Clarendon's policies, and finally led the attack which
drove him from power. How is Clarendon's treatment of
Coventry to be interpreted?

Vale chooses three passages from *Continuation of the
Life* for examination. In them Clarendon makes three
accusations: that Coventry deserted the King's cause in
the Interregnum; that he was chiefly responsible for
precipitating the Dutch War of 1664-65; and that he
extorted money on an unprecedented scale from applicants
for naval offices.

In respect to the first charge, Hyde the *émigré* knew
the facts which would prove it untrue, but these Clarendon the historian forgot.

On naval matters, Clarendon is notoriously unreliable.
The third question is dealt with at length and in detail,
which includes examining Coventry's rebuttal of charges
brought against him before the Commons. He seems to
have been not only a target of disgruntled aspirants to
naval commissions, but also of anti-Clarendonians. The
cause of the animosity of the latter is that he refused
to pursue the utter ruin of Clarendon, being satisfied
with having ousted him from the administration of things
for which he was not fit. Curiously, Coventry's moral
probity, in this and other instances, plus his refusal
to align himself firmly with party interests, brought
about his own displacement from office.

344 Vaughan, Robert. *The History of England under the House of Stuart, Including the Commonwealth.* 2 parts. London: Baldwin and Cradock, 1840.

Political perspective is established in the first sentence of the Preface: "The condition of England under the House of Stuart exhibits that point in our progress as a nation, toward which all the previous changes in English history converged." If that point is well understood, there remains "little to be explained in relation to either the past or the present." This is, therefore, a classic Whig account which treats Clarendon as an enemy of the popular party in the Long Parliament, who sometimes tells the truth when he criticizes Charles I's political truculence, and tells lies when he eulogizes Charles' rule.

There is an interesting passage on Falkland, whose prominence in the history of those times is more a consequence of Clarendon's pen than of anything he himself achieved.

His studies, like those of his friend Clarendon, tended to make him better acquainted with the great names of antiquity, and of the early Church, than with the history of the English constitution; and to this defect, still so common in the education of the same class of persons, some of the most material errors in the conduct of these distinguished men are in part to be attributed.

There is also a characteristically Whig appraisal of the *History.* Compared with Hobbes, Clarendon is highly favorable to religion and freedom. His knowledge of human nature, powers of description, and general literary excellence are sure to preserve his reputation in English literary history. But as an historian he is to be read with caution because of his deployment of prejudices.

A fine account of Clarendon's fall, exile, and death concludes his treatment of that figure.

345 Veatch, Henry B. *Two Logics: The Conflict between Classical and Neo-Analytic Philosophy.* Evanston: Northwestern University Press, 1969.

"A new battle of the books?" This is precisely the ground Veatch wishes to dispute again. A highly stimulating and controversial examination of the "bankruptcy" of modern philosophy (in one of its dominant forms) invokes Clarendon at one point in a novel but not uncongenial context. His account of the fall of Strafford,

along with the character sketch of the Earl, is given as
an example of high achievement in "what-logic" (i.e.,
Aristotelian). It is a superb "achievement of seventeenth century literary art." Veatch is playfully
scathing about the way in which a professor of English
might be transported into raptures over the excellence
of the literary art here displayed, but he is more
interested in how it instructs. With a startling shift
of perspective he asks how modern behavioral science
would depict the same personality, according to the mode
of the California Psychological Inventory (C.P.I.).
Perhaps the Earl would be an undelightful golf partner.
C.P.I. logic is "relating-logic," not "what-logic." In
the event, therefore, Clarendonian analysis is the useful
and valuable one. The modern behavioral account of personality scores poorly in Veatch's rigorous test.

346 Wallace, J.M. *Destiny his Choice: The Loyalism of Andrew
     Marvell.* Cambridge: University Press, 1968.

     Hyde and Marvell are compared as central moderates in
     the political spectrum of the 1640's. Wallace has
     benefitted from Wormald's *Clarendon* [359], which allows
     him to see Hyde's similarity to the subject of his book.

347 Warner, George F. *The Nicholas Papers: Correspondence
     of Sir Edward Nicholas, Secretary of State.* 4 vols.
     Vol. I, 1641-1652, [London]: Camden Society, 1886;
     Vol. II, Jan., 1653-June, 1655, [London]: Camden
     Society, 1892; Vol. III, July, 1655-Dec., 1656,
     [London]: Camden Society, 1897; Vol. IV, 1657-1660,
     London: Camden Society, 1920.

     The letters of Secretary Nicholas to Hyde are comple-
     mentary to *Clarendon State Papers* [155]. Especially
     interesting are those after 1650 when Hyde and others
     competed for eventual control of the policies of
     Charles II's penurious court-in-exile. They throw a
     great deal of light on the plots and machinations of the
     Royalists in their relations with Cromwellian England.

348 Watson, George. "The Reader in Clarendon's *History of
     the Rebellion.*" *Review of English Studies*, 25
     (November, 1974), 396-409.

     This article pursues an unusual and contentious direc-
     tion of inquiry, and draws from it startling conclusions.
     Perhaps its major argument may be summarized in the fol-
     lowing manner (though there are several digressions on

the way): the purposes for which Clarendon wrote the
History remain unclear (see Firth [218]) and Clarendon
himself never discovered with certainty what they were.
One of these purposes is to vindicate the King
(Charles I), but, as Clarendon had persistent doubts
about monarchy, he wrote in such a way as to exclude the
contemporary reader from the meaning of the *History* by
means of impenetrably involved syntax, which followed a
dead Ciceronian pattern he himself imperfectly understood. This uncertainty is especially marked in the
immensely long opening sentence, the structure of which
has baffled editors since Clarendon. Not only is the
reader "secretively" excluded from the "terms of the
debate," but also the author came to lack confidence in
the integrity of his work. Eighteenth-century readers
are said to be baffled also. The result of Clarendon's
confusion and concealment of real motive is one which
Watson seems to reduce to absurdity: Clarendon's appeal
to Providence is his answer to his logical dilemma, and
this posterity found difficult to reconcile to the other
claims he makes. "If God justly punishes prosperity,
why seek prosperity out?"

Trying to put this mass of confusion (partly) to
rights, Watson finds that the *History* "in its very in-
coherence, is an abiding monument to a passionate rather
than a consistent temper of mind."

What is most valuable in the article is its close
analysis of the syntax of the opening sentence, along
with considerations of its relationship to Hooker, whose
judicious temper is (so the argument runs) meant to be
recalled by the mind of the reader (but which?). The
defect of the article is evident in its passionate
desire to find the work consistent, that is, with a
single polemical point of view, without adequate reference to the time span of its composition (this despite
Watson's having consulted Firth). Firth's account drew
attention to changing purpose, and, unfriendly though it
is to Clarendon, understood that change in an historical
context.

Others have argued (*contra* Firth) that the purpose is
consistent according to seventeenth-century notions of
Providential history. Watson seems to want the work to
conform to more recent notions of a literary text to
which, as an object of value in itself, the author is
committed. But in this respect Clarendon is Baconian,
rather than a devotee of "Eng. lit.": usefulness is the
first criterion. No doubt the "reader in ..." type of
literary analysis, now still in vogue (1980), with its

subtle elucidation of strategies used by authors on
readers, had to be applied, sooner or later, to Clarendon.
Its results here are not auspicious, for they minimize
the subtlety of authorial analysis, and the subtlety of
reader response. (Despite what Watson suggests there
was a vast readership which would disagree with Oldmixon,
and which read the *History* unaware of its incomprehen-
sibility.) Works of seventeenth-century historiography
are longer than most works of modern fiction. Their
purposes unfold differently, not in a vacuum, but in
relation to the reader's understanding of political
history.

The *History* is "in the end an angry book," writes
Watson. Perhaps that view depends on the reader in....

349 Weber, Kurt. *Lucius Cary Second Viscount Falkland.*
     New York: AMS Press, 1967. First published New York:
     Columbia University Press, 1940.

     This study of Falkland should be compared with that of
     Murdock [285]. Weber comments on his having accidentally
     trespassed on Murdock's subject. His interest in Falk-
     land concentrates more on his sponsorship of liberal
     thought than on the high-minded statesman who won a
     martyr's crown. Clarendon's accounts are necessarily
     frequently cited, but whenever possible Weber uses the
     edition of Nichol Smith [313]. He reproduces a letter
     of Hyde to Falkland, not previously printed, which con-
     cerns the disposal of the library of Bishop Williams of
     Lincoln, a victim of Laud's Star Chamber. It is a fasci-
     nating document. Hyde requests Falkland's judgment on
     whether he would be morally justified in purchasing items
     from this library (he even offers to buy some for Falk-
     land). There is a fine tension between Hyde's sense of
     moral rectitude and his blossoming passions as a biblio-
     phile. The delicacy of the Hyde-Falkland relationship
     is glowingly illustrated.

350 Wedgwood, C.V. *Seventeenth Century English Literature.*
     London: Oxford University Press, 1950.

     To be a short guide, a kind of general survey rather
     than the incorporation of fresh scholarly inquiry, is the
     modest aim of this work. Nevertheless, the treatment of
     Clarendon is quite surprising. It is a common approach
     (following Firth [218]) to criticize Clarendon's handling
     of narrative, and almost *de rigueur* to praise his charac-
     ter sketches. Wedgwood pronounces that "his real genius
     lies in narrative-exposition." Indeed she advises that

the opening book of the *History* "should be a set subject
for all postulant historians; it is a model of scene-
setting. Every element in the situation, every event,
every personality is 'placed' exactly as Clarendon
wishes." As the foremost exponent of the narrative
historical method, employed in her own accounts of
Caroline history, she is peculiarly well fitted to judge
this matter. The first two works in her trilogy of
Charles I's reign--*The King's Peace* and *The King's War*--
rely to a great extent on Clarendon, and generally
endorse his perception of events. In her pamphlet (co-
authored by Mary Coate, M.A. Thomson, and David Piper)
King Charles I (London: Historical Association, 1949),
she reminds readers that of all writers on Charles I
"Clarendon is infinitely the most important."

Here she recognizes his occasional inaccuracies, but
allows that when he gets his chronology wrong it is of
no importance to the literary critic.

351   Weston, Corinne Comstock. "The Theory of Mixed Monarchy
          under Charles I and After." *English Historical Review,*
          75 (July, 1960), 426-43.

This article argues that the prevailing constitutional
theory in the English Civil War was that of mixed
monarchy, and that its popularity was due to its having
been adopted by Charles I in the Answer to the Nineteen
Propositions. Hobbes' description in *Behemoth* of the
royal councillors being lawyers by profession, and
averse to absolute monarchy as much as to absolute democracy or aristocracy, and therefore in love with mixed
monarchy, is applied to Hyde. Although he had much to
do with the formation of Royalist mixed monarchy doctrines, he did not have a hand in the composition of
this document. (It is one of the very few he did not
compose.) Weston recounts the reasons for his disliking
it, but sees him as accepting it in essence. Warwick,
who thought Hyde was one of its authors, along with
Falkland and Colepeper, disliked it and its effects
very strongly.

The article goes on to describe reactions to it, and
to ascribe the return of Charles II to its influence.

352   Whibley, Charles. *Political Portraits*. London:
          Macmillan, 1917.

The third of fifteen essays is a portrait of Clarendon.
It is extraordinary more for the ferocity of its defense
than for the quality of its research. Its evidence is

largely excerpted from the *Life*, which perhaps accounts
for Whibley's excessive emphasis on Hyde's natural royal-
ism, and the inevitability of the latter's choice of
King over reform. Craik's biography [206] is cited
approvingly, and Gardiner [226] is reproved. In his
assessment of the *History* Whibley takes an uncommon
route in relating the art of portraiture to Theophrastus,
Overbury, and Earle, concluding that Clarendon's development of the art is unparalleled since classical antiquity.
The opening sentences are worthy of note:

> Edward Hyde, Earl of Clarendon, has always stood in
> especial need of defence. The Whigs ... have cast
> upon his character the dust of misunderstanding and
> detraction.... But it is better to look at the hero
> as he was, than to reply to the aspersions of his
> opponents. And if only he be set against the proper
> background of his time, then all men who are not "im-
> partial", with the impartiality of the Whigs, will
> recognize in the portrait a brave, wise, and dignified
> gentleman.

353 Whiteman, Anne. "The Restoration of the Church of
     England." In Geoffrey F. Nuttall and Owen Chadwick,
     eds., *From Uniformity to Unity: 1662-1962*. London:
     S.P.C.K., 1962.

This full-scale essay is a detailed and sensitive
account of the difficulties experienced in trying to
align political and religious priorities. The author
is equally aware of the attendant difficulties of interpretation of what did occur. It is not easy, she
remarks, to elucidate the policies of either Clarendon
or Charles. The ecclesiastical policy of the former
has been a matter of intermittent debate. She reviews
and compares the accounts of Abernathy [164], Bosher
[185], Feiling [215], and Wormald [359], as well as contemporary accounts by Burnet, Baxter, and Clarendon.
In the matter of analyzing Clarendon's role, his actions
are reckoned more useful than his words. It is doubted
(*contra* Bosher) that Clarendon enjoyed the close cooperation of Laudians such as Sheldon, and even Morley, his
close friend, and his own retrospective rationalization
is to be treated with caution. The author is inclined,
even though stressing throughout the uncertainty of evidence, to believe that Clarendon generally favored a
fairly broad comprehension and remained in personal con-
viction under the influence of Great Tew's indifference
to matters indifferent in religion.

354 Wilson, Gayle Edward. "Clarendon's Hamlet: the 'Character' of Lucius Cary, Viscount Falkland." *CLA Journal*,
14 (September, 1970), 171-177.

With a cursory review of the treatment of Clarendon's
characters Wilson concludes that little work has been
done on them. He seems to propose this article as a
more thorough study. It compares point by point Shakespeare's treatment of Hamlet's decline, mirrored out-
wardly by his increasingly slovenly dress and uncommuni-
cative behavior, with Clarendon's depiction of Falkland
just before his death at Newbury.
Why does Clarendon so depict his hero? The answer is
that, as Oldmixon alleged, he wishes to confirm the
reader in his awe of the metaphysical conception of
hierarchical order. The comparison is interesting in
point of verbal resemblances, but Wilson does not imply
that Clarendon knew his Shakespeare and copied. What is
curious in his conclusion is the view that Shakespeare
uses his Hamlet character for dramatic purpose, and
Clarendon for political: the latter is most suspect.
Falkland, on the authority of Marchette Chute (which is
unquestioned), was "a dwarfish little man with a rather
stupid-looking face." So Clarendon cannot be telling
the truth. If, however, he is writing a work of literature, then this treatment of Falkland succeeds.

355 Wilson, Gayle Edward. "'Likeness in his Pictures':
'Characters' in Clarendon's History." *Humanities
Association Bulletin* 21 (Fall, 1970), 20-26.

Wilson believes that there has been only cursory
treatment of the literary qualities of Clarendon, and
cites the general uniformity of modern commentators in
evidence. But there have been great differences of reac-
tion to Clarendon's portraits. Oldmixon thought there
was no "likeness in his pictures," while Evelyn praised
their natural and lively touches. As a test of these
opinions Wilson examines the *History* portraits of
Sir Henry Vane, Jr., and Falkland, and in order to
establish his terms, invokes Overbury's famous "What a
Character Is."
Clarendon's treatment of Vane is compared with Dryden's
Achitophel. In the case of Falkland Clarendon is shown
to downplay physiognomy and to stress repeatedly his
subject's rational and pure mind. In conclusion, he
judges Oldmixon correct in his opinion that the characters are "colour'd with fruitful Fancy"--an opinion
echoed by Coleridge. But whichever way one views them,
the characters show their author's literary skill.

356 Witcombe, D.T. *Charles II and the Cavalier House of
      Commons: 1663-1674.* Manchester: Manchester University
      Press; New York: Barnes & Noble, 1966.

      This is a detailed and closely researched account
      which necessarily assesses Clarendon's politics. The
      course of events leading to his downfall is traced
      particularly in the chapter "Clarendon as Scapegoat."
      Witcombe inclines to the view (expressed by Pepys) that
      his disgrace was brought about as much by his own con-
      duct as by any "skill in management."

357 Woodburn, [Samuel]. *Woodburn's Gallery of Rare Portraits;
      Consisting of Original Plates, by Cecil, Delaram,
      Droeshout, Elstracke, Fairthorne, Loggan, Pass, Payne,
      Vertue, Vandergucht, White, &c. &c. &c. With Fac-simile
      Copies from the Rarest and Most Curious Portraits,
      Illustrative of Granger's Biographical History of
      England, Clarendon's History of the Rebellion, Burnet's
      History of His Own Time, Pennant's London, &c. &c. &c.
      Containing Two Hundred Portraits, of Persons Celebrated
      for their Diplomatic Services, Military or Naval
      Achievements, Literary Acquirements, Eccentric Habits,
      or Some Peculiar Feature in their Lives Deserving the
      Notice of the Historian and Biographer; Particularly
      the very Extraordinary and Unique Equestrian Set of
      Plates in the Illustrated Clarendon, Belonging to the
      Right Hon. Earl Spencer, K.G. With Others from the
      Most Remarkable and Singular Prints, in the Possession
      of Different Noblemen and Gentlemen, Celebrated for
      their Collections of Rare Portraits.* 2 vols. London:
      George Jones, 1816.

      This is in fact a large collection of engraved portraits
      arranged in alphabetical order of subject with no refer-
      ence to the works they illustrate.

358 Wordsworth, Christopher. *"Who Wrote ΕΙΚΩΝ ΒΑΣΙΛΙΚΗ?"
      Considered and Answered, in Two Letters, Addressed to
      his Grace the Archbishop of Canterbury.* London: John
      Murray, 1824.

      Wordsworth's attempt to destroy the claims for Gauden's
      authorship depends to some extent on what he describes
      as the "high principles of the virtuous Clarendon," who
      would have declared the authorship to have been other
      than that of Charles if that had been the case. A number
      of letters to and from Clarendon which are to be found
      in *Clarendon State Papers* [155] are presented as docu-
      mentary evidence.

359 Wormald, B.H.G. *Clarendon: Politics, History & Rebellion, 1640-1660*. Cambridge: Cambridge University Press, 1951.

This work is a milestone in Clarendon studies: no subsequent treatment of his politics can ignore its conclusions. Some have dissented from Wormald's conclusions in particulars, but in general his interpretation, especially of Hyde's political objectives in the Long Parliament, has won widespread acceptance. "Throughout the period from 1641 to the Treaty of Uxbridge, Hyde as a public figure, had but one aim, to heal the breach between the King and the two Houses of Parliament which the earthquake of the Revolution of 1640-1 had created." However, when he came to write the *History* in 1646, and that objective was impossible of success, the argument that the rebellion had been a premeditated plot, which he had used topically as a means of discrediting the violent party in 1642, took hold of the theoretical shape of the *History*.

Wormald considers his study to be "inevitably a critical commentary on the work of S.R. Gardiner" [226]. "It is a singular fact that, whereas that great and indispensable historian made of a mythical Hyde a figure to be severely criticized, the real Hyde, whom he missed, embodies with remarkable exactitude his own ideal of what should have been done and thus provides the standard by which the mythical Hyde is tried and found wanting."

360 Zagorin, Perez. *The Court and the Country: The Beginning of the English Revolution*. New York: Atheneum, 1970.

The main purpose of this book is to trace the inception and rise of a "Country" party from 1620 to the outbreak of hostilities, 1642. Its focus is on the two crucial years before open war. In the modern tradition of post-Whig history, Zagorin is disinclined to accept many of Hyde's details concerning 1641-42. Hyde is regarded as having had a foot in both Court and Country camps, but, in 1642, as if emblematic of the break in ranks of the governing class, Hyde disrupted the Country party to give the King a recognizable and distinct nucleus of support in Parliament. Taking issue with Wormald [359] he sees Hyde as underrating the genuine distrust of Charles I, and regarding the Parliamentary expression of this as Pym's contrivance. There is a discriminating analysis of Hyde's role as penman, of "inestimable value to the refurbishing and renewal of the monarch's public image." The themes of the declarations are nicely summarized, leading to the conclusion that Parliament did

not care to join battle on the first principles which
Hyde propounded.

361 Zagorin, Perez. *A History of Political Thought in the
     English Revolution.* London: Routledge and Kegan Paul,
     1954.

     This is particularly concerned with the Levellers and
     the political ferment from which their ideas arose.
     Treatment of Royalist political thought is less thorough.
     Clarendon's *History* is used to gloss this, but Zagorin
     has no great enthusiasm for it, thinking more highly of
     Harrington. The *History* "is one of the classics of his-
     torical literature. Yet despite Clarendon's political
     experience, his knowledge of concrete circumstances, and
     his masterly portrayal of character, he understood his
     time, its significance, and the forces that had shaped
     it, far less than did the doctrinaire author of *Oceana.*"
     He touches also on Clarendon's dissent from the consti-
     tutional model propounded in the answer to the nineteen
     propositions.

ADDENDUM

362 Bradford, Gamaliel. "A Great English Portrait-Painter."
     In his *A Naturalist of Souls*. Boston and New York:
     Houghton Mifflin Company, 1926, pp. 231-255. First
     published 1917.

Clarendon is England's great portrait painter of the
pen, fit to be compared with the great continental
painters of the seventeenth century. Bradford's account
of Clarendon is meant to follow from the principles of
what he calls "psychography." It is, in fact, a biographical sketch, weighing Clarendon's strengths with his weaknesses. Among the latter is Clarendon's propensity for
playing Polonius to Charles II.

The *History* is adjudged to be very grand, but not read-
able, and there is a plea that the characters be extri-
cated from all the grosser material in which they are
embedded. It is precisely because of his faults in this
regard that the modern generation shuns him. The main
focus of this sketch, however, is to be Clarendon's portraiture. This topic is pursued in the elaborately over-
extended metaphor of painting, with comparisons along
the way to Shakespeare, Tacitus, Saint-Simon, Macaulay,
etc. Having so compared, Bradford is inclined to endorse
Bishop Warburton's estimate that Clarendon "excells all
the Greek and Latin historians put together," and thus
to deny Gardiner's picture of Clarendon's "usual habit
of blundering." Few writers have painted the "mighty
influence of soul over body" so well as he.

There is one thing missing from Clarendon's unequaled
portraits: women. Tacitus and Saint-Simon both portray
women with wonderful power, but Clarendon seems inhibited
in this area, and he is also less successful in depicting
groups of people.

At the close of this fascinating survey Bradford
shrewdly asks what Clarendon's motive might have been.
Perhaps to immortalize himself as much as "celebrating
the memory of eminent and extraordinary persons," but

certainly because of his passion for observing mankind,
reinforced always, despite whatever burden he had to
bear, by a "lasting love of his fellow men."

363 Every, George. "Clarendon and the Popular Front."
     Criterion, 16 (April, 1937), 432-451.

Liberal historians have sought to ignore the gulf
dividing the Long Parliament's legal and conservative
reforms in 1640-41 from its proceedings the following
autumn and winter. Its early concern to prevent English
mixed monarchy from altering to French absolutism changed
into an intention to recast the government into unprecedented moulds. Of contemporary historians and politicians, Hyde was the most alive to the threat of totali-
tarianism, dictatorship, and unitary solutions. (Writing
in 1937 Every's use of these terms has special force.)
He was the founder of a Cavalier party, which, even
though it eventually disowned him, lasted on his principles until the Whig hegemony.

In the Short Parliament Hyde had been a moderate
reformist leader; in the Long Parliament he was rejected
by an extremist majority. His activity in that Parliament
is described and its significance weighed, especially
with reference to his attitude toward the Strafford
impeachment, and the Root and Branch Bill. Hyde is shown
as a friend of the clergy, but more critical than Charles,
and they are both labeled Anglo-Catholic churchmen. This
brand of churchmanship is praised, a "calm faith," compared with the "divine inspiration" of Cromwell.

Hyde's manifestos, examined in some detail, are hailed
as his "political masterpiece," and each is said to be
in some way a first draft of the *History of the Rebellion,*
which in its turn is praised for a style "which defies
boredom," and for the grasp of its subject matter as a
whole. Yet, as Every demonstrates, not all Royalists
were happy with either the style (citing Warwick [105]),
or its repeated theme: mixed monarchy (citing Hobbes'
Behemoth).

The essential characteristics of the Long Parliament
majority are then pinpointed and detailed. They constitute the "Whiggery" of the seventeenth century, which is
the acknowledged father of British, French, and American
democracies. But Fascism and Communism bear close facial
resemblances to it. There follows a brief history of
both Whig and Tory impulses to modern times.

364 Hardacre, P.H. "Clarendon and the University of Oxford, 1660-1667." *British Journal of Educational Studies*, 9 (1961), 117-131.

In October, 1660, on the death of the Marquess of Hertford, who had been removed from his post as Chancellor of the University, and reinstated at the Restoration, Clarendon was elected Chancellor of Oxford. Hardacre says it is not possible to know how popular his election was, but certainly Clarendon was known as a friend to the University, and to learning in general. However, in the *Life* he has very little to say about this role, and the article is intended to supply the deficiency.

This Hardacre does by reference to letters of Clarendon concerning University business, by other contemporary accounts, and by reference to Clarendon's *A Dialogue ... Concerning Education* [152], in which, it may be presumed, his broader views on educational theory and practice may be discovered. Hardacre's method leads to a wide-ranging and detailed investigation.

Clarendon, it seems, took his duties very seriously, "unlike most of the seventeenth-century chancellors," but his contributions to university affairs did not always meet with approbation. Royalist academics ejected during the Protectorate clamored for reinstatement, and others sought rewards in honorary degrees, and dispensation from statutory requirements for degrees. Hardacre finds ample grounds in Clarendon's correspondence for extenuating his motives in making requests of this sort, and cites instances in which he declared himself quite willing to be overruled by the judgments of such members of the University as John Oliver, his old tutor, who had become President of Magdalen College. One of his most notable nominees (November 3, 1666), Mr. John Locke, was refused.

Hardacre notes that Clarendon took care always to nominate for positions of administrative power men of genuine learning, the most celebrated of which was Vice-Chancellor John Fell, whose tenure "is justly regarded as a high-point of the century."

In other matters he did not meddle. For example, he saw no harm in the practice of non-lecturing Professors, many of whom were almost always engaged by business in London. One of the most notable of these was the Professor of Astronomy, Christopher Wren. Nor did he do much to amend the curriculum. He failed also to solve the University's financial crises, although always on the look-out for benefactors. The Sheldonian Theatre,

for example, was financed by a gift of £1000 from
Sheldon, and in it the Press, later Clarendon Press,
his "best-known monument," was housed.
In general, Clarendon's view of the University was
like his view of the Church: "an engine of government."
He fought to preserve its many privileges and laws, but
overrode the University where interests of the Crown
were at stake. He must be judged a traditionalist in
education, although enlightened in his treatment of
Oxford, and if not a "great reformer," he was a "sincere
friend and promoter of learning."

365   M., E. "Lord Clarendon--A Striking Figure in the Legal
      History of England." *American Law Review*, 40 (1906),
      883-895. First published in *Law Times* (London),
      November 11, 1905.

      This is a brief biography of Clarendon, swiftly and
      engagingly narrated. It is taken largely from Clarendon's
      own accounts, but augmented with passages from the
      diarists Evelyn and Pepys. One example of Clarendon's
      allegedly great historical writing is given--the account
      of the attempted arrest of the five members. Clarendon's
      education in the law is given some prominence. E.M.
      judges him to have been "a most able statesman, an ad-
      mirable historian, a great judge," but especially admires
      his wisdom and integrity in the shaping of a difficult
      period in his country's annals.

366   Taylor, Dick, Jr. "Clarendon and Ben Jonson as Witnesses
      for the Earl of Pembroke's Character." In Josephine W.
      Bennett, Oscar Cargill, Vernon Hall, Jr. (eds.),
      *Studies in the English Renaissance Drama: in Memory of
      Karl Julius Holzknecht*. New York: New York University
      Press, 1959, pp. 322-344.

      This remarkable investigation concerns the man who is
      presumed by many to be Mr. W.H. and the young man of
      Shakespeare's sonnets, William Herbert, third Earl of
      Pembroke. It addresses itself specifically to the dis-
      crepancies in the reports given of him. Clarendon's is
      the damaging one, presenting him as a womanizer, although
      in the context of praise for his other qualities. He
      was, wrote Clarendon in the *History*, "immoderately given
      up to women."
      Taylor has asked himself why other portraits and
      accounts of Pembroke do not confirm this view. Not even
      Aubrey, who might normally be relied upon to sniff out
      sexual peccadillos, speaks of him in this vein. The

suggested answer, following a detailed examination of
the extant evidence, is that Clarendon confused William
(the third Earl) with Philip, his brother (the fourth).
Why should he have made this mistake? Clarendon himself
was only twenty-three when, in 1630, William died, and
did not know him at all closely. Furthermore, Clarendon's
family was associated with the Villiers faction, enemies
to Pembroke. To make good his argument, Taylor calls on
the authority of Firth [218] to show how in general
Clarendon can be unreliable, and how, in particular,
this portrait originates in the MS Life, written long
after the death of Pembroke. "Hence Clarendon's portrait
of Pembroke in the 'Life' should not be accepted
uncritically."

Attention is then turned to Philip, showing his scandalous infidelity, which was celebrated in contemporary
lampoons when Clarendon was at work on the MS History in
1646-1648. Such a confusion is not unique to Clarendon:
contemporary writers frequently associated the brothers
together, and told anecdotes capable of being construed
in a misleading way. Sir Henry Craik's biography of
Clarendon [206] does just that. Ben Jonson, in the
event, is a better character witness.

367 Theobald, J. Anwyl. "Clarendon and Machiavelli." *Times
     Literary Supplement*, June 30, 1927.

The point of the letter is to draw attention to the
proposition that Clarendon was one of those who understood Machiavelli's praise of Caesar Borgia. The writer
quotes the well-known passage in the *History of the
Rebellion* (book X) where Clarendon says Machiavelli was
in the right, although he gets an ill report from those
who do not read him for themselves, but accept others'
biased accounts.

INDEX OF TITLES

SHORT FORM OF TITLES DISCUSSED IN SECTIONS A & B
omitting initial *A*, *An* or *The*, in alphabetical order
of words; peculiarities of capitalization ignored;
H.M.s = all variant forms of *His Majesty's*

GENERAL INDEX

References to the Introduction or to section intro-
ductions are italicized and preceded by "*p.*"
All other numbers refer to items, those asterisked*
referring to the named authors and editors of items.

Abbott, Wilbur C., 162*, 245
Abernathy, George R., Jr., *p. 179*, 163*, 164*, 185, 229, 259,
  353
Achitophel, 355
Adam and Eve, 106
Adams, R.M., *p. 180*
Airy, Osmund, 165*
Aldrich, Dr. Henry, Dean of Christ Church, 115, 130, 133, 134,
  135, 137, 150; designs for engravings of *Hist. Reb.*, 106
Allen, J.W., 166*
America: emigration to, 189; North America, colonies, 254
Amsterdam, 112, 112A
Anabaptists, 35A, 38, 49A, 50, 59; Hooker's description of rise
  of Anabaptism, 32A
Andiver, Lord, 37A
Anglican, *p. 5, p. 100*, 163, 176, 215, 229, 278, 305; affairs,
  185; Anglo-Catholic, 363; Church, 103, 179; position, 97;
  Anglicanism, 244, 277, 325; liberal Anglicanism, *p. 180*
Anne, Queen, *p. 149*, 106, 135, 149, 151, 247
Answer to the Nineteen Propositions, *p. 35n*, 166, 351, 361
Aristotle, 303; Aristotelian logic, 345
Arlington, Henry Bennet, Earl of, 88, 104A, 148, 163, 324;
  Bennet-Coventry faction, 236; a character of, 305; as Secre-
  tary of State, 178
Arminian: Dutch, 112; humanism, 303
Army: anti-army ideology, 312; disbanding of, 56, 56A, 56B, 56C,
  58; disbanding of (1660), 78; proclamation to exclude re-
  cusants, 18A
Arnold, Thomas, *p. 180*, 171*
Articles of Cessation, April 1643, 57
Arundel, Earl of: a character of, 106
Asaph (St. Asaph), Thomas, Bishop of, 135

Long, Oliver, 122, 135
Lord, George de F., *p. 111n*
Lord Keeper, Edward Littleton, 14
Louvre, 93, 123
Low (an amanuensis), 106
Lowestoft, battle of, 236
Lowndes, William Thomas, 106C, 106E, 106H
Ludlow, Edmund, 268
Lushington, Thomas, 113*, sermons preached by, 97, 113A, 279

M., E., 365*
Macaulay, Thomas Babington, *p. 182, p. 183*, 219A, 362
MacDiarmid, John, 265*
MacDonald, Hugh, 266*, 290, 332
MacGillivray, Royce, 267*, 268*
Machiavelli, 85, 169, 296, 367
MacKenzie, Robert Jameson, *p. 181*, 269*
Mackworth, Humphrey, 109
Macleane, Rev. Douglas, 270*
Macray, W. Dunn, *p. 102, p. 149, p. 157*, 69, 106, 106X, 169,
    193, 269, 271*, 331, 339
Madan, Francis F., *p. 157*, 60, 66A, 272*, 334
Maidment, James, *p. xiii n*
Malignant(s), *p. 4*, 32A, 52B, 63A, 67B, 136; *Malignants Con-
    venticle, The*, 63D, 65, 66B, 68; mock definition of, 65;
    party, 33, 35A, 38, 42
Manchester, Earl of, 52B
Manning, Brian, 273*
Marie, Princess, 11
Marprelate, Martin, 97
Marriott, J.A.R., 274*
Marvell, Andrew, 258, 346
Mason, John E., 275*
Matthews, William, 246, 276*
May, Thomas, *p. xiii, p. xiv, p. 5*
Mazarin, Jules, Cardinal, 195
McAdoo, H.R., 277*
McCormick, Charles, 157
McGee, J. Sears, 278*
McLachlan, H. John, 279*
Mercurius Aulicus, 63
Mersey, 2nd Viscount. *See* Bigham, Charles Clive
Micah, 72
Militia, 28, 29, 32A, 312; control of, 10, 11, 14, 17, 22, 25;
    of London, 15; ordinance of, 37, 44
Milk-street, 66D
Miller, Amos C., 280*
Miller, John, *p. 180*, 281*
Millward, J.S., 282*
Milton, John, *p. xv, p. 74*, 177, 239, 319, 329, 333, 334, 342;
    Eikonoklastes, 280

DATE DUE

HIGHSMITH 45-220